The Complete
Christmas
Book

Transcontinental Books
1100 René-Lévesque Boulevard West
24th floor
Montreal, Que. H3B 4X9
Tel. : (514) 340-3587
Toll-free: 1-866-800-2500
www.canadianliving.com

Bibliothèque et Archives nationales du Québec and Library and
Archives Canada cataloguing in publication

Main entry under title:
The complete Christmas book: the all-you need guide to a memorable Christmas,
with recipes, crafts and decorating ideas

At head of title: Canadian Living
ISBN 978-0-9738355-7-1
1. Christmas cookery. 2. Christmas decorations. I. Title: Canadian living.
TX739.2.C45C65 2007   641.5'686   C2007-941270-X

Project editor: Beverley Renahan
Copy editor: Karen Campbell-Sheviak
Indexer: Gillian Watts
Art direction and cover design: Michael Erb
Designer: Vickie Rowden
Production coordinator: Christina Anson Mine

Printed in Canada
© Transcontinental Books, 2007
Legal deposit — 3rd quarter 2007
National Library of Quebec
National Library of Canada
ISBN 978-0-9738355-7-1

We acknowledge the financial support of our publishing activity by
the Government of Canada through the BPDIP program of the Department
of Canadian Heritage, as well as by the Government of Quebec through
the SODEC program Aide à la promotion.

For information on special rates for corporate libraries
and wholesale purchases, please call 1-866-800-2500.

Canadian Living

The Complete Christmas Book

The All-You-Need Guide to a Memorable Christmas,
with Recipes, Crafts and Decorating Ideas

BY THE EDITORS OF CANADIAN LIVING MAGAZINE

Transcontinental Books

Remember when your biggest worry at Christmastime was whether you'd made Santa's "good" or "bad" list? Now you wonder how you're going to cook a perfectly bronzed turkey for 12, wrap all the presents and get enough sleep that the kids' excited 5 a.m. wake-up call doesn't kill you.

Relax. It's time to get back the joy and merriment that you've been missing during the holidays. *The Complete Christmas Book* has everything you need to have a happy festive season, plus tips and shortcuts that will help you make it all happen with a minimum of fuss.

We've assembled our best holiday recipes – a memorable Christmas dinner menu for 12, a laid-back brunch for eight and our tastiest cocktail party appetizers among them – so planning is easy. Our Test Kitchen has tested the recipes till they're perfect so you don't have to worry. Plus, they've added work plans that will help you get some of the steps done ahead of time, leaving you more time to enjoy the party and catch up with family and friends.

Christmas wouldn't be complete without a houseful of your favourite holiday decorations. So we've tucked in plenty of creative craft and decor ideas throughout the book. We'll help you spruce up old ornaments, make some pretty new ones, decorate the perfect tree and set a sparkling table. We'll show you how to weave together old family traditions and start new ones of your own.

We wish you a very merry Christmas and a happy new year filled with the joys of family and friends.

> – *Susan Antonacci, editor-in-chief,*
> *and the editors of* Canadian Living *Magazine*

※ *acknowledgments*

A team of talented people helped us put together all the perfect recipes, decor ideas and crafts to make this Christmas delicious, glittering, fun and doable.

First, thanks go to The Canadian Living Test Kitchen: food section editor Gabrielle Bright; senior home economist Heather Howe; senior food specialist Alison Kent; food specialists Kate Dowhan, Rheanna Kish and Adell Shneer; and contributing editor Andrew Chase. Adding their creative recipes were a number of food writers (see page 233), many of whom are alumnae of The Canadian Living Test Kitchen.

A book with this many beautiful crafts and decor ideas is not possible without the input of leading craft and decorating experts from across Canada, including our own contributing editor for decor and style, Karen Kwinter. Kudos and thanks to them. Credits for their work are on page 233. You'll also find the talented photographers, illustrators, and food and props stylists who created the inspiring visuals on page 234.

Big behind-the-scenes credit goes to senior editor Beverley Renahan, the book's project editor, who steered it through every design and production stage, making sure every deadline was met while she simultaneously edited all the recipes with precision and clarity. Assisting her were copy editor Karen Campbell-Sheviak, art production coordinator Erin Poetschke, registered dietitian Sharyn Joliat of Info Access and indexer Gillian Watts.

Creative director Michael Erb made this book not only beautiful but also user-friendly. Thanks to his team: designer Vickie Rowden, who translated broad strokes into fine detail; senior associate art director June Anderson; associate art director Miguel Cea; and former associate art director John Edney.

Our cheeriest thanks go to *Canadian Living* group publisher Lynn Chambers; Transcontinental Books publisher Jean Paré; and our colleagues at Random House Canada, Duncan Shields, Janet Joy Wilson and Frances Bedford.

A book always starts with an idea and passion. Lighting the fire under this book was *Canadian Living* Magazine editor-in-chief Susan Antonacci, who is always the first to put up her Christmas tree, crank up the carols and invite friends and family over to share in the blessings of the season.

– *Elizabeth Baird, executive food editor*
Jo Calvert, crafts and gardening editor
Karen Kirk, decor editor

Chapter One

HOLIDAY CHEER

Shrimp and Avocado Salad Phyllo Cups

Vibrant fresh flavours are the features of this filling.

48	Phyllo Cups (recipe, page 5)	48
FILLING:		
8 oz	cooked medium shrimp (48)	250 g
⅓ cup	chopped fresh coriander	75 mL
2 tbsp	each vegetable oil and cider vinegar	25 mL
1 tbsp	grainy mustard	15 mL
1	clove garlic, minced	1
¼ tsp	each salt, pepper and hot pepper sauce	1 mL
Half	mango, peeled and diced	Half
1	green onion, finely chopped	1
1	avocado, peeled and diced	1

● **FILLING:** In bowl, toss together shrimp, coriander, oil, vinegar, mustard, garlic, salt, pepper, hot pepper sauce, mango, green onion and avocado. Spoon into phyllo cups.

MAKES 48 PIECES.

PER PIECE: about 36 cal, 1 g pro, 2 g total fat (1 g sat. fat), 2 g carb, trace fibre, 12 mg chol, 49 mg sodium. % RDI: 2% iron, 2% vit A, 2% vit C, 3% folate.

VARIATION

Tomato Goat Cheese Salad Phyllo Cups:
Omit filling. In bowl, whisk 2 tbsp (25 mL) extra-virgin olive oil; 1 tbsp (15 mL) wine vinegar; 1 clove garlic, minced; 2 tsp (10 mL) chopped fresh thyme; and ¼ tsp (1 mL) each salt and pepper. Add 2 cups (500 mL) cherry tomatoes, quartered; and 2 tbsp (25 mL) chopped fresh parsley. Spoon half tube (4.5 oz/130 g tube) goat cheese, softened, into phyllo cups; top with tomato mixture.

Roast Beef and Horseradish Phyllo Cups

These intriguing bites taste best made with rare roast beef.

48	Phyllo Cups (recipe, page 5)	48
FILLING:		
⅔ cup	spreadable cream cheese	150 mL
2 tbsp	prepared horseradish	25 mL
1½ tsp	grainy or Dijon mustard	7 mL
½ tsp	Worcestershire sauce	2 mL
48	thin slices English cucumber (about 4 inches/10 cm long)	48
8 oz	shaved rare roast beef	250 g

● **FILLING:** In small bowl, blend together cream cheese, horseradish, mustard and Worcestershire sauce; set aside.
● Cut cucumber slices in half. Trim any fat from beef; cut into forty-eight 2- x 1½-inch (5 x 4 cm) pieces.
● Spoon cheese mixture by rounded ½ tsp (2 mL) into phyllo cups. Arrange 2 cucumber pieces on either side of each cup. Fold each piece of beef in half lengthwise; crumple loosely and fit into cup between cucumber.

MAKES 48 PIECES.

PER PIECE: about 40 cal, 2 g pro, 3 g total fat (2 g sat. fat), 2 g carb, trace fibre, 11 mg chol, 46 mg sodium. % RDI: 1% iron, 2% vit A, 1% folate.

From left:
Shrimp and Avocado
Salad Phyllo Cups,
Roast Beef and
Horseradish Phyllo
Cups, Thai Crab Salad
Phyllo Cups

Thai Crab Salad Phyllo Cups

The fresh taste and cool colours of this salad filling lend glamour to the appetizer.

48	Phyllo Cups (recipe, this page)	48
2 tbsp	finely chopped peanuts	25 mL
FILLING:		
3 tbsp	vegetable oil	50 mL
3 tbsp	lime or lemon juice	50 mL
2 tbsp	granulated sugar	25 mL
2 tsp	fish sauce or soy sauce	10 mL
1½ tsp	peanut butter	7 mL
1	clove garlic, minced	1
Dash	hot pepper sauce	Dash
8 oz	crabmeat (fresh or thawed)	250 g
⅔ cup	each finely chopped English cucumber and sweet red pepper	150 mL
3 tbsp	finely chopped green onion	50 mL
3 tbsp	finely chopped fresh basil or mint	50 mL

• **FILLING:** In large bowl, whisk together oil, lime juice, sugar, fish sauce, peanut butter, garlic and hot pepper sauce until sugar is dissolved. Gently squeeze any excess liquid from crabmeat. Add to bowl along with cucumber, red pepper, green onion and basil; toss to combine.

• Spoon filling into phyllo cups. Sprinkle with peanuts.

MAKES 48 PIECES.

PER PIECE: about 37 cal, 2 g pro, 2 g total fat (1 g sat. fat), 3 g carb, trace fibre, 6 mg chol, 79 mg sodium. % RDI: 2% iron, 2% vit A, 8% vit C, 3% folate.

Phyllo Cups

Flaky phyllo cups hold impressive party hors d'oeuvres. Or for dessert, fill with ice cream and fruit or nuts or chocolate sauce. Muffin cups that are about ¾ inch (2 cm) deep are better than shallower ones.

6	sheets phyllo pastry	6
¼ cup	butter, melted	50 mL

• Lightly grease 24 mini muffin or tart tins; set aside.

• Place 1 sheet of phyllo on work surface, covering remainder with plastic wrap then damp towel. Brush with butter. Top with second sheet; brush with butter. Top with third sheet; brush with butter. Cut lengthwise into 4 strips and crosswise into 6 strips to make 24 squares.

• Press each square into prepared cup. Bake in centre of 400°F (200°C) oven until golden, about 5 minutes. Let cool in pan on rack. Repeat with remaining phyllo. *(Make-ahead: Freeze in single layer in airtight container for up to 1 month; recrisp in 350°F/180°C oven for 3 minutes.)*

MAKES 48 CUPS.

PER CUP: about 18 cal, trace pro, 1 g total fat (1 g sat. fat), 2 g carb, 0 g fibre, 3 mg chol, 25 mg sodium. % RDI: 1% iron, 1% vit A, 1% folate.

Cheddar Shorties

Three-year-old Cheddar is the secret to making these cocktail biscuits truly zingy.

2 cups	shredded extra-old Cheddar cheese	500 mL
¼ cup	butter, softened	50 mL
½ tsp	each dry mustard and salt	2 mL
¼ tsp	each cayenne pepper and ground nutmeg	1 mL
1 cup	all-purpose flour	250 mL
½ tsp	baking powder	2 mL
2 tbsp	poppy seeds or black sesame seeds	25 mL

• Line rimless baking sheet with parchment paper; set aside.

• In food processor, whirl together cheese, butter, mustard, salt, cayenne pepper and nutmeg until smooth and fluffy. Add flour, baking powder and 1 tbsp (15 mL) water; pulse until incorporated, scraping down side of bowl occasionally.

• Transfer to lightly floured surface; knead just until dough comes together. Shape into 1½-inch (4 cm) diameter log.

• Spread poppy seeds on waxed paper; roll log in seeds to coat. Wrap and refrigerate until firm, about 4 hours. *(Make-ahead: Refrigerate for up to 4 days.)*

• Cut log into ¼-inch (5 mm) thick slices; place on prepared pan. Bake in centre of 275°F (140°C) oven until golden, 40 to 45 minutes. Let cool on rack. *(Make-ahead: Store in airtight container for up to 5 days or freeze for up to 1 month.)*

MAKES ABOUT 38 PIECES.

PER PIECE: about 49 cal, 2 g pro, 3 g total fat (2 g sat. fat), 3 g carb, trace fibre, 10 mg chol, 83 mg sodium. % RDI: 5% calcium, 1% iron, 3% vit A, 2% folate.

Anchovy Puff Pastry Straws

Crunchy golden straws make perfect party munchies with a glass of bubbly.

8	anchovy fillets (4 inches/10 cm long)	8
¼ tsp	cayenne pepper	1 mL
1	egg	1
Half	pkg (450 g pkg) frozen butter puff pastry, thawed and cold	Half

• Line large rimless baking sheet with parchment paper; set aside.

• Rinse anchovies and pat dry. In bowl, toss anchovies with cayenne pepper; set aside. In separate small bowl, whisk egg with 1 tbsp (15 mL) water; set aside.

• Unroll pastry onto prepared baking sheet; brush lightly with some of the egg wash. Starting at right side of pastry, arrange anchovies horizontally in rows about ½ inch (1 cm) apart so 1 end touches edge of pastry and anchovies extend to centre of sheet. Fold left half of pastry over to meet right edge of pastry. Press firmly to remove air and seal. Freeze until firm, about 15 minutes.

• Brush pastry with egg wash. Using knife or pizza cutter, trim edges; cut lengthwise into 12 strips and separate to leave some space among strips.

• Bake in centre of 425°F (220°C) oven until golden, about 15 minutes. *(Make-ahead: Store in airtight container for up to 2 days. Recrisp in 425°F/220°C oven for 5 minutes.)*

MAKES 12 PIECES.

PER PIECE: about 86 cal, 2 g pro, 5 g total fat (2 g sat. fat), 7 g carb, 1 g fibre, 25 mg chol, 162 mg sodium. % RDI: 1% calcium, 5% iron, 3% vit A, 1% folate.

> Ornamental Wreath

Easy but elegant, this eye-catching wreath – which showcases about two dozen vintage ornaments – can be used year after year. Fold 78¾-inch (2 m) length of 2¼-inch (56 mm) wide wire-edged satin ribbon in half so ends are even, forming loop. Thread loop through centre of 14-inch (35.5 cm) cylindrical Styrofoam wreath base; slide ends through loop and tighten at top. With glue gun, secure loop to base, then tie ends in bow to make hanging loop and cut notch in each end. Working counterclockwise from top and leaving spaces for vintage ornaments, glue 2-inch (5 cm) diameter ball ornaments (about 75) all over sides, then front, of base (glue balls to each other, as well as to base, to secure); glue on vintage ornaments. To fill spaces between ornaments, glue on 1-inch (2.5 cm) ball ornaments (about 30) and glass beads.

> How to Hang a Wreath

You can decorate your door without making a hole-y mess. Modern doors that thwart burglars and drafts often inhibit wreath hanging, too. Unless you have a wooden door adorned with enough dents and scuffs to hide yet another hole, more cunning tools are needed than a mere hammer and nail.

A windowed door with extensive glazing might seem like a real challenge, but a two-part hanger consisting of an outside knob held against the glass by a strong magnet placed on the inside, such as the

Hanger Knob from Lee Valley, will hold up to three pounds (1.5 kg), so you can simply suspend the wreath from the knob with ribbon.

If you've got a wooden door, hammer a flat-headed metal tack into the top edge (check that the door still opens and closes as usual). As you tap in the tack, punch through one end of a length of wide, festive ribbon (fold the end over to avoid a tear), then tie it in a bow around your wreath.

Peppery Anchovy Puff Pinwheels

Puff pastry canapés are always impressive. With our Quick Puff Pastry (or store-bought already-rolled frozen butter equivalent), the canapés are professional looking and surprisingly easy to make.

	Quick Puff Pastry (recipe, this page)	
FILLING:		
3 tbsp	butter, melted	50 mL
3 tbsp	anchovy paste or minced anchovies	50 mL
¼ cup	each chopped fresh parsley and chives	50 mL
3 tbsp	chopped fresh basil or oregano	50 mL
1 tsp	pepper	5 mL

• Line rimless baking sheet with parchment paper; set aside.
• On lightly floured surface, roll out pastry to two 10-inch (25 cm) squares.
• **FILLING:** Mix butter with anchovy paste; spread over pastry. Sprinkle with parsley, chives, basil and pepper.
• Starting at edge, roll up pastry. With serrated knife, cut into ¼-inch (5 mm) thick slices; arrange, about 1 inch (2.5 cm) apart, on prepared pan.
• Bake in centre of 425°F (220°C) oven until golden, 10 to 15 minutes. Let cool on pan on rack. *(Make-ahead: Store, layered between waxed paper, in airtight container for up to 2 days. Or freeze for up to 2 weeks; reheat frozen in 375°F/190°C oven for 5 to 10 minutes.)*

MAKES ABOUT 48 PIECES.

PER PIECE: about 58 cal, 1 g pro, 5 g total fat (3 g sat. fat), 3 g carb, trace fibre, 13 mg chol, 69 mg sodium. % RDI: 2% iron, 5% vit A, 5% folate.

VARIATION

Smoked Salmon Puff Pinwheels: Omit filling. Blend ⅔ cup (150 mL) cream cheese; ¼ cup (50 mL) finely chopped smoked salmon; 4 tsp (20 mL) chopped fresh dill; and ¼ tsp (1 mL) pepper. Spread over pastry, leaving ½-inch (1 cm) border on all sides.

Quick Puff Pastry

1 cup	cold unsalted butter	250 mL
1⅔ cups	all-purpose flour	400 mL
¾ tsp	salt	4 mL
⅓ cup	cold water	75 mL

• Cut butter into ½-inch (1 cm) cubes; set aside ¾ cup (175 mL) in refrigerator.
• In food processor, blend flour with salt. Sprinkle with remaining butter; pulse until blended, about 10 seconds. Sprinkle with reserved butter; pulse 4 or 5 times to cut into pea-size pieces.
• Pour water evenly over top (not through feed tube). Pulse 6 to 8 times to form loose ragged dough (do not let form ball). Transfer to floured waxed paper; press into rectangle. Dust with flour; top with waxed paper. Roll into 15- x 12-inch (38 x 30 cm) rectangle.
• Remove top paper. Starting at long edge and using bottom paper to lift pastry, fold over one third; fold opposite long edge over top, bringing flush with edge of first fold to make 15- x 4-inch (38 x 10 cm) rectangle. Starting from 1 short end, roll up firmly; flatten into 5-inch (12 cm) square. Wrap and refrigerate until firm, about 1 hour. *(Make-ahead: Refrigerate for up to 5 days or freeze in airtight container for up to 2 weeks.)*

MAKES 1 LB (500 G).

Caramelized Onion Pizza Wedges

Pizza, everybody's favourite food, becomes the perfect party snack when cut into bite-size wedges.

1 lb	pizza dough	500 g
TOPPING:		
4 tsp	extra-virgin olive oil	20 mL
2	Spanish onions, thinly sliced	2
2	sweet red peppers, thinly sliced	2
3	cloves garlic, sliced	3
1 tbsp	dried oregano	15 mL
Pinch	granulated sugar	Pinch
1 tbsp	balsamic or wine vinegar	15 mL
24	oil-cured black olives, pitted and sliced	24
2 tbsp	chopped anchovies (optional)	25 mL
1½ cups	shredded Gruyère or Parmesan cheese	375 mL
¼ cup	chopped fresh parsley	50 mL

• Lightly grease 2 rimmed baking sheets; set aside.

• **TOPPING:** In skillet, heat oil over medium heat; fry onions, red peppers, garlic, oregano and sugar, stirring occasionally, until softened and onions are golden, about 20 minutes. Stir in vinegar. *(Make-ahead: Refrigerate in airtight container for up to 2 days.)*

• Meanwhile, punch down dough; knead gently. Divide in half; roll each into log. Cut each log into 6 pieces; roll each into ball. Cover and let rest for 20 minutes.

• On lightly floured surface, roll out each ball to 5-inch (12 cm) circle; place on prepared pans. Divide onion mixture over top, spreading to edge. Sprinkle with olives, and anchovies (if using); sprinkle with cheese. *(Make-ahead: Cover lightly and refrigerate for up to 1 hour.)*

• Bake in centre of 450°F (230°C) oven until lightly browned, about 15 minutes. Sprinkle with parsley. Cut each into 6 wedges.

MAKES 72 PIECES.

PER PIECE: about 36 cal, 1 g pro, 2 g total fat (1 g sat. fat), 4 g carb, trace fibre, 3 mg chol, 65 mg sodium. % RDI: 3% calcium, 1% iron, 2% vit A, 10% vit C, 2% folate.

VARIATIONS

Porcini Pizza Wedges: Omit topping. Soak 2 pkg (14 g each) dried porcini mushrooms in hot water for 20 minutes. Drain and squeeze, saving liquid for another use. In skillet, heat 1 tsp (5 mL) extra-virgin olive oil over medium heat; fry mushrooms; 2 cloves garlic, minced; and pinch each salt and pepper until dry and slightly crispy, about 5 minutes.

• Spread pizza circles with 2 tbsp (25 mL) basil pesto. Divide mushroom mixture over top. Sprinkle with 1½ cups (375 mL) shredded mozzarella or provolone cheese. Sprinkle baked pizzas with 2 tbsp (25 mL) chopped fresh basil or parsley.

Puttanesca Pizza Wedges: Omit topping. Drain 1 can (28 oz/796 mL) diced tomatoes, saving juice for another use. In skillet, heat 1 tsp (5 mL) extra-virgin olive oil; tomatoes; 1 cup (250 mL) diced eggplant; ½ cup (125 mL) black olives, pitted and quartered; 3 cloves garlic, minced; 1 tbsp (15 mL) capers; 1 tsp (5 mL) dried oregano; and ¼ tsp (1 mL) each salt and pepper. Simmer until juices are evaporated, 5 minutes. Divide among pizzas. Sprinkle with 1½ cups (375 mL) shredded mozzarella cheese.

Mushroom Cheesecakes

The mini individual cheesecake pan is essential for these rounds, but for squares, all you need is an 8-inch (2 L) square metal cake pan. Either as rounds or squares, the cheesecakes are a fine sit-down appetizer course with a drizzle of hazelnut oil and a bed of lightly dressed mixed greens or watercress.

1	pkg (8 oz/250 g) cream cheese, softened	1
1	egg	1
½ tsp	hot pepper sauce	2 mL
¼ tsp	each salt and pepper	1 mL
⅔ cup	sour cream	150 mL

HAZELNUT CRUST:

¼ cup	butter, softened	50 mL
½ cup	all-purpose flour	125 mL
¼ cup	finely chopped hazelnuts	50 mL
¼ tsp	salt	1 mL

MUSHROOM TOPPING:

1 tbsp	butter	15 mL
3 cups	thinly sliced shiitake mushroom caps (8 oz/250 g)	750 mL
1	shallot (or half onion), finely chopped	1
1	clove garlic, minced	1
½ tsp	crumbled dried sage	2 mL
¼ tsp	salt	1 mL
1 tbsp	minced fresh parsley	15 mL
2 tbsp	hazelnut oil (optional)	25 mL

● **HAZELNUT CRUST:** In bowl, beat butter until light; stir in flour, hazelnuts and salt. Press into twelve 4-oz (125 mL) mini-cheesecake cups. Bake in centre of 350°F (180°C) oven until golden, about 10 minutes; let cool on rack.

● In large bowl, beat cream cheese until fluffy. Beat in egg, hot pepper sauce, salt and pepper; beat in sour cream. Pour over each base. Bake in centre of 325°F (160°C) oven until edges are set but centres still jiggle slightly, about 12 minutes.

● Run hot wet knife around sides; let cool on rack. Cover and refrigerate until set, about 2 hours. *(Make-ahead: Refrigerate for up to 2 days.)*

● **MUSHROOM TOPPING:** In large skillet, melt butter over medium-high heat; sauté mushrooms, shallot, garlic, sage and salt until no liquid remains, about 3 minutes. Stir in parsley. *(Make-ahead: Cover and set aside for up to 4 hours.)* Spoon over cheesecakes. Drizzle with hazelnut oil (if using).

MAKES 12 SERVINGS.

PER SERVING: about 180 cal, 4 g pro, 16 g total fat (9 g sat. fat), 7 g carb, 1 g fibre, 59 mg chol, 270 mg sodium. % RDI: 4% calcium, 6% iron, 15% vit A, 2% vit C, 11% folate.

VARIATION

Mushroom Cheesecake Squares: Bake base in parchment paper–lined 8-inch (2 L) square metal cake pan for 18 minutes. Pour filling over cooled base; bake for 35 minutes. Let cool and chill. Cut into squares, wiping knife between cuts.

❯ *A Frosty Fireplace*

Light from pillar candles set on tall white candlesticks washes the creamy walls with a golden glow. More candles – votives held by the curvy, wrought-iron screen – animate the faux fireplace. The mosaic surround uses pieces of vintage china. Symmetrically placed trees, a garland and a wreath stand out against the pale backdrop.

❯ *Cranberry Candles*

Light up the table with a festive centrepiece you can make in minutes. Into an odd number of glass or crystal containers, pour dried or fresh cranberries until each is about one-quarter full. Set votive candle in each, adding a few berries around side.

Mushroom Tenderloin Cubes

Ground dried wild mushrooms intensify the flavour of these beef-and-mushroom bites. Porcini mushrooms are the most flavourful, but dried morel or shiitake mushrooms are also sumptuous.

1¼ lb	beef tenderloin or strip loin grilling steak	625 g
2 tbsp	brandy	25 mL
2 cups	small white mushrooms (about 8 oz/250 g)	500 mL
1	pkg (14 g) dried porcini mushrooms	1
½ tsp	each salt and pepper	2 mL
2 tbsp	butter	25 mL
1 tsp	chopped fresh thyme	5 mL
2 tsp	soy sauce	10 mL
¼ tsp	granulated sugar	1 mL
1 tbsp	chopped fresh chives	15 mL

• Cut beef into 1-inch (2.5 cm) cubes; place in bowl. Mix in half of the brandy; let stand for 10 minutes. Trim stems off white mushrooms; set mushrooms aside.

• In spice grinder, clean coffee grinder or using mortar and pestle, grind porcini mushrooms to fine powder. Transfer to shallow dish; stir in salt and pepper. Drain beef; coat, a few pieces at a time, in porcini mixture.

• In large skillet, melt 1 tbsp (15 mL) of the butter over medium-high heat; sear beef all over, in batches. Transfer to plate. Wipe out pan.

• In same pan, melt remaining butter over medium heat; fry white mushrooms and thyme, stirring, for 3 minutes. Add soy sauce, sugar and remaining brandy; simmer, stirring, until glazed and no liquid remains, about 30 seconds. Let cool.

• For each piece, thread 1 mushroom and 1 beef cube onto toothpick. *(Make-ahead: Place on rimmed baking sheet; cover and refrigerate for up to 8 hours. Bake in 450°F/230°C oven until heated through, about 5 minutes.)* Transfer to warmed serving platter; garnish with chives.

MAKES ABOUT 38 PIECES.

PER PIECE: about 32 cal, 3 g pro, 2 g total fat (1 g sat. fat), 1 g carb, trace fibre, 9 mg chol, 63 mg sodium. % RDI: 4% iron, 1% vit A, 1% folate.

Quick Hors d'Oeuvres

❯ Halve cherry tomatoes, sandwich around small bocconcini balls then thread onto short skewers. Set out a small bowl of balsamic vinegar mixed with extra-virgin olive oil for dipping.

❯ Wrap thin slices of prosciutto around pitted honey dates or dried figs. If desired, grill until prosciutto is crisp.

❯ Cube chicken breasts and toss with prepared honey-garlic sauce. Broil until no longer pink inside. Skewer chicken cube along with cube of pineapple, mango or cantaloupe.

❯ Stuff halved mini-pitas with prepared hummus or baba ghanoush, an eggplant dip. Top with finely diced cucumber and tomato.

❯ Top toasted baguette slices with a slice of Brie cheese and either a slice of strawberry, a slice of fresh fig or a dab of mango chutney. Top with a toasted pecan half.

Sweet-and-Sour Pork Meatballs

Freezing already-sauced meatballs a few days or weeks ahead makes them a convenient appetizer. You can substitute lean ground beef or chicken for the pork.

1	egg	1
¼ cup	dry bread crumbs	50 mL
¼ cup	finely chopped green onions	50 mL
2 tbsp	grated carrot	25 mL
1 tsp	grated gingerroot	5 mL
¼ tsp	each salt and pepper	1 mL
1 lb	lean ground pork	500 g

SWEET-AND-SOUR SAUCE:

1 cup	pineapple juice	250 mL
⅓ cup	ketchup	75 mL
¼ cup	cider vinegar	50 mL
¼ cup	maple syrup	50 mL
1 tbsp	cornstarch	15 mL
1 tbsp	extra-virgin olive oil	15 mL
1	small onion, finely chopped	1
1	clove garlic, minced	1
2 tsp	grated gingerroot	10 mL

● Line large rimmed baking sheet with foil; set aside.

● In large bowl, beat egg; stir in bread crumbs, 2 tbsp (25 mL) of the green onions, carrot, ginger, salt and pepper. Mix in pork. Roll by 1 tbsp (15 mL) into balls; place on prepared pan.

● Bake in centre of 375°F (190°C) oven until digital rapid-read thermometer inserted in centre of several reads 160°F (71°C), about 15 minutes.

● **SWEET-AND-SOUR SAUCE:** Meanwhile, in bowl, whisk together pineapple juice, ketchup, vinegar, maple syrup and cornstarch; set aside.

● In large saucepan, heat oil over medium heat; fry onion, garlic and ginger, stirring often, for 4 minutes. Stir in pineapple juice mixture and bring to boil; reduce heat and simmer, stirring occasionally, until thickened, about 5 minutes.

● Add meatballs, stirring to coat. *(Make-ahead: Transfer to airtight container. Let cool, uncovered, for 30 minutes; refrigerate until cold. Place plastic wrap directly on surface; cover and freeze for up to 2 weeks. Thaw in refrigerator. Add 5 minutes to baking time.)*

● Transfer to ovenproof serving dish. Cover and bake in 350°F (180°C) oven, stirring once, for 25 minutes. Sprinkle with remaining green onions.

MAKES ABOUT 34 PIECES.

PER PIECE: about 52 cal, 3 g pro, 3 g total fat (1 g sat. fat), 4 g carb, trace fibre, 13 mg chol, 64 mg sodium. % RDI: 1% calcium, 2% iron, 2% vit A, 3% vit C, 2% folate.

Rosemary Lemon Lamb Chops

With their very own built-in handles, lamb chops are ideal finger food. Frozen frenched lamb racks are supermarket available. For fresh lamb, ask the butcher to french them, or french them yourself by cutting away the meat at the ends of bones to expose them. Serve with a small bowl of sea salt for sprinkling.

18	frenched rib lamb chops (2 lamb racks or about 2 lb/1 kg)	18

MARINADE:

3 tbsp	extra-virgin olive oil	50 mL
2 tbsp	finely chopped fresh rosemary (or 2 tsp/10 mL crumbled dried)	25 mL
2 tsp	grated lemon rind	10 mL
2 tbsp	lemon juice	25 mL
3	cloves garlic, minced	3
½ tsp	pepper	2 mL
½ tsp	salt	2 mL

● MARINADE: In glass baking dish, whisk together oil, rosemary, lemon rind and juice, garlic and pepper. Add lamb chops, turning to coat. Cover and refrigerate for 2 hours, turning occasionally. *(Make-ahead: Refrigerate for up to 12 hours.)*

● Sprinkle chops with salt; place on broiler pan or foil-lined rimmed baking sheet. Broil, 6 inches (15 cm) from heat and turning once, until medium-rare, 6 to 8 minutes, or until desired doneness.

MAKES 18 PIECES.

PER PIECE: about 105 cal, 6 g pro, 9 g total fat (3 g sat. fat), trace carb, trace fibre, 24 mg chol, 62 mg sodium. % RDI: 1% calcium, 4% iron, 2% vit C, 2% folate.

Party Planner

› Choose the Format

For an informal drop-in evening with friends, serve two or three simple finger foods and easy-pouring soft drinks, wine and beer. At a more formal open house, offer coffee, tea and punch (nonalcoholic and spiked versions) and hors d'oeuvres and cookies without going all-out as you would for a cocktail party. The classic cocktail party format is traditional but flexible enough to reflect the host's personal style. Serve guests lots of finger foods and a range of nonalcoholic and alcoholic drinks, according to the budget.

› Supplies for Large Events

● GLASSES: Prepare enough glasses that each guest can exchange a used one for a clean one at least once.

● ICE: Allow 8 oz (250 g) of ice per person for the first two hours and 1 lb (500 g) per person for a party that will last three or more hours.

● TABLEWARE: You will need about three paper napkins and three small appetizer-size plates per person.

● HANDY GADGETS: Look at party or dollar stores for glass holders that clip onto plates so guests can simultaneously mingle and eat without juggling. Wineglass charms – store-bought or homemade – are handy to help guests keep track of their glasses.

› Plan the Menu

● FOOD SELECTION: Offer foods that match well with the drinks on the menu. Feature a variety of hors d'oeuvres and remember the principle of balance: variations in colour, texture and temperature make for interesting eating.

● THINK SMALL: Serve one or two bite-size items that are easy to eat while balancing a glass in the other hand.

Whether you're hosting a cocktail party or a casual drop-in, here's how to map out the menu and the mood.

- PLAN FOR ALLERGIES: The two most common food allergies people have are to nuts and seafood. If possible, check with guests before planning the menu and warn them about dishes that contain these common allergy triggers.
- DRINKS SELECTION: Serve a variety of nonalcoholic beverages – sparkling waters, juices, pop, eggnog and/or punch. If you're serving wine, choose crowd-pleasing whites, such as Chardonnay or Sauvignon Blanc, and reds, such as Merlot or Cabernet Sauvignon. Stock the bar for made-to-order cocktails or serve pitchers of mixed drinks – guests are usually excited to try a new cocktail, especially if it's just waiting to be poured.

> Set the Mood

- ENCOURAGE MINGLING: Set up food tables and the bar well away from the door. Encourage guests to mix and meet by placing drinks and food at opposite ends of the room or in different rooms.
- CIRCULATE: There are always guests who want to help out, so enlist them to circulate with plates of foods – people involved in conversations will certainly appreciate it. Guests can ask questions about each dish and will sample more if the food comes to them.
- STRIKE UP THE BAND: Music – recorded or live – is an essential part of any party: it sets the tone, provides energy and brings people together. Pick your favourite CDs or ask a friend to play DJ.

> Stir Up Some Drinks

- HOW MUCH: If you are serving primarily wine, plan for at least half a bottle per person. If you're serving wine, beer and Champagne, plan to serve guests one or two glasses each. For cocktails, plan on two per person per hour during the first two hours and one per person per hour for every hour thereafter.

> Serve the Food

- HOW MUCH? For a cocktail party, provide five hors d'oeuvres per person per hour. If you're just whetting guests' appetites before dinner, serve two to five pieces per person.
- START THE PARTY WITH DISHES YOU CAN SERVE STRAIGHT FROM THE FRIDGE: Welcome guests with spreads, dips and crudités, seasoned nuts and hors d'oeuvres that you can arrange hours ahead and that won't go soggy in the fridge.
- AS THE PARTY GETS GOING: Serve hors d'oeuvres that require last-minute arranging. Surround pâtés or terrines with crackers and breads or cut and arrange on crackers, then garnish. Fill pastry cups with savoury fillings and start passing them around.
- WHEN THE PARTY IS ROLLING: Serve piping hot hors d'oeuvres. When choosing hot dishes, read recipes carefully and finish certain components ahead. Then simply heat, reheat or broil the final dishes prior to serving.
- PRESENTATION: Arrange hors d'oeuvres on plates rather than platters. Put out fresh plates as food disappears (or after no more than two hours) and don't refill plates.
- GARNISH: Adorn serving plates with grapes, fresh herbs, cherry tomatoes, cherries, pomegranates, starfruit, blood oranges, melon, kiwifruits or kumquats. If you can find them, geraniums are edible and add a shot of colour.

> Send Guests Off in Style

- OFFER A SWEET GOODBYE: Bid guests adieu beautifully: serve coffee and set out decadent truffles or squares in bonbon cases for them to take home.
- RIDE SAFE: If you serve alcohol, make sure that guests get home safely: send them home with a designated driver or in a cab.

Sumac Chicken Skewers with Lemon Yogurt Sauce

These "waves" of chicken are spiced with sumac, a tart flavouring available in Middle Eastern and specialty markets. You can substitute 1 tsp (5 mL) each lemon rind and paprika.

2 tbsp	extra-virgin olive oil	25 mL
1 tbsp	each ground sumac and chopped fresh parsley	15 mL
2	cloves garlic, minced	2
Pinch	cayenne pepper	Pinch
12 oz	boneless skinless chicken breasts	375 g
¼ tsp	salt	1 mL

LEMON YOGURT SAUCE:

1 cup	Balkan-style plain yogurt	250 mL
1 tbsp	chopped fresh parsley	15 mL
½ tsp	grated lemon rind	2 mL
1 tsp	lemon juice	5 mL
¼ tsp	each salt and pepper	1 mL

• **LEMON YOGURT SAUCE:** Line sieve with double thickness cheesecloth; set over bowl. Spoon in yogurt; cover and let drain in refrigerator for 1 hour to make about ½ cup (125 mL).
• In bowl, whisk together drained yogurt, parsley, lemon rind and juice, salt and pepper. *(Make-ahead: Cover and refrigerate for up to 2 days.)*
• Line rimmed baking sheet with foil; grease foil. Set aside.
• In separate bowl, whisk together oil, sumac, parsley, garlic and cayenne pepper. Cut chicken crosswise into ¼-inch (5 mm) thick strips; add to oil mixture and toss to coat. Thread 1 strip onto each of about twenty 6- or 8-inch (15 or 20 cm) soaked wooden skewers. *(Make-ahead: Cover and refrigerate for up to 4 hours.)*
• Place skewers on prepared pan. Broil, 6 inches (15 cm) from heat, until no longer pink inside, about 5 minutes. Sprinkle with salt. Serve with Lemon Yogurt Sauce.

MAKES 20 PIECES.

PER PIECE: about 44 cal, 4 g pro, 2 g total fat (1 g sat. fat), 1 g carb, 0 g fibre, 12 mg chol, 73 mg sodium. % RDI: 2% calcium, 1% iron, 2% vit A, 2% vit C, 1% folate.

Smoky Wings with Caper Lemon Mayonnaise

These wings are redolent with the fragrance of Spanish smoked paprika. If you prefer them mild, omit the cayenne pepper from both the wings and mayonnaise.

2 tbsp	dry sherry	25 mL
1 tbsp	lemon juice	15 mL
1 tbsp	extra-virgin olive oil	15 mL
2 tsp	smoked or sweet paprika	10 mL
½ tsp	each salt and dried thyme	2 mL
¼ tsp	cayenne pepper	1 mL
2	cloves garlic, minced	2
2 lb	chicken wings, tips removed	1 kg
	Caper Lemon Mayonnaise, recipe follows	

• Line rimmed baking sheet with foil; set aside.
• In large bowl, mix together sherry, lemon juice, oil, paprika, salt, thyme, cayenne and garlic. Add chicken wings; toss to coat well. Cover and marinate in refrigerator for 2 hours. *(Make-ahead: Refrigerate for up to 24 hours.)*

• Arrange wings on rack on prepared pan. Roast in 400°F (200°C) oven for 20 minutes. Turn and roast until juices run clear when chicken is pierced, about 15 minutes. Broil, turning once, until crisp and browned, 1 to 2 minutes per side. Serve with Caper Lemon Mayonnaise.

MAKES 25 TO 30 PIECES.

PER EACH OF 30 PIECES: about 45 cal, 3 g pro, 3 g total fat (1 g sat. fat), 1 g carb, 0 g fibre, 10 mg chol, 68 mg sodium. % RDI: 1% iron, 2% vit A, 2% vit C.

Caper Lemon Mayonnaise

¼ cup	light mayonnaise	50 mL
¼ tsp	grated lemon rind	1 mL
4 tsp	lemon juice	20 mL
2 tsp	chopped capers	10 mL
1	clove garlic, minced	1
¼ tsp	smoked or sweet paprika	1 mL
Pinch	cayenne pepper	Pinch

• In small serving bowl, mix together mayonnaise, lemon rind and juice, capers, garlic, paprika and cayenne.

MAKES ABOUT ⅓ CUP (75 ML).

PER 1 TSP (5 ML): about 12 cal, 0 g pro, 1 g total fat (0 g sat. fat), 1 g carb, 0 g fibre, 1 mg chol, 38 mg sodium. % RDI: 2% vit C.

Smoked Salmon Bites

Garnish with dill sprigs or salmon roe.

7	slices white bread	7
1 tbsp	extra-virgin olive oil	15 mL
26	capers	26
¼ cup	light mayonnaise	50 mL
2 tsp	finely chopped fresh dill (or ½ tsp/2 mL dried)	10 mL
1 tsp	lemon juice	5 mL
¼ tsp	pepper	1 mL
5	thin slices smoked salmon	5
1	piece (3 inches/8 cm) English cucumber	1

• With rolling pin, flatten each slice of bread. Using 2¼-inch (5.5 cm) round cookie cutter, cut out 20 shapes. Lightly brush both sides of each with oil; press each into cup of mini-muffin pan.
• Bake in centre of 350°F (180°C) oven until golden and crisp, about 12 minutes. Remove from pan; let cool on rack. *(Make-ahead: Store in airtight container for up to 5 days or freeze for up to 1 month; recrisp in oven.)*
• Remove 20 capers; set aside. Chop remaining capers; place in bowl. Mix in mayonnaise, dill, lemon juice and pepper.
• Cut salmon into 1½- x ½-inch (4 x 1 cm) strips; roll into rosettes. Quarter cucumber lengthwise; thinly slice crosswise. *(Make-ahead: Cover and refrigerate salmon, cucumber, capers and sauce separately for up to 8 hours.)*
• Spoon ½ tsp (2 mL) mayonnaise mixture into each cup. Tuck in 1 salmon rosette and cucumber slice; garnish with caper.

MAKES ABOUT 20 PIECES.

PER PIECE: about 49 cal, 2 g pro, 2 g total fat (trace sat. fat), 5 g carb, trace fibre, 3 mg chol, 157 mg sodium. % RDI: 1% calcium, 3% iron, 4% folate.

Potted Shrimp

This splendid pâté is so irresistible that you may want to make double. You can set one of the shrimp aside for garnish.

1 lb	large raw shrimp	500 g
½ cup	butter	125 mL
½ cup	chopped shallots	125 mL
2	cloves garlic, chopped	2
½ tsp	salt	2 mL
1	bay leaf	1
1 tbsp	lemon juice	15 mL
1 tbsp	vodka (optional)	15 mL
¼ tsp	prepared horseradish	1 mL
¼ cup	softened cream cheese, cubed	50 mL
1 tbsp	minced fresh chives	15 mL

• Peel and devein shrimp; rinse shells and pat dry. Set aside.

• In large skillet, melt butter over medium heat; fry shells, stirring, until pink, about 4 minutes. Scrape shells and butter into food processor; chop coarsely. Strain through fine sieve into bowl, pressing shells.

• Pour strained butter into large clean skillet. Add shallots, garlic, salt and bay leaf; fry over medium heat, stirring, until shallots are translucent, about 4 minutes. Add shrimp; fry until pink, about 3 minutes. Discard bay leaf.

• In food processor, coarsely chop together shrimp mixture, lemon juice, vodka (if using) and horseradish. Add cream cheese; whirl until incorporated and shrimp are still slightly chunky. Let cool. Scrape into terrine or bowl; smooth top. Cover and refrigerate until firm, about 4 hours. *(Make-ahead: Refrigerate for up to 2 days.)* Garnish with chives.

MAKES ABOUT 1¼ CUPS (300 mL).

PER 1 TBSP (15 mL): about 71 cal, 4 g pro, 6 g total fat (4 g sat. fat), 1 g carb, 0 g fibre, 44 mg chol, 139 mg sodium. % RDI: 1% calcium, 4% iron, 7% vit A, 2% vit C, 1% folate.

To peel shrimp, pull off shells, then cut down back and pull out the vein.

> Ribbon Wreath

Lustrous ribbons tie into a shimmery wreath. For a lush look, plump up each loop in every bow. From scraps of 1½-inch (39 mm) wide wire-edge ribbon, cut about eighty 24-inch (61 cm) lengths; wrap each around 12-inch (30.5 cm) embroidery hoop (or cylindrical Styrofoam wreath base) and tie in bow at front. With sharp scissors, diagonally trim ends.

> Wine Cooler

Chill out – beautifully – with this easy, attractive cooler (fits a standard 750 mL bottle).

• Two days before you need cooler, fill clean 2 L milk or juice carton with water to 1-inch (2.5 cm) depth; freeze overnight. Centre empty 750 mL wine bottle on ice; pour water between carton and bottle to 4- to 6-inch (10 to 15 cm) depth. Set sprigs of leaves, berries or flowers, cut ends down, into water (if desired, leaves can extend above water as shown); freeze overnight.

• Pour warm water into bottle to loosen; pull out. Peel away carton. Set cooler on saucer to catch drips; set full 750 mL wine bottle in cooler.

Sesame Shrimp with Wasabi Sauce

These are delicious hot and crisp from the broiler, but you can prepare the sauce, shrimp and coating ahead. Look for wasabi paste in the Asian section of supermarkets, or buy it in powdered form and mix 4 tsp (20 mL) with 2 tsp (10 mL) water.

½ cup	sesame seeds	125 mL
½ cup	fine fresh bread crumbs	125 mL
¼ tsp	salt	1 mL
2	egg whites	2
1 lb	large raw shrimp (about 30), peeled and deveined (with tails)	500 g
SAUCE:		
½ cup	light mayonnaise	125 mL
2 tsp	wasabi paste	10 mL
1 tbsp	lime juice	15 mL
1 tsp	each finely chopped fresh chives and sesame oil	5 mL

• Grease rimmed baking sheet; set aside.
• SAUCE: In small bowl, stir 1 tbsp (15 mL) of the mayonnaise with wasabi until smooth. Stir in remaining mayonnaise, 1 tbsp (15 mL) at a time. Stir in lime juice, chives and oil. Set aside.
• In shallow dish, stir together sesame seeds, bread crumbs and salt; set aside.
• In separate bowl, beat egg whites until foamy; add shrimp and turn to coat. One at a time, press shrimp into sesame mixture to coat all over; place on prepared pan.
• Broil, 4 inches (10 cm) from heat, until pink and coating is golden, about 2 minutes per side. Serve with sauce.

MAKES ABOUT 30 PIECES.

PER PIECE: about 44 cal, 3 g pro, 3 g total fat (trace sat. fat), 1 g carb, trace fibre, 19 mg chol, 74 mg sodium. % RDI: 1% calcium, 4% iron, 1% vit A, 2% folate.

Prosciutto-Wrapped Scallops

This appetizer is both quick to make and make-ahead. The wrap-in-prosciutto-and-broil theme works as well with shrimp, figs and dates.

4	thin slices prosciutto (about 2 oz/60 g)	4
20	sea scallops (about 12 oz/375 g)	20
2 tbsp	lemon juice	25 mL
2 tbsp	liquid honey	25 mL

• Line rimmed baking sheet with foil; set aside.
• Stack prosciutto slices; cut crosswise into 5 stacks to make 20 strips. Pat scallops dry. Place scallop at 1 end of each strip; roll up to cover side. Skewer with toothpick. *(Make-ahead: Cover and refrigerate for up to 4 hours.)* Place on prepared pan.
• In small bowl, mix lemon juice with honey; brush over roll-ups. Bake in 425°F (220°C) oven until scallops are opaque and prosciutto is crisp, about 10 minutes.

MAKES 20 PIECES.

PER PIECE: about 26 cal, 3 g pro, trace total fat (0 g sat. fat), 2 g carb, 0 g fibre, 7 mg chol, 64 mg sodium. % RDI: 1% iron.

VARIATIONS

Prosciutto Shrimp: Substitute large peeled deveined shrimp for the scallops.
Prosciutto Figs: Omit scallops. Pour boiling water over 20 plump dried fig halves; let stand for 5 minutes. Drain well. Cut off tips. Continue with recipe.
Prosciutto Dates: Omit scallops. Pour boiling water over 20 pitted plump dates; let stand for 5 minutes. Drain well. Continue with recipe.

Oysters on the Half Shell

Oysters signal a celebration and are a wonderful way to whet appetites. Serve them with lemon wedges and hot pepper sauce or with our simple garnishes.

• Plan on at least 3 or 4 oysters for each guest. If you don't want to shuck oysters to order, you can shuck them up to 1 hour before serving. Place in bottom shells on tray of chipped ice (with some seaweed, if available) or coarse salt to hold the shells; cover with plastic wrap and refrigerate.
• Spoon generous ¼ tsp (1 mL) golden Canadian whitefish caviar onto each oyster; top with a few finely shaved rings of green onion. Serve with lemon wedges.

TIPS
❯ Whitefish caviar is available at specialty shops and usually comes in 125 g jars, enough for about 4 dozen oysters.
❯ To chip your own ice, place cubes in strong bag; hit with bottom of heavy pot until crushed.

Two Sauces for Oysters

From the Blue Water Cafe & Raw Bar in Vancouver, these sauces suit lobster and shrimp as well.

Raspberry Mignonette Sauce

2	small shallots, minced	2
½ cup	good-quality raspberry vinegar	125 mL
¼ tsp	each salt and pepper	1 mL

• In small bowl, combine shallots, vinegar, salt and pepper; cover and set aside for up to 24 hours.

MAKES ABOUT ⅔ CUP (150 ML).

PER 1 TBSP (15 ML): about 3 cal, 0 g pro, 0 g total fat (0 g sat. fat), 1 g carb, 0 g fibre, 0 mg chol, 54 mg sodium. % RDI: 1% iron.

Blue Water Cocktail Sauce

½ cup	chopped fresh tomatoes	125 mL
½ cup	drained oil-packed sun-dried tomatoes	125 mL
2 tbsp	prepared horseradish	25 mL
1 tbsp	lemon juice	15 mL
½ tsp	granulated sugar	2 mL
Pinch	each salt and pepper	Pinch
½ cup	vegetable oil	125 mL

• In food processor, purée together fresh and sun-dried tomatoes, horseradish, lemon juice, sugar, salt and pepper. With motor running, slowly drizzle in oil. Scrape into small bowl. *(Make-ahead: Cover and refrigerate for up to 1 week.)*

MAKES 1 CUP (250 ML).

PER 1 TBSP (15 ML): about 70 cal, trace pro, 7 g total fat (1 g sat. fat), 1 g carb, trace fibre, 0 mg chol, 12 mg sodium. % RDI: 1% vit A, 8% vit C, 1% folate.

Pour It On – with Style

Dramatically popping a Champagne cork is both wasteful and potentially dangerous. A slow release of pressure (known as the lover's sigh) prevents wine from gushing out or the cork from popping off in all directions. Here are tips for an elegant pour.

> Serve Champagne and sparkling wine chilled (about 7°C). To chill wine quickly, place in a bucket with equal parts ice and cold water.

> Remove foil and cage while pointing bottle in a safe direction and keeping thumb firmly on the cap.

> Cover cork with a towel. While holding cork in one hand, gently twist bottle until cork eases out, tilting slightly to allow gas pressure to escape out one side with a gentle "poof" or "sigh" (not pop).

> Wrap bottle in a clean napkin when pouring so water or condensation from chilling doesn't drip on the table or into the glass.

> Serve wine in flutes to best admire and retain bubbles, pouring about halfway full.

Roasted Stuffed Jalapeños

Since the seeds and membranes (which hold most of the heat) are removed, these stuffed peppers are not nearly as hot as you might expect.

10	fresh jalapeño peppers (8 oz/250 g)	10
½ cup	shredded Cheddar cheese	125 mL
¼ cup	light cream cheese, softened	50 mL
¼ cup	salsa	50 mL
¾ cup	fresh bread crumbs	175 mL
2 tbsp	chopped fresh parsley	25 mL
2 tbsp	butter, melted	25 mL

• Wearing rubber gloves to protect hands, cut jalapeño peppers in half lengthwise, leaving stems intact. With small knife, scrape out seeds and membranes.

• In bowl, combine Cheddar cheese, cream cheese and salsa; blend in ¼ cup (50 mL) of the bread crumbs. Spoon evenly into each pepper half. Arrange on rimmed baking sheet.

• In small bowl, toss together remaining bread crumbs, parsley and butter; spoon onto each filling. *(Make-ahead: Cover and refrigerate for up to 24 hours.)*

• Bake in 375°F (190°C) oven until topping is golden and crisp, about 20 minutes.

MAKES 20 PIECES.

PER PIECE: about 74 cal, 3 g pro, 4 g total fat (2 g sat. fat), 9 g carb, 1 g fibre, 11 mg chol, 78 mg sodium. % RDI: 4% calcium, 8% iron, 83% vit A, 302% vit C, 8% folate.

Baked Brie with Caramelized Pear

There's no denying the appeal of baked Brie. Serve with sliced baguette, crispbreads or flatbreads.

1	round (8 oz/250 g) Brie cheese	1
1 tbsp	slivered almonds, toasted	15 mL
CARAMELIZED PEAR:		
2 tsp	butter	10 mL
1	shallot, thinly sliced	1
1	pear, peeled, cored and thinly sliced	1
Pinch	each salt and pepper	Pinch
¼ cup	pear or apple juice	50 mL
1 tbsp	brandy or pear juice	15 mL
2 tsp	chopped fresh thyme (or ½ tsp/2 mL dried)	10 mL
1 tsp	packed brown sugar	5 mL

• **CARAMELIZED PEAR:** In small skillet, melt butter over medium heat; fry shallot, pear, salt and pepper until shallot is softened, about 5 minutes.

• Add pear juice, brandy, thyme and sugar; bring to boil. Boil, stirring occasionally, until no liquid remains and pear is softened, 5 minutes. *(Make-ahead: Let cool; refrigerate in airtight container for up to 24 hours.)*

• Place Brie on small heatproof serving plate or in small cake pan; top with pear mixture. Bake in 350°F (180°C) oven until cheese is softened, about 10 minutes. Let stand for 5 minutes. Sprinkle with nuts.

MAKES 8 TO 10 SERVINGS.

PER EACH OF 10 SERVINGS: about 111 cal, 5 g pro, 8 g total fat (5 g sat. fat), 4 g carb, 1 g fibre, 27 mg chol, 166 mg sodium. % RDI: 5% calcium, 2% iron, 6% vit A, 5% vit C, 8% folate.

Gorgonzola and Black Mission Fig Cups

With spectacular flavour and virtually no labour, this hors d'oeuvre was inspired by Nigel Didcock of the Granite Club in Toronto. If Black Mission figs are unavailable, use any other fresh fig.

¾ cup	Gorgonzola cheese, softened (about 6 oz/175 g)	175 mL
2 tbsp	whipping cream	25 mL
2	fresh Black Mission figs	2
1 tbsp	port	15 mL
2 tsp	maple syrup	10 mL
1	pkg (1.4 oz/40 g) 1-inch (2.5 cm) croustade cups	1

• In small bowl, mash Gorgonzola with cream until smooth; set aside.
• Cut figs into 12 wedges each; place in shallow dish. Add port and maple syrup; stir to coat. Let stand for 10 minutes. *(Make-ahead: Cover and refrigerate cheese and figs separately for up to 24 hours; let stand at room temperature for 30 minutes before continuing.)*
• Using spoon or piping bag with large star tip, fill each croustade cup with mounded 1 tsp (5 mL) cheese mixture; top with fig wedge.

MAKES 24 PIECES.

PER PIECE: about 47 cal, 2 g pro, 3 g total fat (2 g sat. fat), 2 g carb, trace fibre, 10 mg chol, 149 mg sodium. % RDI: 5% calcium, 1% iron, 3% vit A, 2% folate.

Fig and Wine Conserve

This glossy spiced conserve is particularly good on a cheese platter, especially one that stars creamy blue cheese and old Cheddar. See Great Canadian Cheese Platter, page 35.

1 lb	dried light-colour figs	500 g
1½ cups	white wine	375 mL
1 cup	granulated sugar	250 mL
2	cinnamon sticks, broken	2
4	cardamom pods, crushed	4
2	whole cloves	2

• Trim tough tips off figs; quarter. In saucepan, bring wine and sugar to boil. Tie cinnamon, cardamom and cloves in cheesecloth; add to syrup along with figs. Reduce heat and simmer until thickened and syrupy and figs are tender, about 25 minutes. *(Make-ahead: Let cool to room temperature; refrigerate in airtight container for up to 2 weeks.)*

MAKES 3 CUPS (375 ML).

PER 1 TBSP (15 ML): about 47 cal, trace pro, trace total fat (0 g sat. fat), 10 g carb, 1 g fibre, 0 mg chol, 1 mg sodium. % RDI: 1% calcium, 1% iron, 2% vit C.

Mini Golden Latkes

Top these mini latkes with sour cream and smoked salmon.

5	large potatoes, peeled (about 2½ lb/1.25 kg)	5
1	onion, quartered	1
1	egg	1
¼ cup	matzo meal or finely crushed unsalted crackers (such as Saltine)	50 mL
¾ tsp	salt	4 mL
¼ tsp	pepper	1 mL
	Vegetable oil for frying	

• By hand or in food processor using shredder blade, grate potatoes alternating with onion.

• In large bowl, whisk together eggs, matzo meal, salt and pepper. Add potatoes and onion; toss to mix.

• Pour enough oil into each of 2 large heavy skillets to come ¼ inch (5 mm) up side; heat over medium-high heat until hot but not smoking. Using 2 tbsp (25 mL) lightly packed potato mixture per latke, add to pan, leaving 1 inch (2.5 cm) between each; flatten slightly. Fry, turning once, until edges are golden and crisp, about 6 minutes. Drain on paper towel–lined racks.

• With sieve, remove any potato pieces from oil and discard. Repeat with remaining latke mixture, heating more oil as necessary. *(Make-ahead: Let cool. Cover and refrigerate on paper towel–lined rimmed baking sheet for up to 8 hours. Recrisp on unlined baking sheets in 450°F/230°C oven for 4 minutes.)*

MAKES ABOUT 36 MINI LATKES.

PER LATKE: about 65 cal, 1 g pro, 5 g total fat (1 g sat. fat), 6 g carb, 1 g fibre, 5 mg chol, 51 mg sodium. % RDI: 1% calcium, 1% iron, 1% vit A, 4% vit C, 2% folate.

Black Olives with Orange and Fennel

The medium-coarse side of a box grater or a zester is ideal for shredding the orange rind.

½ tsp	each coriander and fennel seeds	2 mL
2 tbsp	extra-virgin olive oil	25 mL
2 tsp	coarsely shredded orange rind	10 mL
4 tsp	orange juice	20 mL
¼ tsp	hot pepper flakes	1 mL
1½ cups	oil-cured black olives (8 oz/250 g)	375 mL

• Place coriander and fennel seeds in sturdy plastic bag. Using bottom of pan, lightly crush seeds. In jar, combine seeds, oil, orange rind and juice and hot pepper flakes.

• Add olives; seal and turn upside down a few times to coat. Refrigerate for 24 hours. *(Make-ahead: Refrigerate for up to 1 week, turning jar upside down occasionally.)*

MAKES ABOUT 1½ CUPS (375 ML).

PER 2 TBSP (25 ML): about 79 cal, trace pro, 8 g total fat (1 g sat. fat), 2 g carb, 1 g fibre, 0 mg chol, 556 mg sodium. % RDI: 1% calcium, 2% iron, 2% vit C.

Port and Peppercorn Pâté

Decorated with a colourful mixed peppercorn crust, this pâté looks festive. It is lighter than most traditional pâtés since some of the butter is replaced by light cream cheese.

1 tbsp	butter	15 mL
1	onion, chopped	1
2	cloves garlic, minced	2
¼ tsp	dried thyme	1 mL
1 lb	chicken livers, halved and trimmed	500 g
¼ cup	port or brandy	50 mL
¼ cup	light cream cheese	50 mL
½ tsp	dry mustard	2 mL
¼ tsp	each ground cloves, allspice, salt and pepper	1 mL
1 tbsp	mixed peppercorns, coarsely cracked	15 mL
1 tbsp	finely chopped fresh parsley	15 mL

• In skillet, melt butter over medium heat; fry onion, garlic and thyme, stirring often, until softened, about 3 minutes.
• Add chicken livers; fry, stirring often, just until slightly pink inside, about 8 minutes. Remove from heat; let cool for 5 minutes.
• In food processor, purée together liver mixture, port, cheese, mustard, cloves, allspice, salt and pepper until smooth. Scrape into bowl. Place plastic wrap directly on surface; refrigerate until firm, 4 hours. *(Make-ahead: Refrigerate for up to 24 hours.)* Sprinkle with peppercorns and parsley.

MAKES 2 CUPS (500 ML).

PER 1 TBSP (15 ML): about 29 cal, 3 g pro, 1 g total fat (1 g sat. fat), 1 g carb, 0 g fibre, 68 mg chol, 34 mg sodium. % RDI: 1% calcium, 7% iron, 52% vit A, 3% vit C, 37% folate.

Smoked Salmon Spread

This is tasty on baguette slices, endive spears or cucumber squares.

6 oz	smoked salmon	175 g
1	stalk celery heart	1
½ cup	each light sour cream and light mayonnaise	125 mL
3 tbsp	finely chopped fresh chives or green onions	50 mL
1 tbsp	minced fresh dill (or ½ tsp/2 mL dried dillweed)	15 mL
½ tsp	finely grated lemon rind	2 mL
1 tsp	lemon juice	5 mL
Pinch	salt	Pinch
Dash	hot pepper sauce	Dash

• Finely chop salmon and celery; place in serving bowl. Stir in sour cream, mayonnaise, chives, dill, lemon rind and juice, salt and hot pepper sauce. *(Make-ahead: Cover and refrigerate for up to 2 days.)*

MAKES ABOUT 2 CUPS (500 ML).

PER 1 TBSP (15 ML): about 22 cal, 1 g pro, 2 g total fat (trace sat. fat), 1 g carb, 0 g fibre, 3 mg chol, 73 mg sodium. % RDI: 1% calcium, 1% iron, 1% vit A.

TIP

❯ To make cucumber squares, cut English cucumber in half crosswise. Trim off narrow end. Cut off 4 sides, leaving green tip at each corner. Cut into ¼-inch (5 mm) thick slices.

> *Magical Mantelscapes*

Transform a simple mantel into a trio of dazzling
displays using fragrant greenery, family heirlooms,
holiday-best accessories and favourite ornaments.

Traditional

• Symmetry creates a balanced, uncluttered
look. Centre the main element, then work
out to each end, mirroring the objects on
either side.
• Give life to your creation with sprays of
greenery or fresh flowers. You can change
the look with the seasons, using spring
flowers, seashells and colourful gourds.

Filling the room with the heady scent of
Christmas are all things fresh and fragrant
in this stunning mantelscape of evergreens,
seeded eucalyptus and plump white roses.
The tiny bouquet of roses is simply arranged
in a shimmery silver rosebud vase. Single
buds rest in a pair of antique silver nosegay
cones tucked beneath the boughs. Silver
candle spheres that look like gazing balls
and silver reindeer candlesticks make it all
shine with holiday cheer.

> **Don't have a fireplace?
Decorate a table, sideboard
or windowsill with one
of these fabulously festive
arrangements.**

Vintage

• Layering allows you to display more objects, but group similar styles or colours together to avoid a cluttered look. Vary the heights by setting objects on stacked books.
• Arrange tall, large items – such as mirrors, trays and candlesticks – along the back or against the wall.

Start with a backdrop of antique mirrors in ornately carved frames, set against a soft mocha brown wall. Aged red leather–bound books, brilliant teal antique glass Christmas balls and 1930s-style snowy white bottle-brush trees create a wintry scene. A pair of exquisitely attired German Belsnickles Santas cheerfully lends a delightful touch of nostalgia and tradition.

Contemporary

• Leave space between objects or small groups of objects for more impact.
• Keep it simple. Clear glass and mirrored objects make a dramatic statement that sparkles against the rich, red background.

Tweak an existing mantelscape by adding just a touch of seasonal glitz. Here, an unassuming glazed bowl brimming with miniature pinecones and pomegranates is made to shine with the addition of uniquely shaped silver and black ornaments set in three tall, slender glass candlesticks. A chunkier pair at either end lends flickers of light to this elegant holiday look.

Herbed Crab Dip

Serve this make-ahead dip with cracker bread, Belgium endive leaves, radishes and blanched cauliflower and broccoli florets. To blanch, immerse the vegetables in boiling salted water for 30 seconds; drain and chill in cold water. Immediately drain well.

1	pkg (7 oz/200 g) frozen crabmeat, thawed	1
2 tbsp	extra-virgin olive oil	25 mL
¼ cup	minced shallots or onion	50 mL
4	cloves garlic, minced	4
½ tsp	salt	2 mL
¼ tsp	pepper	1 mL
¼ tsp	mace or nutmeg	1 mL
⅓ cup	dry white wine or dry white vermouth	75 mL
1 tbsp	lemon juice	15 mL
½ tsp	crumbled dried tarragon	2 mL
¾ cup	light cream cheese, cubed and softened	175 mL
¼ cup	light sour cream	50 mL
¼ cup	each minced fresh parsley and chives	50 mL
¼ cup	diced roasted or fresh sweet red pepper	50 mL

• Place crab in sieve; pick through and remove any cartilage. Gently squeeze out moisture; set aside.

• In small skillet, heat oil over medium-low heat; fry shallots, garlic, salt, pepper and mace, without browning, until softened and fragrant, about 4 minutes.

• Add wine, lemon juice and tarragon; boil over medium heat until reduced by half, about 3 minutes. Let cool.

• In bowl and using fork, blend cream cheese with sour cream. Add shallot mixture, crabmeat, parsley, chives and red pepper; mix well. Scrape into serving dish. *(Make-ahead: Cover and refrigerate for up to 2 days.)*

MAKES 2 CUPS (500 ML).

PER 1 TBSP (15 ML): about 30 cal, 2 g pro, 2 g total fat (1 g sat. fat), 1 g carb, 0 g fibre, 6 mg chol, 120 mg sodium. % RDI: 1% calcium, 1% iron, 2% vit A, 5% vit C, 1% folate.

VARIATION

Herbed Smoked Salmon Dip: Omit salt. Use 8 oz (250 g) smoked salmon, finely chopped, instead of crabmeat.

Shropshire Walnut Spread on Belgian Endive Spears

Though you could also mound this nutty spread onto toasted raisin bread or into celery stalks, endive is glamorous and adds a pleasant edge of bitterness. If you can't find Shropshire, use 1/4 cup (50 mL) each crumbled blue cheese and cold-pack Cheddar (such as MacLaren's Imperial).

½ cup	chopped walnut halves	125 mL
½ cup	crumbled Shropshire blue cheese	125 mL
Half	pkg (8 oz/250 g pkg) cream cheese, softened	Half
2 tbsp	tawny or white (not ruby) port or 10% cream	25 mL
¼ tsp	pepper	1 mL
¼ cup	finely chopped fresh chives	50 mL
2	large Belgian endives	2

• On rimmed baking sheet, bake walnuts in 350°F (180°C) oven until lightly toasted, about 6 minutes. Let cool.
• In food processor, blend Shropshire and cream cheeses, port and pepper until smooth; scrape into bowl. Stir in ⅓ cup (75 mL) of the walnuts and 3 tbsp (50 mL) of the chives. *(Make-ahead: Cover and refrigerate for up to 24 hours.)*
• Slice about 1 inch (2.5 cm) from root ends of Belgian endives; separate leaves. Mound heaping 1 tbsp (15 mL) cheese mixture on each leaf; sprinkle with remaining walnuts and chives.

MAKES ABOUT 24 PIECES.

PER PIECE: about 47 cal, 1 g pro, 4 g total fat (2 g sat. fat), 1 g carb, trace fibre, 8 mg chol, 55 mg sodium. % RDI: 2% calcium, 1% iron, 3% vit A, 3% folate.

Roasted Carrot Dip

This colourful dip highlights the most ordinary ingredient you're sure to have in the crisper. The secret to the dip's unique rich flavour is roasting the carrots. Serve with seeded lavash or toasted pita chips.

10	carrots, peeled (1½ lb/750 g)	10
4	cloves garlic	4
2 tbsp	vegetable oil	25 mL
½ cup	light mayonnaise	125 mL
¼ cup	light sour cream	50 mL
2 tsp	wine vinegar	10 mL
Pinch	each granulated sugar, salt and pepper	Pinch

• Slice carrots lengthwise into ½-inch (1 cm) thick widths. In large bowl, toss together carrots, garlic and oil. Spread on rimmed baking sheet; roast in bottom third of 425°F (220°C) oven for 20 minutes. Remove garlic and set aside.
• Turn carrots; roast until tender, about 20 minutes longer.
• In food processor, purée carrots with garlic until smooth. Add mayonnaise, ¼ cup (50 mL) water, sour cream, vinegar, sugar, salt and pepper; pulse to blend. Transfer to serving dish. *(Make-ahead: Cover and refrigerate for up to 24 hours.)*

MAKES 2 CUPS (500 ML).

PER 1 TBSP (15 ML): about 30 cal, trace pro, 2 g total fat (trace sat. fat), 3 g carb, 1 g fibre, 0 mg chol, 39 mg sodium. % RDI: 1% calcium, 1% iron, 48% vit A, 2% vit C, 1% folate.

Deli Meat Platter

Whether for snacks at a cocktail party or a filling for sandwiches, this combination of meats offers a taste for everyone. As a rule of thumb, offer 2 oz (60 g) meat per person for a snacking platter or 4 oz (125 g) per person for a sandwich-building platter. Serve with grainy Dijon or a sweet mustard.

6 oz	thinly sliced prosciutto	175 g
1 lb	thinly sliced roast beef	500 g
6 oz	thinly sliced smoked turkey	175 g
6 oz	thinly sliced salami	175 g
Half	cantaloupe, seeded	Half
4	figs	4
1 cup	black and green olives	250 mL
½ cup	pickled onions	125 mL

• Scrunch prosciutto slices and arrange in centre of platter. Arrange beef, turkey and salami, fanning slices slightly, around prosciutto. *(Make-ahead: Cover with plastic wrap; refrigerate for up to 8 hours.)*
• Peel cantaloupe and cut into ¾-inch (2 cm) thick wedges; nestle among prosciutto. Cut figs into quarters. Scatter attractively around platter along with olives and onions.

MAKES ABOUT 18 APPETIZERS.

PER SERVING: about 102 cal, 10 g pro, 5 g total fat (2 g sat. fat), 5 g carb, 1 g fibre, 24 mg chol, 508 mg sodium. % RDI: 2% calcium, 7% iron, 6 vit A, 12 vit C, 3 folate.

Great Canadian Cheese Platter

Canada produces excellent cheese from coast to coast. Though some are from large, high-quality factories, there are many small-scale cheese makers perfecting artisanal cheeses.

❯ Specialty cheeses are best eaten shortly after purchase. Cheese needs air, so if you must store it, wrap it in paper or the original wrapping – not plastic wrap – or place in a sealed plastic bag with plenty of air in it.

❯ As a rule, buy 1 to 1½ oz (30 to 45 g) of each type of cheese you're serving per person. Here's a guideline to the perfect platter:
   • SOFT OR SEMISOFT CHEESE (such as Brie, Camembert or Oka)
   • FIRM OR HARD CHEESE (such as old Cheddar or Gouda). Or flavoured cheese (such as Gouda with cumin seeds or Verdelait with cracked pepper)
   • BLUE CHEESE (such as Bleu Bénédictin, Borgonzola, Bleubry or le Ciel de Charlevoix)
   • GOAT CHEESE

❯ At least 1 hour before serving, arrange cheeses on platter. Supply knife for each cheese and add a bowl of Fig and Wine Conserve (recipe, page 27), fresh grapes and nuts.

Vanilla Eggnog

Think of this fireside favourite as a smooth alternative to dessert. If you don't have a vanilla bean, add 1 tsp (5 mL) vanilla to the cooled eggnog instead. If you like, sprinkle with 1 tsp (5 mL) grated nutmeg instead of the chocolate.

1	vanilla bean	1
2 cups	10% cream	500 mL
½ cup	granulated sugar	125 mL
6	egg yolks	6
2¾ cups	milk	675 mL
TOPPINGS:		
1 cup	whipping cream	250 mL
¼ cup	grated milk or bittersweet chocolate	50 mL

• Split vanilla bean in half lengthwise. In large saucepan, heat vanilla bean, 10% cream and sugar over medium heat, stirring occasionally, until steaming and sugar is dissolved. Remove vanilla bean.

• Using tip of knife, scrape out seeds and set aside. Reserve pod for another use, such as flavouring sugar.

• In bowl, whisk egg yolks until light. Whisk in 1 cup (250 mL) of the hot cream mixture; pour back into pan. Cook over medium-low heat, whisking constantly, until thick enough to coat back of spoon, 5 to 7 minutes.

• Strain into clean bowl; whisk in milk and reserved vanilla seeds. Let cool, whisking occasionally, for 10 minutes. Place plastic wrap directly on surface; refrigerate until cold, about 2 hours. *(Make-ahead: Refrigerate for up to 2 days.)*

• TOPPINGS: Whip cream. Pour eggnog into chilled punch bowl or glasses. Top with whipped cream and chocolate.

MAKES 12 TO 16 SERVINGS.

PER EACH OF 16 SERVINGS: about 157 cal, 4 g pro, 11 g total fat (6 g sat. fat), 11 g carb, 0 g fibre, 108 mg chol, 42 mg sodium. % RDI: 9% calcium, 2% iron, 13% vit A, 6% folate.

VARIATIONS

White Chocolate Vanilla Eggnog: Reduce milk to 2 cups (500 mL); add ¾ cup (175 mL) white chocolate liqueur, such as Godet.

Irish Cream Vanilla Eggnog: Reduce milk to 2 cups (500 mL); add 1 cup (250 mL) Irish cream liqueur.

Coffee Vanilla Eggnog: Reduce milk to 2 cups (500 mL); add ¾ cup (175 mL) coffee-flavoured liqueur or strong brewed coffee. Garnish with chocolate-covered espresso beans.

Orange Vanilla Eggnog: Stir in 2 tbsp (25 mL) orange juice concentrate, or reduce milk to 2 cups (500 mL) and add ¾ cup (175 mL) orange-flavoured liqueur.

White Cranberry Mulled Wine

Grocery stores offer two kinds of cranberry cocktail: white, made from berries when only a blush of pink colours them, and red, made from fully ripe, ruby-red berries.

4	cardamom pods	4
4 cups	white cranberry cocktail	1 L
1	bottle (750 mL) white wine	1
6	whole allspice or cloves	6
2	sticks (each 3 inches/ 8 cm) cinnamon	2
1	strip (2 inches/5 cm long) lemon rind	1
2 tbsp	granulated sugar (approx)	25 mL

• Using side of large knife, gently press cardamom pods just until pods crack.
• In large saucepan, combine cranberry cocktail, wine, allspice, cinnamon, lemon rind, 2 tbsp (25 mL) of the sugar and the cardamom; cover and warm over medium-low heat until steaming and spices are infused, about 30 minutes. Add more sugar if desired. Strain into warmed mugs.

MAKES 8 SERVINGS.

PER SERVING: about 105 cal, 0 g pro, 0 g total fat (0 g sat. fat), 21 g carb, 0 g fibre, 0 mg chol, 8 mg sodium. % RDI: 1% calcium, 3% iron, 43% vit C.

VARIATION

Red Cranberry Mulled Wine: Replace white wine with red wine and white cranberry cocktail with red cranberry cocktail. Add 1 strip (2 inches/5 cm long) orange rind along with lemon rind.

Mulled Apple Cider

Snuggle up with this cosy nonalcoholic holiday treat on a cold day. Serve each mug with a cinnamon stick for stirring.

8 cups	apple cider	2 L
1	red-skinned apple, sliced	1
3	sticks cinnamon	3
6	whole cloves	6
1	strip (2 inches/5 cm) orange rind	1

• In saucepan, combine apple cider, apple, cinnamon, cloves and orange rind. Heat over medium-low heat until steaming; reduce heat to low and simmer until spices are infused, about 30 minutes.
• Strain into warmed mugs.

MAKES 8 SERVINGS.

PER SERVING: about 124 cal, trace pro, 0 g total fat (0 g sat. fat), 34 g carb, 0 g fibre, 0 mg chol, 7 mg sodium. % RDI: 1% calcium, 9% iron, 3% vit C.

Champagne Cocktail

Make this time-tested classy aperitif with any dry sparkling wine.

¼ cup	brandy	50 mL
2 tsp	granulated sugar	10 mL
¼ tsp	bitters	1 mL
1	orange, thinly sliced	1
1	bottle (750 mL) Champagne or other dry white sparkling wine, chilled	1

• In pitcher, stir together brandy, sugar and bitters. Add orange slices; pour in Champagne.

MAKES 6 SERVINGS.

PER SERVING: about 122 cal, trace pro, 0 g total fat (0 g sat. fat), 5 g carb, trace fibre, 0 mg chol, 6 mg sodium. % RDI: 2% calcium, 3% iron, 1% vit A, 20% vit C, 3% folate.

Classic Dry Martini

This is the popular dry version, but for the original martini, double the vermouth. If guests choose just cocktail onions for the garnish, they will have the classic Gibson.

2 cups	gin or vodka	500 mL
¼ cup	dry white vermouth	50 mL
	Green olives, lemon rind strips and/or cocktail onions	

• In pitcher, stir gin with vermouth. Top with ice; stir until well chilled.
• Set out bowls of olives, lemon rind strips and onions for guests to spear on cocktail picks and place in glasses. Strain martini into glasses.

MAKES 8 SERVINGS.

PER SERVING: about 138 cal, 0 g pro, 0 g total fat (0 g sat. fat), trace carb, 0 g fibre, 0 mg chol, 2 mg sodium.

TIP

❯ To make the Champagne Cocktail, the Classic Dry Martini and the Cosmopolitan ahead, mix ingredients up to the point of adding any sparkling liquid or ice; just cover and refrigerate and add those ingredients just before serving.

Cosmopolitan

This rosy cocktail has taken North America by storm over the last few years.

1½ cups	vodka	375 mL
½ cup	pure cranberry juice	125 mL
¼ cup	orange-flavoured liqueur	50 mL
2 tbsp	lime juice	25 mL
24	frozen cranberries	24
8	green maraschino cherries or lime wedges	8

• In pitcher, stir together vodka, cranberry juice, orange liqueur and lime juice. Top with ice; stir until well chilled.
• Strain into glasses garnished with 3 cranberries each and cherry or lime wedge.

MAKES 8 SERVINGS.

PER SERVING: about 144 cal, trace pro, trace total fat (0 g sat. fat), 8 g carb, trace fibre, 0 mg chol, 1 mg sodium. % RDI: 1% iron, 5% vit C.

White Cranberry Raspberry Punch

This makes a festive, colourful drink for any holiday buffet or open house.

4 cups	cold white cranberry cocktail	1 L
2	bottles (each 750 mL) chilled sparkling white wine or soda water	2
1	can (355 mL) frozen raspberry cocktail concentrate	1

• In punch bowl, stir together cranberry cocktail, wine and raspberry cocktail.

MAKES 12 CUPS (3 L), OR 16 SERVINGS.

PER SERVING: about 143 cal, trace pro, trace total fat (0 g sat. fat), 21 g carb, 0 g fibre, 0 mg chol, 6 mg sodium. % RDI: 1% calcium, 3% iron, 38 vit C, 1% folate.

No Thanks

A gracious host does not push drinks on a guest or press for refills. Remember that as host, you should ensure that guests do not drive if they have had too much to drink. Always have a selection of nonalcoholic alternatives available.

Chapter Two

CELEBRATION
MENUS

A Memorable Christmas Dinner for 12

There are two secrets for a gracious Christmas dinner. The first, invite family to share in the preparation to the make-ahead stages in these recipes. The hosting family can deal with the turkey, while others bring starters, side dishes or dessert. The second secret is to teach an eager person how to carve the turkey, then assign that job permanently. So while the last-minute gravy, vegetables and stuffing fandango plays out on the stove and in the microwave and oven, the turkey is in safe hands.

....

- **Roasted Pears and Greens with Pear Vinaigrette**

- **Sage Butter Turkey with Shallot Sausage Stuffing**

- **Clementine Cranberry Sauce** (recipe, page 219)

- **Sweet Potato Strudel with Balsamic Mushroom Sauce**

- **Make-Ahead Mashed Potatoes**

- **Turnip and Apple Bake**

- **Steamed Sugar Snap Peas** (recipe not included)

- **Ice-Cream Christmas Pudding** (recipe, page 121) **or** **Plum and Carrot Pudding** (recipe, page 114)

....

Roasted Pears and Greens with Pear Vinaigrette

This salad is lovely with a small wedge of blue cheese or aged Gouda on each plate.

9	small ripe pears	9
⅓ cup	vegetable oil	75 mL
3 tbsp	packed light brown sugar	50 mL
3 tbsp	lemon juice	50 mL
12 cups	torn mixed salad greens	3 L
6 cups	torn radicchio	1.5 L
¾ cup	roasted almonds, coarsely chopped	175 mL
PEAR VINAIGRETTE:		
⅓ cup	pear or cider vinegar	75 mL
¼ cup	vegetable oil	50 mL
4 tsp	minced shallots	20 mL
¼ tsp	each salt and pepper	1 mL

• Peel and halve pears; core, if desired. Place, cut side up, in 13- x 9-inch (3 L) glass baking dish. In small bowl, whisk together oil, sugar and lemon juice; brush all over pears. Roast in 425°F (220°C) oven, basting once, until caramelized and tender, about 40 minutes. Let cool in pan.

• **PEAR VINAIGRETTE:** Transfer 1 tsp (5 mL) of the pan juices to glass measuring cup; whisk in vinegar, oil, shallots, salt and pepper. *(Make-ahead: Cover and refrigerate pears and vinaigrette separately for up to 2 days. Let pears come to room temperature.)*

• In large bowl, toss together salad greens, radicchio and vinaigrette; divide among plates. Top with pears; sprinkle with chopped almonds.

MAKES 12 SERVINGS.

PER SERVING: about 176 cal, 3 g pro, 11 g total fat (1 g sat. fat), 20 g carb, 5 g fibre, 0 mg chol, 20 mg sodium. % RDI: 6% calcium, 7% iron, 12% vit A, 22% vit C, 30% folate.

Christmas Dinner Countdown

Up to a week ahead

❯ Check that dishes, glasses, cutlery, linens and serving items are sufficient for the crowd. Make sure you have the necessary pots, pans and other equipment.

❯ Make Clementine Cranberry Sauce.

❯ Make Ice-Cream Christmas Pudding and Chocolate Orange Sauce.

❯ Leave enough time for turkey to thaw: in refrigerator, 5 hours per pound (10 hours per kilogram); or covered well in cold water, 1 hour per pound (2 hours per kilogram), changing water every hour.

Two days before

❯ Prepare pears and vinaigrette for salad.

❯ Make potato and turnip dishes.

❯ Simmer turkey stock, if desired.

One day before

❯ Prepare stuffing and butter for turkey.

❯ Assemble strudel and make sauce.

❯ Trim ends and strings from sugar snap peas (4 to 6 per person), wrap in towels to store in plastic bag in crisper.

Christmas Day

❯ Stuff turkey and roast.

❯ Forty-five minutes before sitting down:
  • Arrange salad.
  • Add peas to steamer insert; cover.

❯ When turkey comes out of oven:
  • Pop strudel and extra stuffing into oven.
  • Make gravy.
  • Serve salads.

❯ Finishing touches:
  • Reheat sauce for strudel.
  • Remove stuffing to warm bowl and cover. Carve turkey.
  • Heat potatoes and turnip in microwave.
  • Steam peas; toss with butter, salt and pepper.

Sage Butter Turkey with Shallot Sausage Stuffing

For the traditionalist, see the variation, Old-Fashioned Sage Stuffing.

1	turkey (about 16 lb/7.2 kg)	1
½ tsp	each salt, pepper and crumbled dried sage	2 mL
STUFFING:		
2 tbsp	extra-virgin olive oil	25 mL
2 cups	quartered shallots	500 mL
1	stalk celery, chopped	1
2	cloves garlic, minced	2
1 tbsp	each chopped fresh sage and thyme (or 1 tsp/5 mL dried)	15 mL
½ tsp	each salt and pepper	2 mL
4	mild Italian sausages (about 1 lb/500 g)	4
12 cups	cubed day-old Italian or French bread	3 L
¼ cup	chopped fresh parsley	50 mL
1¼ cups	sodium-reduced chicken stock or Turkey Stock (recipe, page 44)	300 mL
SAGE BUTTER:		
⅓ cup	butter, softened	75 mL
4	cloves garlic, minced	4
1	shallot, finely chopped	1
1 tbsp	each grated lemon rind and crumbled dried sage	15 mL
½ tsp	each salt and pepper	2 mL
GRAVY:		
⅓ cup	all-purpose flour	75 mL
2 cups	sodium-reduced chicken stock or Turkey Stock (recipe, page 44)	500 mL
1 tbsp	wine vinegar	15 mL

• STUFFING: In large skillet, heat oil over medium-high heat; fry shallots, stirring occasionally, until deep golden, 10 minutes.
• Add celery, garlic, sage, thyme, salt and pepper; fry until celery is softened, about 3 minutes. Transfer to large bowl.
• Remove sausages from casings. In same skillet, fry sausages over medium-high heat, breaking up with fork, until browned, about 5 minutes. Drain off fat. Add to shallot mixture along with bread and parsley. Drizzle with stock; toss to combine. Let cool.
• SAGE BUTTER: In small bowl, mix together butter, garlic, shallot, lemon rind, sage, salt and pepper; set aside. *(Make-ahead: Cover and refrigerate stuffing and butter separately for up to 24 hours.)*
• Remove giblets and neck from turkey; reserve for stock, if desired. Pat turkey dry inside and out. Easing fingers under skin, carefully loosen skin over breasts and thighs. Spread half of the sage butter under skin, massaging to cover breasts and thighs.
• Loosely stuff neck and body cavities with about 6 cups (1.5 L) of the stuffing. Skewer cavities shut. Tie legs together; tuck wings under back. Place on rack in roasting pan. Spread remaining sage butter over skin. Sprinkle with salt, pepper and thyme. Place remaining stuffing in greased 11- x 7-inch (2 L) glass baking dish; cover and refrigerate.
• Tent turkey with foil, tucking in sides but leaving ends open. Roast in 325°F (160°C) oven for 3 hours. Uncover and roast until meat thermometer inserted into thickest part of thigh registers 185°F (85°C), 1 to 1½ hours. Transfer to carving board and tent with foil; let stand for 20 to 30 minutes before carving.
• Meanwhile, increase heat to 400°F (200°C). Bake stuffing in dish for 20 minutes; uncover and bake until top is crisp, about 10 minutes.

• GRAVY: Meanwhile, skim fat from pan juices. Whisk in flour; cook, stirring, over medium heat for 1 minute. Whisk in stock and vinegar; bring to boil, stirring and scraping up brown bits from bottom of pan. Reduce heat and simmer, stirring often, until thickened, about 8 minutes; strain. Serve with turkey and stuffing.

MAKES 12 TO 16 SERVINGS.

PER EACH OF 16 SERVING: about 595 cal, 67 g pro, 26 g total fat (9 g sat. fat), 19 g carb, 1 g fibre, 183 mg chol, 892 mg sodium. % RDI: 9% calcium, 38% iron, 7% vit A, 5% vit C, 24% folate.

VARIATION
Old-Fashioned Sage Stuffing:

¾ cup	butter	175 mL
2½ cups	chopped onions	625 mL
1 cup	each chopped celery and fennel (or 2 cups/ 500 mL celery)	250 mL
4 tsp	dried sage	20 mL
1 tsp	each salt, dried savory, marjoram and pepper	5 mL
½ tsp	dried thyme	2 mL
14 cups	cubed white bread	3.5 L
1 cup	chopped fresh parsley	250 mL

• In skillet, melt butter over medium heat; fry onions, celery, fennel, sage, salt, savory, marjoram, pepper and thyme until tender, 10 to 12 minutes. Transfer to bowl. Toss with bread and parsley.

MAKES ABOUT 14 CUPS (3.5 L).

Secrets to Perfect Gravy

Perfect gravy starts with good stock. While you can use purchased chicken stock, making your own with the turkey neck and giblets promotes a waste-not approach to Christmas dinner — and tastes grand. Freeze any leftover for soups later in the season.

Turkey Stock

1	each turkey neck, gizzard and heart	1
2	onions (unpeeled), quartered	2
2	stalks celery with leaves, chopped	2
2	carrots, chopped	2
2	cloves garlic	2
6	sprigs fresh parsley	6
3	stalks fresh thyme (or ½ tsp/2 mL dried)	3
2	bay leaves	2
1 tsp	each salt and peppercorns	5 mL

• Chop turkey neck into 6 pieces; cut gizzard and heart in half. In saucepan, bring 12 cups (3 L) cold water, neck, gizzard and heart to boil; skim off foam.
• Add onions, celery, carrots, garlic, parsley, thyme, bay leaves, salt and peppercorns; cover and simmer over low heat for 2 hours. Strain into container. *(Make-ahead: Let cool; refrigerate for up to 2 days or freeze for up to 1 month.)*

MAKES ABOUT 8 CUPS (2 L).

PER 1 CUP (250 mL): about 39 cal, 5 g pro, 1 g total fat (trace sat. fat), 1 g carb, 0 g fibre, 1 mg chol, 318 mg sodium. % RDI: 1% calcium, 4% iron, 2% folate.

Perfect Gravy

½ cup	all-purpose flour	125 mL
½ tsp	each salt and pepper	2 mL
6 cups	Turkey Stock (recipe, this page) or chicken stock	1.5 L

• Skim fat from pan juices in turkey roasting pan. Whisk flour, salt and pepper into juices; cook over medium-high heat, stirring and scraping up brown bits, for 1 minute.
• Gradually whisk in stock and bring to boil; reduce heat and simmer, stirring, until thickened, about 5 minutes. Strain through fine sieve.

MAKES 8 CUPS (2 L).

PER ½ CUP (125 mL): about 65 cal, 3 g pro, 4 g total fat (1 g sat. fat), 3 g carb, trace fibre, 10 mg chol, 242 mg sodium. % RDI: 4% iron, 1% vit A, 5% folate.

Flavourings

❯ Replace 1 cup (250 mL) stock with 1 cup (250 mL) red wine. Or add a splash of bourbon or rye.
❯ Whisk in 2 tbsp (25 mL) jelly, such as red currant, apple or sweet red pepper.
❯ Stir in 2 tbsp (25 mL) minced fresh parsley.

Lump-Free Gravy

❯ It is important to gradually whisk stock into pan.
❯ Whisk constantly with flat whisk.
❯ Strain gravy through fine sieve into large measuring cup. No one will ever know if there were lumps — and you can reheat the gravy in the microwave to refill the gravy boat as needed.

❯ *Holiday Tablescapes*

Casual

Classic and cheerful, Christmas candy canes inspire this casual table setting. Plain white dinnerware pairs up with French porcelain bowls and mugs patterned with stripes and polka dots. Footed glass bowls filled with colourfully wrapped candies and two red glass Christmas trees serve as the centrepiece.

Formal

Inspired by holiday horticulture, this table setting achieves its elegance from the simple scheme of white, green and silver. Some of the beautiful bone-china plates are wreathed with green, others each sport a single topiary. Graceful lead crystal wineglasses feature a seamless pulled stem and a towering profile. White linens and shining silver flatware and napkin rings add to the elegance. In the centre of the table, a mix of seasonal greens and hypericum berries spills over the edge of a low rectangular glass vase.

Sweet Potato Strudel with Balsamic Mushroom Sauce

This flavourful winter vegetable strudel works double duty. It's an impressive side dish and an elegant way to satisfy vegetarian friends and family.

1 tbsp	extra-virgin olive oil	15 mL
2	sweet onions, sliced	2
3	cloves garlic, sliced	3
1½ tsp	dried thyme	7 mL
1 tsp	salt	5 mL
½ tsp	pepper	2 mL
5 cups	cremini or white mushrooms, sliced	1.25 L
10 cups	thinly sliced peeled sweet potatoes	2.5 L
2 tbsp	chopped fresh parsley	25 mL
1 tbsp	balsamic vinegar	15 mL
8	sheets phyllo pastry	8
½ cup	butter, melted	125 mL
2 tbsp	whole parsley leaves	25 mL

BALSAMIC MUSHROOM SAUCE:

1	pkg (14 g pkg) dried porcini mushrooms	1
1 tbsp	extra-virgin olive oil	15 mL
½ tsp	dried thyme	2 mL
¼ tsp	each salt and pepper	1 mL
4 tsp	all-purpose flour	20 mL
1 tbsp	balsamic vinegar	15 mL

• Line rimmed baking sheet with parchment paper; set aside.
• In large Dutch oven, heat oil over medium heat; fry onions, garlic, thyme, salt and pepper until deep golden, about 10 minutes.
• Add mushrooms; fry until softened, about 5 minutes. Add sweet potatoes and ¼ cup (50 mL) water; cover and simmer, stirring often, until potatoes are tender, 10 minutes. Stir in chopped parsley and vinegar. Let cool to room temperature, about 20 minutes
• Place 1 sheet of phyllo on work surface, covering remainder with damp towel to prevent drying out. Brush lightly with butter; arrange half of the whole parsley leaves over phyllo. Top with 3 sheets of phyllo, brushing first 2 with butter.
• Spoon half of the potato mixture along long side of phyllo, leaving 2-inch (5 cm) border at each end. Fold over ends and roll up to form long roll. Place on prepared pan. Brush all over with half of the remaining butter. With sharp knife, score top diagonally through phyllo into 6 servings. Repeat with remaining ingredients to make second roll. *(Make-ahead: Cover with plastic wrap; refrigerate for up to 24 hours.)*
• Bake in 400°F (200°C) oven until golden, about 20 minutes. With serrated knife and using score marks as guide, cut into slices.
• **BALSAMIC MUSHROOM SAUCE:** Meanwhile, in bowl, soak mushrooms in 1½ cups (375 mL) boiling water until softened, about 20 minutes. Reserving soaking liquid, strain mushrooms; squeeze out liquid and pat dry.
• In small saucepan, heat oil over medium heat; fry mushrooms, thyme, salt and pepper, stirring, until softened, about 2 minutes. Stir in flour; cook, stirring, for 1 minute. Stir in mushroom soaking liquid until combined. Bring to boil; reduce heat and simmer until thickened, about 2 minutes. Stir in vinegar. *(Make-ahead: Let cool; refrigerate in airtight container for up to 24 hours. Reheat.)* Serve with strudel.

MAKES 12 SERVINGS.

PER SERVING: about 242 cal, 4 g pro, 11 g total fat (5 g sat. fat), 33 g carb, 3 g fibre, 24 mg chol, 413 mg sodium. % RDI: 4% calcium, 11% iron, 121% vit A, 25% vit C, 17% folate.

Make-Ahead Mashed Potatoes

Even with a gaggle of helpers, the prerequisite spuds are best done ahead and reheated in the microwave — just one less pot to wash.

12	Yukon Gold potatoes (about 5 lb/2.2 kg)	12
1	pkg (4 oz/125 g) cream cheese	1
1½ cups	hot milk	375 mL
⅓ cup	butter	75 mL
1 tsp	salt	5 mL
¼ tsp	pepper	1 mL
½ cup	finely diced sweet red pepper	125 mL
⅓ cup	minced fresh parsley or chives	75 mL

• Peel and cube potatoes. In large pot of boiling salted water, cover and cook potatoes until tender, about 25 minutes. Drain and return to low heat for about 30 seconds to dry.
• Press potatoes through ricer or mash well. Mash in cheese, milk, butter, salt and pepper until smooth. Stir in red pepper and parsley. *(Make-ahead: Transfer to microwaveable serving dish, smoothing top; cover with plastic wrap and refrigerate for up to 2 days. Reheat in microwave at high for about 8 minutes.)*

MAKES 12 SERVINGS.

PER SERVING: about 217 cal, 4 g pro, 9 g total fat (6 g sat. fat), 30 g carb, 2 g fibre, 28 mg chol, 622 mg sodium. % RDI: 6% calcium, 5% iron, 12% vit A, 25% vit C, 8% folate.

TIP

❯ For a festive touch, cut a tree shape out of cardboard to make a stencil; place on potatoes and sprinkle parsley to fill shape.

Turnip and Apple Bake

There can be no turkey dinner without turnip, correctly known today as rutabaga. It's a vegetable that's best when mellowed with sweet apple and onion.

1	rutabaga (about 3 lb/1.5 kg)	1
2	apples	2
1	large onion, chopped	1
2 tbsp	butter	25 mL
1 tbsp	liquid honey	15 mL
½ tsp	salt	2 mL
¼ tsp	pepper	1 mL

• Peel and cube rutabaga to make about 10 cups (2.5 L). In large pot of boiling salted water, cover and cook rutabaga until tender, about 20 minutes. Drain, reserving ¾ cup (175 mL) of the liquid. Return rutabaga and reserved cooking liquid to pot.
• Meanwhile, peel, core and chop apples; add to rutabaga along with onion. Simmer, covered, over medium heat, stirring occasionally, until almost no liquid remains, about 20 minutes.
• In food processor, purée rutabaga mixture, in batches if necessary; return to pot. Stir in butter, honey, salt and pepper. *(Make-ahead: Spoon into 8-inch/2 L square glass baking dish or shallow ovenproof casserole; cover and refrigerate for up to 3 days. Reheat in microwave at high for 8 minutes or in 400°F/200°C oven for about 20 minutes.)*

MAKES 12 SERVINGS.

PER SERVING: about 76 cal, 1 g pro, 2 g total fat (1 g sat. fat), 14 g carb, 3 g fibre, 5 mg chol, 392 mg sodium. % RDI: 5% iron, 4% iron, 2% vit A, 42% vitamin C, 9% folate.

❯ *Set a Formal Table*

Forgotten where everything goes? Here's a quick refresher:

Helpful hints for young diners:

• Use the utensils farthest away from the plate first, then work in.

• Return your butter knife back to the bread-and-butter plate after you've buttered your roll.

• When you finish each course, place your utensil(s), singly or side by side in the four-o'clock position on the plate, to signal that you're done.

• Special tools for dessert (a spoon for soft desserts, such as ice cream or pudding, and a fork for more solid foods, such as cake or pie) lie above your plate. Once you've used your soup spoon, salad fork, and main-course knife and fork, and they've been removed from the table, replace them with the dessert spoon on the right-hand side and the dessert fork on the left.

• And, after you've helped yourself, remember to put the serving utensils back in their bowls or on their platters.

> Monogrammed Ornaments

Take plain ball ornaments and put on the glitz.

• With white craft glue in fine-nozzled applicator, write initial freehand onto ornament side (hold with hanging loop up), ensuring glue line is at least ⅛-inch (3 mm) wide; immediately sprinkle with glitter. Let dry (set in cup to dry, if desired).

• With artist's paintbrush, gently brush off excess glitter. If desired, spray with coat of clear acrylic sealer.

• From ⅜-inch (9 mm) wide wire-edge ribbon, cut short length; thread through hanging loop and tie into bow.

> Beaded Initials

These elegant beaded initials can be used more than once for returning guests or given to each person as a take-away keepsake. Choose clear seed beads and a few slightly larger beads in a colour that coordinates with your china.

• With pencil, draw initial on scrap of paper for pattern.

• From 26-gauge hobby wire, cut short length, then, with needle-nose pliers, tightly twist one end. Shape, following pattern, by threading remaining end through desired beads until first swirl and stroke of initial is complete, then bend angle. Continue threading and shaping in same manner until initial is complete.

• Tightly twist end to secure beads, then trim off excess wire.

> Embroidered Table Linens

Embroidered in seasonal colours or classic white-on-white, simple stitches add special-occasion style to table linens.

• Preshrink and press linens. With dressmaker's chalk pencil, lightly outline stem, leaves and berries.

• With 3 strands of embroidery floss, stemstitch stems, lazy daisy–stitch leaves and French-knot berries.

• For napkin tie, cut 33½-inch (85 cm) length of ⅜-inch (9 mm) wide grosgrain ribbon. Press under ⅛ inch (3 mm) along each end; fold, right side out, and tack corners together, stitching on small jingle bell.

Welcome Home for 8

Gather family and friends together for
a dinner that's just as special as they are.

....

- **Corn and Saffron Bisque**

- **Tear-and-Share Checkerboard Rolls**
  (recipe, page 171)

- **Crown Roast of Pork with
  Mushroom Pilaf**

- **Green Beans with Lemon and Hazelnuts**

- **Creamy Carrot Purée**
  (recipe, page 97)

- **Earl Grey Pots de Crème**
  (recipe, page 99) **or**
  Whisky Chocolate Mousse
  (recipe, page 119)

....

Corn and Saffron Bisque

*A small cup of this velvety golden soup is an
elegant start to a holiday meal. For best
colour, use yellow corn.*

1 tbsp	vegetable oil	15 mL
2	stalks celery, diced	2
1	onion, diced	1
2	cloves garlic, minced	2
1	bay leaf	1
¼ tsp	saffron threads	1 mL
¼ tsp	ground coriander	1 mL
¼ tsp	salt	1 mL
4 cups	frozen corn kernels	1 L
½ cup	grated peeled Yukon Gold potato	125 mL
3 cups	sodium-reduced chicken stock	750 mL
⅓ cup	crème fraîche or sour cream	75 mL

PARSLEY OIL:

⅓ cup	chopped fresh parsley	75 mL
¼ cup	vegetable oil	50 mL

SAFFRON OIL:

1 tsp	saffron threads	5 mL
¼ cup	vegetable oil	50 mL

- In large saucepan, heat oil over medium heat; fry celery, onion, garlic, bay leaf, saffron, coriander and salt, stirring often, until onion is softened, about 6 minutes.
- Add corn and potato. Pour in stock and 3 cups (750 mL) water; bring to boil. Reduce heat, cover and simmer until potato is tender, 15 minutes. Let cool for 10 minutes.
- **PARSLEY OIL:** Meanwhile, in blender, purée parsley with oil until bright green; let stand for 10 minutes. Strain through coffee filter into small bowl, pressing to extract oil.
- **SAFFRON OIL:** In small bowl, combine saffron with 1 tsp (5 mL) hot water; let stand for 10 minutes. Whisk in oil. Let stand for 10 minutes; strain through coffee filter into small bowl. *(Make-ahead: Cover and refrigerate oils for up to 24 hours; whisk.)*
- Discard bay leaf from soup. In blender, purée soup, in batches, until smooth. Strain into clean pot, adding up to ¼ cup (50 mL) water for thinner consistency if desired. *(Make-ahead: Let cool for 30 minutes; refrigerate, uncovered, in airtight container until cold. Cover and refrigerate for up to 2 days. Rewarm, stirring occasionally.)*
- Ladle into bowls. Garnish each with dollop of crème fraîche and drizzle each of parsley and saffron oils.

MAKES 8 SERVINGS.

PER SERVING: about 236 cal, 4 g pro, 17 g total fat (2 g sat. fat), 19 g carb, trace fibre, 4 mg chol, 316 mg sodium. % RDI: 3% calcium, 5% iron, 5% vit A, 13% vit C, 17% folate.

Crown Roast of Pork with Mushroom Pilaf

A crown roast of pork makes a stunningly elegant holiday entrée. You'll need some of the mushroom soaking liquid from the pilaf for the gravy.

1	pork loin rib half crown roast (12 bones), about 6½ lb (3 kg)	1
¾ cup	sodium-reduced chicken stock	175 mL
	Mushroom Pilaf (recipe follows)	

DIJON HERB RUB:

1 cup	fresh parsley leaves	250 mL
¼ cup	Dijon mustard	50 mL
2 tbsp	extra-virgin olive oil	25 mL
2 tbsp	lemon juice	25 mL
2 tsp	dried thyme	10 mL
1 tsp	each salt and pepper	5 mL
2	cloves garlic, minced	2

WINE GRAVY:

½ cup	white wine	125 mL
2 tbsp	all-purpose flour or cornstarch	25 mL
½ cup	mushroom soaking liquid (or sodium-reduced chicken stock)	125 mL

• **DIJON HERB RUB:** In food processor, whirl together parsley, mustard, oil, lemon juice, thyme, salt and pepper until paste. Stir in garlic. Rub all over pork, excluding bones. Place roast, bones up, on rack in roasting pan. Wrap bone ends in foil; stuff centre with foil ball. Pour stock into pan.

• Roast in 325°F (160°C) oven until meat thermometer registers 160°F (71°C), 2½ to 3 hours, adding up to 1½ cups (375 mL) water if necessary to maintain juices in pan. Transfer to serving platter and remove foil ball; tent with foil and let stand for 20 minutes.

• **WINE GRAVY:** Meanwhile, skim fat from pan juices. Place pan over medium heat. Pour in wine, stirring and scraping up brown bits from bottom of pan. Whisk flour into mushroom soaking liquid; whisk into pan and cook, whisking, until thickened, about 2 minutes. Strain.

• Spoon some of the pilaf into centre of roast. Transfer remainder to serving bowl. Carve roast between bones.

MAKES 12 SERVINGS.

PER SERVING: about 436 cal, 37 g pro, 19 g total fat (6 g sat. fat), 28 g carb, 3 g fibre, 80 mg chol, 536 mg sodium. % RDI: 6% calcium, 19% iron, 23% vit A, 23% vit C, 14% folate.   >

Welcome Home Countdown

One day before:

> Make bisque.

> Make rub for pork roast.

> Toast hazelnuts and blanch green beans.

> Make carrot purée.

> Bake Tear-and-Share Checkerboard Rolls. Cool and wrap in foil.

Up to four hours ahead

> Make and chill desserts.

> Prepare and roast pork.

> Make pilaf.

Just before dinner

> Reheat soup.

> Rewarm rolls.

> Remove roast from oven to rest.

> Reheat carrot purée.

For dinner

> Serve soup and rolls.

> Reheat green beans.

> Fill roast cavity with pilaf and scoop remainder into warmed bowl with lid.

> Serve and enjoy – the dessert's in the fridge.

Mushroom Pilaf

1	pkg (14 g) dried mushrooms (such as porcini or morel)	1
2 tbsp	vegetable oil	25 mL
2	cloves garlic	2
1	leek (white and light green parts only), finely chopped	1
1 cup	diced carrots	250 mL
1 tsp	dried thyme	5 mL
1⅓ cups	brown basmati rice	325 mL
⅔ cup	wild rice	150 mL
½ tsp	salt	2 mL
¼ tsp	pepper	1 mL
1½ cups	each sodium-reduced chicken stock and water	375 mL
¼ cup	chopped fresh parsley	50 mL
¼ cup	finely diced sweet red pepper	50 mL

• Soak mushrooms in 1 cup (250 mL) boiling water for 30 minutes. Strain through sieve, reserving ½ cup (125 mL) soaking liquid for gravy. Chop mushrooms.

• In skillet, heat oil over medium heat; fry garlic, leek, carrots, thyme and mushrooms, stirring occasionally, until leeks are softened, about 5 minutes.

• Stir in basmati and wild rice, salt and pepper. Add stock and water, scraping up brown bits from bottom of pan; bring to boil. Reduce heat, cover and simmer until rice is tender and liquid is absorbed, about 40 minutes. *(Make-ahead: Cover and keep warm for up to 30 minutes.)* Stir in parsley and red pepper.

MAKES ABOUT 8 CUPS (2 L).

PER ⅔ CUP (150 ML) SERVING: about 141 cal, 4 g pro, 3 g total fat (trace sat. fat), 25 g carb, 2 g fibre, 0 mg chol, 183 mg sodium. % RDI: 2% calcium, 6% iron, 18% vit A, 13% vit C, 8% folate.

Green Beans with Lemon and Hazelnuts

Toasted almonds are equally suited to these make-ahead green beans.

2 lb	green beans, trimmed and halved diagonally	1 kg
¼ cup	sliced or chopped hazelnuts	50 mL
¼ cup	extra-virgin olive oil	50 mL
2 tsp	grated lemon rind	10 mL
2 tbsp	lemon juice	25 mL
½ tsp	salt	2 mL
¼ tsp	pepper	1 mL

• Fill large bowl with ice water; set aside. In large pot of boiling salted water, cook green beans, in 2 batches, until tender-crisp, about 3 minutes. With tongs, transfer to ice water; stir until beans are cold. Remove immediately and pat dry. *(Make-ahead: Wrap in towel; enclose in plastic bag and refrigerate for up to 24 hours.)*

• In large skillet, toast hazelnuts over medium heat, stirring often, until fragrant and golden, about 3 minutes. Remove from pan and set aside. *(Make-ahead: Let cool; store in airtight container for up to 3 days.)*

• Add oil and lemon rind and juice to skillet; bring to boil. Add green beans. Sprinkle with salt and pepper; toss until hot, about 1 minute. Sprinkle with hazelnuts.

MAKES 8 SERVINGS.

PER SERVING: about 117 cal, 2 g pro, 9 g total fat (1 g sat. fat), 9 g carb, 4 g fibre, 0 mg chol, 369 mg sodium. % RDI: 4% calcium, 6% iron, 7% vit A, 20% vit C, 16% folate.

Sugared Fruit

❯ In saucepan, bring 1 cup (250 mL) granulated sugar and ¾ cup (175 mL) water to boil; boil for 1 minute. Let cool to room temperature. Pour into glass measure.

❯ Place ½ cup (125 mL) granulated sugar in small bowl.

❯ Dip small bunches of grapes, mint leaves or cranberries in syrup. Drain in sieve, shaking gently to remove excess syrup.

❯ Place in sugar; shake bowl to roll fruit until coated. Transfer to waxed paper–lined rimmed baking sheet. Let dry, about 30 minutes. *(Make-ahead: Store at room temperature for up to 24 hours.)*

> *Napkin Flair*

Set a gracious table with cleverly folded cloth napkins. For best results, start with crisply starched white damask or plain-weave linen or cotton, 20 to 30 inches (50.8 to 76 cm) square and lightly press finished folds, if desired.

A) The Lazy Butler

1. Lay napkin flat, right side down, then fold top and bottom edges over centre, along broken lines.

2. Fold each side edge to bold line at centre, along broken line.

3. Fold top edge of each corner to bold line at centre, along broken line.

4. Folded napkin looks like this.

5. Turn over.

6. Pick up folded napkin and tuck corner A between folds at bottom edge at corner B. Flip over onto plate so point sits at centre front.

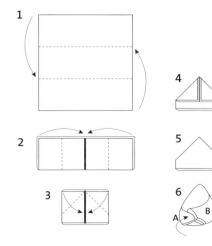

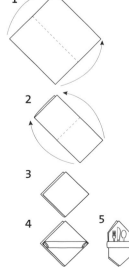

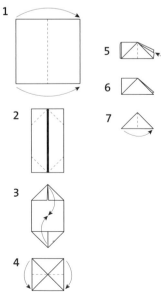

B) The Pocket

1. Lay napkin flat, right side down and with points at top and bottom, then fold in half, along broken line.

2. Fold in half again, along broken line.

3. Folded napkin looks like this.

4. Pick up 2 top points; holding together, roll halfway down folded napkin.

5. Holding roll against napkin, fold each side corner to back; insert cutlery under roll and into pocket.

C) The Christmas Tree

1. Lay napkin flat, right side down, then fold in half, along broken line.

2. Fold each corner to bold line at centre, along broken line.

3. Fold top, then bottom point to centre.

4. Fold in half, to back, along broken line.

5. With just-folded edge along top, push right-hand top corner between layers so right-hand edges are angled and even.

6. Napkin looks like this. Repeat Step 5 with left-hand side.

7. Fold in half, along broken line; firmly press folds. Set napkin upright then open out folds into tree shape and top with adhesive-backed bow or star napkin ring.

D) The Lily

1. Lay napkin flat, right side down and with points at top and bottom, then fold in half, along broken line.

2. Fold in half again, along broken line.

3. Folded napkin looks like this.

4. Fold in half diagonally, along dotted line.

5. Accordion-pleat, along broken lines; with points up, set in wine glass, then separate points and arrange as shown in photo.

E) The Tuxedo

1. Lay napkin flat, right side down and with points at top and bottom, then fold in half, along broken line.

2. Fold each top corner down to bottom point, along broken line, so top edge is even with bold line at centre.

3. Folded napkin looks like this.

4. Roll back folded edge from left-hand side, up around tip and down right-hand side to create "collar," then fold bottom and each side corner to back, along broken lines. From black card stock, cut out "bow-tie;" with silver, fine-tip metallic marker, label with guest's name. Centre on bottom edge of folded napkin.

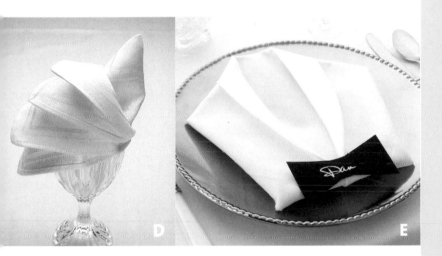

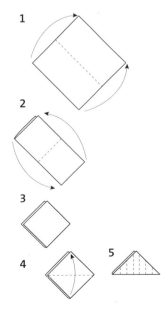

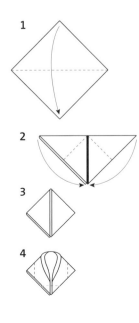

Leisurely Brunch for 8

Brunch will never go out of style. It takes place when everyone is at his or her brightest – especially the kids. And the late-morning invite allows hosts time to put together a crowd-pleasing affordable meal and still have time to relax and enjoy the company.

- **Tropical Fruit Smoothies**
- **Holiday Fruit Salad**
- **Raspberry Almond Spiral Biscuits**
- **Bacon and Gouda Quiche**
- **Sparkling Mimosas**
  (See countdown below)

Leisurely Brunch Countdown

Two weeks ahead
➤ Bake and freeze quiche.
➤ Make and freeze spiral biscuits ready to bake.

One day ahead
➤ Toast coconut for fruit salad.
➤ Chill sparkling wine.

A few hours ahead
➤ Prepare fruit salad.
➤ Organize ingredients for fruit smoothies on tray; refrigerate.

Just before brunch
➤ Bake spiral biscuits; glaze.
➤ In order, add syrup then berries and bananas to fruit.
➤ Reheat quiche.
➤ Get ready to buzz up the smoothies and pour the mimosas (half freshly squeezed orange juice and half sparkling wine).

Tropical Fruit Smoothies

Buzz up more of this tasty drink as needed.

2 cups	frozen tropical fruit mix	500 mL
1 cup	milk	250 mL
½ cup	Balkan-style plain yogurt	125 mL
1 tbsp	liquid honey (optional)	15 mL

• In blender, blend fruit, milk, yogurt, and honey (if using) until smooth and frothy.

MAKES 3 CUPS (750 mL), OR 2 SERVINGS.

PER SERVING: about 218 cal, 8 g pro, 6 g total fat (4 g sat. fat), 33 g carb, 3 g fibre, 21 mg chol, 85 mg sodium. % RDI: 24% calcium, 3% iron, 63% vit A, 95% vit C, 4% folate.

Holiday Fruit Salad

Ginger accents this refreshing fruit combo. Feel free to vary the fruit.

¼ cup	sweetened shredded coconut	50 mL
2	large ruby red grapefruit	2
2	large oranges	2
2 tbsp	granulated sugar	25 mL
4	slices gingerroot	4
2 cups	pineapple wedges	500 mL
2	kiwifruit, peeled and cut into wedges	2
1 cup	green grapes, halved	250 mL
1 cup	blueberries	250 mL
1 cup	strawberries, halved	250 mL
2	bananas, sliced	2

• In small skillet, toast coconut over medium heat, stirring, until golden, about 3 minutes. *(Make-ahead: Set aside in airtight container for up to 24 hours.)*

• Cut off rind and outer membranes of grapefruit and oranges. Working over large sieve set over bowl, cut between membrane and pulp to release fruit into sieve, squeezing membranes to extract juice. Pour ¾ cup (175 mL) juice into saucepan, using any remaining juice for another use.

• Add sugar and ginger to saucepan; bring to boil over medium-high heat. Boil, stirring, until sugar is dissolved; reduce heat and simmer, stirring occasionally, for 2 minutes. Let cool. Discard ginger.

• In large shallow bowl, combine grapefruit mixture, pineapple, kiwifruit, grapes and blueberries. *(Make-ahead: Cover and refrigerate juice mixture and fruit separately for up to 12 hours.)* Drizzle juice mixture evenly over fruit; cover and let stand for 1 hour.

• Add strawberries and bananas, spooning juice mixture over top. Sprinkle with coconut.

MAKES 8 SERVINGS.

PER SERVING: about 161 cal, 2 g pro, 2 g total fat (1 g sat. fat), 39 g carb, 5 g fibre, 0 mg chol, 10 mg sodium. % RDI: 4% calcium, 4% iron, 4% vit A, 177% vit C, 21% folate.

Raspberry Almond Spiral Biscuits

Bake these biscuits right from the freezer.

2½ cups	all-purpose flour	625 mL
2 tbsp	granulated sugar	25 mL
2½ tsp	baking powder	12 mL
½ tsp	each baking soda and salt	2 mL
½ cup	cold butter, cubed	125 mL
1 cup	buttermilk	250 mL
1	egg	1
3 tbsp	seedless raspberry jam	50 mL
¼ cup	sliced almonds	50 mL
GLAZE:		
¼ cup	icing sugar	50 mL
4 tsp	whipping cream	20 mL
Dash	almond extract	Dash

• Line 13- x 9-inch (3.5 L) metal cake pan with parchment paper (double-line if freezing) or grease. Set aside.

• In large bowl, whisk together flour, sugar, baking powder, baking soda and salt. Using pastry blender, cut in butter until in coarse crumbs. In small bowl, whisk buttermilk with egg; add to flour mixture, stirring with fork to make soft dough.

• Turn out onto lightly floured surface; pat into rectangle. Roll out to 10- x 6-inch (25 x 15 cm) rectangle. Spread with jam, leaving ½-inch (1 cm) border at 1 long side. Sprinkle with half of the almonds. Starting at long side with filling, roll up; pinch to seal. Using serrated knife, cut into 12 slices.

• Arrange slices, cut side down, in prepared pan. Sprinkle with remaining almonds. *(Make-ahead: Wrap in plastic wrap then heavy-duty foil; freeze for up to 2 weeks. Increase baking time by 10 minutes.)*

• Bake in centre of 400°F (200°C) oven until golden, about 20 minutes. Remove from pan to rack. Let cool for 15 minutes.

• **GLAZE:** In bowl, whisk together icing sugar, cream and almond extract; drizzle over warm biscuits.

MAKES 12 BISCUITS.

PER BISCUIT: about 227 cal, 4 g pro, 10 g total fat (6 g sat. fat), 30 g carb, 1 g fibre, 39 mg chol, 295 mg sodium. % RDI: 6% calcium, 10% iron, 8% vit A, 2% vit C, 26% folate.

Bacon and Gouda Quiche

Aged Gouda has a nutty sherry flavour that marries well with bacon.

Single-Crust Really Flaky
Pastry (recipe follows)

FILLING:

4	thick strips bacon, chopped	4
1 tbsp	vegetable oil	15 mL
6	shallots, quartered	6
2	cloves garlic, minced	2
¼ tsp	each dried thyme and pepper	1 mL
Pinch	salt	Pinch
½ cup	chopped roasted red pepper	125 mL
2 tbsp	chopped fresh chives	25 mL
¾ cup	shredded aged Gouda cheese	175 mL
3	eggs	3
¾ cup	milk	175 mL

• On lightly floured surface, roll out pastry to scant ¼-inch (5 mm) thickness; fit into 9-inch (23 cm) quiche dish or pie plate. Trim edge to leave 1-inch (2.5 cm) overhang; fold inside rim. Flute edge if using pie plate. Prick all over with fork. Refrigerate for 30 minutes.

• Line pie shell with foil; fill with pie weights or dried beans. Bake in bottom third of 400°F (200°C) oven until rim is light golden, about 15 minutes. Remove weights and foil; let cool on rack.

• **FILLING:** In large skillet, sauté bacon over medium-high heat until crisp, about 5 minutes. With slotted spoon, transfer to paper towel. Drain fat from pan.

• Heat oil in pan over medium heat; fry shallots, garlic, thyme, pepper and salt until shallots are softened, about 10 minutes. Transfer to bowl and let cool. Add bacon, red pepper and chives to bowl.

• Sprinkle ½ cup (125 mL) of the cheese over pastry shell. Spread with bacon mixture. In bowl, whisk eggs with milk; pour over bacon mixture. Sprinkle with remaining cheese.

• Bake in centre of 375°F (190°C) oven until knife inserted in centre comes out clean, about 35 minutes. Let cool in pan on rack for 10 minutes. *(Make-ahead: Let cool for 30 minutes; refrigerate until cold. Wrap in plastic wrap; refrigerate for up to 24 hours or overwrap in heavy-duty foil and freeze for up to 2 weeks. Thaw in refrigerator; reheat in 350°F/180°C oven for 20 minutes.)*

MAKES 8 SERVINGS.

PER SERVING: about 287 cal, 10 g pro, 20 g total fat (9 g sat. fat), 17 g carb, 1 g fibre, 126 mg chol, 391 mg sodium. % RDI: 11% calcium, 10% iron, 16% vit A, 33% vit C, 25% folate.

Single-Crust Really Flaky Pastry

1½ cups	all-purpose flour	375 mL
½ tsp	salt	2 mL
¼ cup	each cold butter and lard, cubed	50 mL
1	egg yolk	1
1 tsp	vinegar	5 mL
	Ice water	

• In bowl, whisk flour with salt. Using pastry blender or 2 knives, cut in butter and lard until in crumbs with a few larger pieces.

• In liquid measure, whisk egg yolk with vinegar; add enough ice water to make ⅓ cup (75 mL). Drizzle over flour mixture, tossing with fork until ragged dough forms.

• Press into disc. Wrap and refrigerate until chilled, about 30 minutes. *(Make-ahead: Refrigerate for up to 3 days.)*

MAKES ENOUGH PASTRY FOR 1 SINGLE-CRUST 9-INCH (23 CM) PIE.

❯ *How to Decorate a Tree*

You only do it once a year, but Kate Seaver of Kate's Garden in Markham, Ont., professionally decorates dozens of trees every holiday season. Here are her top tips for decorating a safe and perfect tree.

❯ Choose energy-efficient LED lights to curb energy use and costs (an average home uses 27 per cent more lighting in December).

❯ When choosing, cutting and setting up tree, ensure 2 feet (61 cm) of space all around side that faces room, and between tree topper and ceiling.

❯ Secure tree firmly in stand, then place lightweight tree topper on tip.

❯ Have strand of 100 lights for each vertical foot (30.5 cm) of tree (or up it to 200 for extra wow). Plug in and ensure they're all working.

❯ Visually divide tree into pie slices, with tip of slices meeting at top of tree. Starting at tree top (and wearing safety glasses, gloves and long sleeves, if desired), zig zag lights down each slice midway out from trunk (to leave branch tips free for ornaments).

❯ If desired, and working with 4- to 5-foot (1.2 to 1.5 m) lengths of 3- to 4-inch (7.5 to 10 cm) wide, wire-edged ribbon, weave ribbon in and out around tree. For added sparkle, repeat with beaded garlands.

❯ Have 20 to 30 ornaments in various shapes and sizes for each vertical foot (30.5 cm) of tree, choosing ornaments that coordinate with colours in room.

❯ Place largest ornaments first, tucking some midway along branches to light up dark spots in the tree.

❯ For impact, add remaining ornaments in clusters of odd-numbered ornaments, interspersing sentimental and homemade decorations throughout.

> *Recycle and Refresh Old Ornaments*

Inspiring Words
Freshen up old ornaments. With chisel-tip permanent marker, write Peace, Hope or Joy on each, or label with names of family and friends, then tie on hanging loop of fine gold cord or ribbon.

Glitter Faux Fruit
Recycle artificial fruit from old wreaths or centrepieces. Push short length of medium-gauge wire through vertical centre of each fruit. Spray with glue, then roll in glitter (or spray with metallic paint); push wire into block of floral foam to hold fruit until dry. Remove wire; with glue gun, fasten ribbon hanging loop, tied in bow, to top.

Starry Pinecones
With glue gun, fasten foil stars to pinecones. With fine wire, cord or narrow ribbon, tie hanging loop.

Christmas Eve for 8

Oh, the anticipation of it all! Even if the 25th is the big feast, the night before has a lock on our hearts long after we've hung our last stocking. Because of Canada's French heritage, a luscious chicken pie is the centrepiece, but if a traditional tourtière is in order, see Mushroom Tourtière, recipe, page 87.

....

- **Shrimp Cocktail**

- **Braised Chicken Pie with Caramelized Onions, Mushrooms and Chestnuts**

- **Endive and Lettuce Salad with Sherry Vinaigrette**

- **Cherry Panna Cotta** (recipe, page 124)

- **Christmas cookies (share some with Santa)**

....

Shrimp Cocktail

Here's an update on a classic that everyone loves.

1½ cups	ketchup	375 mL
3 tbsp	prepared horseradish	50 mL
1½ tsp	lemon juice	7 mL
1½ tsp	hot pepper sauce	7 mL
1 tsp	salt	5 mL
½ tsp	pepper	2 mL
1½ lb	large raw shrimp, peeled and deveined (with tails)	750 g
4 tsp	extra-virgin olive oil	20 mL
4 cups	shredded romaine lettuce	1 L
1	avocado, peeled, pitted and chopped	1

• In bowl, combine ketchup, horseradish, lemon juice, hot pepper sauce, salt and pepper. *(Make-ahead: Cover and refrigerate for up to 24 hours.)*

• In bowl, toss shrimp with oil. Place on foil-lined rimmed baking sheet: broil, turning once, until pink, about 6 minutes.

• On salad plates, layer lettuce, avocado and cocktail sauce; top with shrimp.

MAKES 8 SERVINGS.

PER SERVING: about 179 cal, 15 g pro, 7 g total fat (1 g sat. fat), 16 g carb, 3 g fibre, 97 mg chol, 894 mg sodium. % RDI: 5% calcium, 16% iron, 21% vit A, 27% vit C, 29% folate.

Braised Chicken Pie with Caramelized Onions, Mushrooms and Chestnuts

This puff pastry–topped pie is festive with tiny onions and chestnuts. To use canned chestnuts instead of the fresh, add these already-cooked nuts when adding the mushroom mixture. To use dried chestnuts, rehydrate and use as for fresh chestnuts.

1 lb	fresh chestnuts	500 g
¾ cup	all-purpose flour	175 mL
1 tsp	salt	5 mL
½ tsp	pepper	2 mL
3 lb	boneless skinless chicken breasts, cubed	1.5 kg
⅓ cup	vegetable oil (approx)	75 mL
3	carrots, diagonally sliced	3
2	onions, chopped	2
6	cloves garlic, sliced	6
2 tsp	dried thyme	10 mL
4 cups	chicken stock	1 L
5 cups	button mushrooms (about 14 oz/400 g)	1.25 L
4 cups	pearl onions (1¼ lb/625 g), peeled	1 L
½ cup	chopped fresh parsley	125 mL

TOPPING:

1	pkg (450 g) frozen butter puff pastry, thawed and cold	1
1	egg yolk	1

• Cut X in flat side of each chestnut. In saucepan of boiling water, cook chestnuts, 4 at a time, until skins can be easily peeled off, about 2 minutes. Set aside.

• In large bowl, combine flour, salt and pepper. In batches, toss chicken in flour mixture, reserving any unused mixture. In Dutch oven, heat 2 tbsp (25 mL) of the oil over medium-high heat; brown chicken, in batches and adding up to 2 tbsp (25 mL) more oil as needed. Remove and set aside.

• Add carrots, chopped onions, garlic and thyme to pan; cook over medium-low heat, stirring often, for 5 minutes. Sprinkle with any remaining flour mixture; stir well.

• Return chicken to pan. Add stock and bring to boil, stirring. Reduce heat to low; cover and simmer for 15 minutes. Add chestnuts; simmer until chicken is no longer pink inside, about 15 minutes.

• Meanwhile, in large skillet, heat remaining oil over medium heat; fry mushrooms and pearl onions, stirring often, until onions are tender and no liquid remains, about 25 minutes. Add to chicken mixture; cook for 5 minutes. *(Make-ahead: Refrigerate in shallow airtight container, uncovered, until cool. Cover and refrigerate for up to 2 days or freeze for up to 2 weeks; thaw to continue.)*

• Stir parsley into chicken mixture. Transfer to deep oval 12-inch (30 cm) gratin dish or 13- x 9-inch (3 L) glass baking dish.

• **TOPPING:** On lightly floured surface, unroll 1 sheet of the puff pastry and roll out slightly larger than dish. With cookie cutter, cut out small star in centre for vent hole. Drape over filling, without sealing to edge; trim. Unroll remaining pastry; cut out different-size stars. Brush egg yolk over pastry top; arrange cutouts on pastry and brush again with egg yolk. *(Make-ahead: Cover and refrigerate for up to 4 hours.)*

• Place dish on rimmed baking sheet; bake in 400°F (200°C) oven until bubbly and pastry is puffed and golden, 45 to 60 minutes. Let stand for 10 minutes.

MAKES 8 TO 10 SERVINGS.

PER EACH OF 10 SERVINGS: about 576 cal, 40 g pro, 26 g total fat (4 g sat. fat), 44 g carb, 5 g fibre, 101 mg chol, 742 mg sodium. % RDI: 6% calcium, 28% iron, 58% vit A, 27% vit C, 30% folate.

Christmas Eve Countdown

Two weeks ahead
➤ Make filling for chicken pie.

One day ahead
➤ Make panna cotta and sauce.
➤ Whisk up sherry vinaigrette.
➤ Prepare cocktail sauce for shrimp.
➤ Wash, spin dry and wrap all greens separately in towels. Store in plastic bag in crisper.

Four hours ahead
➤ Peel and devein shrimp; toss with oil.
➤ Shred lettuce for shrimp; cover with damp towel and refrigerate.
➤ Cover chicken pie with pastry topping; refrigerate.
➤ Arrange endive salad ingredients on plates; cover with damp towel and refrigerate.

One-and-one-quarter hours ahead
➤ Put chicken pie in oven.
➤ Unmould panna cottas onto dessert plates; cover lightly and return to fridge.

Just before sitting down
➤ Broil shrimp.
➤ Peel and pit avocado; assemble shrimp cocktail.
➤ The rest is easy. Let pie rest for a few minutes before serving. Drizzle salads with vinaigrette. Spoon sauce around panna cottas when ready to serve.
➤ Set out cookies for Santa and see if you can wait up late enough for his arrival – and eat the offerings.

Endive and Lettuce Salad with Sherry Vinaigrette

This composed salad is refreshing served as a separate course after the chicken pie. You can use any wine vinegar or cider vinegar instead of sherry vinegar.

2	heads Belgian endive	2
Half	sweet yellow pepper	Half
8 cups	torn Boston lettuce (1 head)	2 L
12	grape tomatoes, halved	12
SHERRY VINAIGRETTE:		
¼ cup	extra-virgin olive oil	50 mL
2 tbsp	sherry vinegar	25 mL
1	shallot or green onion, minced	1
1½ tsp	Dijon mustard	7 mL
½ tsp	salt	2 mL
¼ tsp	pepper	1 mL

• **SHERRY VINAIGRETTE:** In small bowl, whisk together oil, vinegar, shallot, mustard, salt and pepper. *(Make-ahead: Cover and refrigerate for up to 24 hours.)*
• Separate leaves of endives. Seed, core and cut yellow pepper in half crosswise; thinly slice lengthwise. *(Make-ahead: Cover with damp towel and refrigerate for up to 4 hours.)*
• Arrange endives on salad plates or in bowls; arrange lettuce, yellow pepper and tomatoes over top. Drizzle with vinaigrette.

MAKES 8 SERVINGS.

PER SERVING: about 78 cal, 1 g pro, 7 g total fat (1 g sat. fat), 4 g carb, 1 g fibre, 0 mg chol, 162 mg sodium. % RDI: 2% calcium, 4% iron, 7% vit A, 38% vit C, 23% folate.

❯ Keep Crystal Shining

There is an ongoing debate about the wisdom of washing crystal or leaded glass in a dishwasher, but expert Jackie Chiesa (of William Ashley China in Toronto) is a proponent. Like some other experts, she blames most breakage on clumsy human hands. Other crystal afficionados, however, say washing by machine will scratch and cloud your crystal. The bottom line? Intense heat and harsh detergents can damage lead crystal, but if the dishwasher has a low-heat or fine-china setting – and you can arrange racks to protect the crystal pieces and prevent them from rattling against one another during the wash – your machine may be the safest way to clean leaded glass. If not, gently hand-wash in warm water and mild dishwashing liquid.

❯ Pinecone Place Cards and Bow-Tied Chairs

With fine-tip artist's paintbrush, dab scale tips of large, flat-bottomed pinecones with white acrylic paint to resemble snow; let dry. For place cards, set each pinecone on plate; tuck small card labeled with guest's name between scales at top. Tie 59-inch (1.5 m) length of ribbon around each chair back at top. With 6-inch (15 cm) length of fine-gauge floral or craft wire, wire painted pinecone onto bow.

Wintry Party for 8

The gang could have been skating, hiking, tobogganing or even snowshoeing and now everyone is home ready for the finale – a wonderful supper. The offerings include a snack as part of the outdoor fun, and the at-home menu is guaranteed to send the winter athletes away smug about their exertion and well satisfied by their supper. (This is fine cold-weather menu for nonatheletes, too – no exercise required.)

....

AT THE RINK
- **Malted Hot Chocolate**
- **Sugar Cookie Mittens**
  (recipe, page 138)

AT HOME
- **Layered Guacamole**
- **Baked Tortillla Chips**
- **Slow Cooker Pulled Pork**
- **Sweet Pepper Slaw**
- **No-Bake Lime Cheesecake Squares**

....

Malted Hot Chocolate

Pour this warming treat into a heated vacuum bottle to take along outdoors. Whipped cream and crushed chocolate-covered malt balls would make it even more special. Quality chocolate gives the creamiest texture.

8 cups	milk	2 L
¼ cup	granulated sugar	50 mL
⅓ cup	powdered chocolate malt (such as Ovaltine)	75 mL
4 oz	bittersweet chocolate, finely chopped	125 g

- In saucepan, bring milk with sugar just to boil over medium-high heat, stirring often. Remove from heat.
- Whisk in malt powder and chocolate until smooth. *(Make-ahead: Let cool. Refrigerate in airtight container for up to 2 days; reheat.)*

MAKES 8 SERVINGS.

PER SERVING: about 251 cal, 10 g pro, 10 g total fat (6 g sat. fat), 31 g carb, 1 g fibre, 18 mg chol, 122 mg sodium. % RDI: 28% calcium, 5% iron, 12% vit A, 2% vit C, 4% folate.

Winter Party Countdown

Up to a month ahead
❯ Make cookies.

Two days ahead
❯ Make hot chocolate.
❯ Decorate cookies.
❯ Assemble cheesecake squares.

One day ahead
❯ Bake tortilla chips.
❯ Make pulled pork in slow cooker.
❯ Prepare slaw.

Four hours ahead
❯ Prepare guacamole.
❯ Place toppings for pulled pork in serving bowls.
❯ Cut cheesecake squares and garnish .

Just before serving
❯ Reheat pulled pork.
❯ Set out buns and toppings.

Layered Guacamole

Chunks of green avocado topped with diced red tomato give this guacamole a festive look. Surround it with Baked Tortilla Chips (recipe follows) to scoop up every last bit.

4	ripe avocados	4
½ cup	minced red onion	125 mL
2 tbsp	minced jalapeño pepper	25 mL
2 tbsp	lime juice	25 mL
2 tbsp	extra-virgin olive oil	25 mL
3	cloves garlic, minced	3
¾ tsp	each salt and pepper	4 mL
1	plum tomato, diced	1
2 tbsp	minced fresh coriander	25 mL

• Pit and peel avocados; cube neatly. In serving bowl, gently toss together avocados, onion, jalapeño pepper, lime juice, 1 tbsp (15 mL) of the oil, garlic and ½ tsp (2 mL) each of the salt and pepper. (*Make-ahead: Cover and refrigerate for up to 4 hours.*)
• In separate bowl, toss tomato with coriander and remaining oil, salt and pepper; sprinkle over avocado mixture.

MAKES 3 ½ CUPS (875 mL).

PER 1 TBSP (15 mL): about 29 cal, trace pro, 3 g total fat (trace sat. fat), 1 g carb, 1 g fibre, 0 mg chol, 32 mg sodium. % RDI: 1% iron, 1% vit A, 3% vit C, 4% folate.

Baked Tortilla Chips
• Brush 5 small flour tortillas with 1 tbsp (15 mL) vegetable oil; cut each into 12 wedges. Bake on rimmed baking sheet in 375°F (190°C) oven until crisp and golden, about 10 minutes. (*Make-ahead: Store in airtight container for up to 24 hours.*)

MAKES 60 PIECES.

Slow Cooker Pulled Pork

Tender enough to be shredded with a fork, pulled pork makes an easy buffet mainstay. Offer buns (to pile high with pork), pickled jalapeño peppers, shredded Cheddar cheese and light sour cream.

3½ lb	pork shoulder blade roast	1.75 kg
¾ tsp	each salt and pepper	4 mL
2 tbsp	vegetable oil	25 mL
2	onions, diced	2
4	cloves garlic, minced	4
2 tbsp	chili powder	25 mL
2 tsp	ground coriander	10 mL
2	bay leaves	2
¼ cup	tomato paste	50 mL
1	can (14 oz/398 mL) tomato sauce	1
2 tbsp	each packed brown sugar and cider vinegar	25 mL
2 tbsp	Worcestershire sauce	25 mL
2	green onions, thinly sliced	2

• Sprinkle pork with salt and pepper. In Dutch oven, heat oil over medium-high heat; brown pork all over. Transfer to slow cooker.

• Add onions, garlic, chili powder, coriander and bay leaves to Dutch oven; fry, stirring occasionally, until onions are softened, about 5 minutes.

• Add tomato paste; cook, stirring, until darkened, about 2 minutes. Add tomato sauce, sugar, vinegar and Worcestershire sauce, scraping up any brown bits. Pour into slow cooker. Cover and cook on low until pork is tender, 8 to 10 hours.

• Transfer pork to cutting board and tent with foil; let stand for 10 minutes. With two forks, shred or "pull" pork.

• Meanwhile, pour liquid from slow cooker into large saucepan; skim off fat. Bring to boil over high heat; boil vigorously until reduced to 3 cups (750 mL), about 15 minutes. Discard bay leaves. Add pork. *(Make-ahead: Let cool for 30 minutes. Refrigerate, uncovered, in airtight container until cold. Cover and refrigerate for up to 12 hours.)*

• Heat through, stirring often. Sprinkle with green onions.

MAKES 8 SERVINGS.

PER SERVING: about 342 cal, 43 g pro, 12 g total fat (3 g sat. fat), 13 g carb, 2 g fibre, 118 mg chol, 735 mg sodium. % RDI: 7% calcium, 27% iron, 14% vit A, 22% vit C, 10% folate.

VARIATION

Slow-Braised Pulled Pork: Return pork to Dutch oven. Cover and braise in 300°F (150°C) oven, basting every 30 minutes and turning once with 2 wooden spoons, until pork is tender, 3½ to 4 hours.

Sweet Pepper Slaw

Use a mandoline for paper-thin slices.

2 cups	shredded green or Napa cabbage	500 mL
1 cup	thinly sliced red onion	250 mL
1	each sweet red, yellow and green pepper, thinly sliced	1
2 tbsp	white wine vinegar	25 mL
2 tbsp	extra-virgin olive oil	25 mL
½ tsp	each salt and pepper	2 mL

• In large bowl, combine cabbage, onion and red, yellow and green peppers.
• Add vinegar, oil, salt and pepper; toss to coat. *(Make-ahead: Cover and refrigerate for up to 24 hours.)*

MAKES 8 SERVINGS.

PER SERVING: about 50 cal, 1 g pro, 4 g total fat (trace sat. fat), 5 g carb, 1 g fibre, 0 mg chol, 146 mg sodium. % RDI: 1% calcium, 3% iron, 10% vit A, 122% vit C, 8% folate.

No-Bake Lime Cheesecake Squares

You can make this dessert in just a few minutes, but guests will think you spent hours, so there's no excuse not to get outdoors with the gang.

1 tbsp	each finely slivered lemon and lime rind	15 mL
1½ cups	chocolate cookie crumbs	375 mL
⅓ cup	butter, melted	75 mL
3	pkg (each 4 oz/125 g) cream cheese, softened	3
⅔ cup	sweetened condensed milk	150 mL
½ cup	whipping cream	125 mL
2 tsp	finely grated lime rind	10 mL
¼ cup	lime juice (2 limes)	50 mL
1 tbsp	granulated sugar	15 mL

• Line 8-inch (2 L) square metal cake pan with parchment paper, leaving 1-inch (2.5 cm) overhang on 2 opposite sides. Set aside.
• Place lemon and lime slivers in bowl of ice water; refrigerate.
• In bowl, combine cookie crumbs with butter; press evenly into prepared pan. Refrigerate until firm, about 30 minutes.
• In large bowl, beat cream cheese at medium-high speed until smooth. Add condensed milk, ¼ cup (50 mL) of the cream, grated lime rind and juice and sugar; beat until smooth. Scrape over chilled base; smooth with spatula. Refrigerate until set, about 4 hours. *(Make-ahead: Cover with plastic wrap; refrigerate for up to 2 days.)*
• Using paper overhang as handles, transfer cheesecake from pan to cutting board. Using hot knife and wiping blade clean after each cut, cut into squares.
• Whip remaining cream; spoon or pipe about 1 tsp (5 mL) onto each square. Drain lemon and lime slivers and pat dry; arrange on whipped cream.

MAKES 16 SQUARES.

PER SQUARE: about 230 cal, 4 g pro, 17 g total fat (10 g sat. fat), 16 g carb, trace fibre, 52 mg chol, 208 mg sodium. % RDI: 6% calcium, 7% iron, 16% vit A, 5% vit C, 2% folate.

Beaded Napkin Ring

Create a quick napkin ring with sparkle and style.

• Fold napkin in half, then tightly roll up; wrap with 26-inch (66 cm) length of sheer, wire-edged ribbon and knot. Coil ribbon ends as desired; cut notch in each end.

• Cut 26-inch (66 cm) length of 26-gauge beading wire. One at a time, thread faceted crystal beads onto wire: Thread first bead to midpoint, then tightly twist wire ends together to form short "branch," ⅜ to 1 inch (1 to 2.5 cm) long; working out along each end, create more beaded branches in same manner, leaving 3 inches (7.5 cm) free at each end.

• Twist wire ends around ribbon knot and trim.

Beribboned Cutlery

Use holiday ribbon scraps to tie up each set of cutlery, then set atop a snow-white napkin at each placesetting.

Christmas Crackers

A snap to make, customized Christmas crackers can be personalized for each of your guests.

• Cut empty paper-towel roll to 4½-inch (11.5 cm) length. Stuff with snapper (available at some craft and party stores), and favours (such as paper hat; handwritten poem, message or wish; chocolates; windup toy and/or tiny bottle of liqueur).

• Centre roll along edge of 12-inch (30.5 cm) square of gift wrap, tissue, paper ribbon or foil. Roll up, then tie each end with thin cord, twine, ribbon or raffia (threaded with bead, button or tiny jingle bell, if desired).

• Wrap ribbon or band of contrasting paper around centre; adhere with glue stick.

• Use dimensional paint or metallic fine-tip marker to label with name.

Chapter Three

CREATIVE ENTERTAINING

Cauliflower Bisque

Holiday meals don't need big appetizers. Just a small bowl of elegant soup will invite everyone to the table.

2 tbsp	butter or canola oil	25 mL
1	large onion, chopped	1
1	potato, peeled and chopped	1
½ tsp	curry paste	2 mL
1	cauliflower (about 2 lb/1 kg)	1
4 cups	chicken or vegetable stock	1 L
2 cups	18% cream or milk	500 mL
¼ tsp	each salt and hot pepper sauce	1 mL
¼ cup	thin strips red onion	50 mL
¼ cup	chopped fresh coriander	50 mL

• In large saucepan, melt butter over low heat. Add onion, potato and curry paste; cover and cook, stirring occasionally, until onion is translucent, about 6 minutes.
• Meanwhile, trim cauliflower and chop coarsely. Add to pan along with stock; bring to boil. Cover, reduce heat and simmer until vegetables are tender, about 10 minutes. Let cool slightly.
• In blender in batches, or using immersion blender, purée cauliflower mixture until smooth. Strain through sieve into clean saucepan. *(Make-ahead: Let cool for 30 minutes; refrigerate, uncovered, in airtight container until cold. Cover and refrigerate for up to 24 hours.)*

• Stir in cream, salt and hot pepper sauce; heat over low heat, stirring often, until hot. Ladle into warmed soup bowls. Garnish with onion and coriander.

MAKES 12 SERVINGS.

PER SERVING: about 130 cal, 4 g pro, 10 g total fat (6 g sat. fat), 7 g carb, 2 g fibre, 30 mg chol, 357 mg sodium. % RDI: 5% calcium, 3% iron, 8% vit A, 37% vit C, 12% folate.

Canadian Living Cooking and Baking Basics

❯ Read the recipe through before starting.

❯ The size of fresh food (such as fruits and vegetables) and equipment is medium.

❯ Sizes of pans and dishes are given when essential to a recipe.

❯ All foods requiring washing are washed before preparation.

❯ Foods such as apples, onions and bananas are peeled.

❯ Eggs are large and are shelled.

❯ Butter is salted unless otherwise stated.

❯ All-purpose flour, icing sugar and cocoa powder are not sifted before measuring.

❯ Pepper is black and freshly ground.

❯ Dried herbs are crumbled, not ground.

❯ Ovens are preheated. Items are baked in the centre of oven unless otherwise noted.

❯ Saucepans are uncovered unless noted.

❯ Generic names for ingredients (for example, hot pepper sauce for Tabasco and others) are used unless a specific brand is essential to the recipe.

Holiday Soup

Impromptu dinner parties are no problem with this festive stylish soup — you can whip it up at a moment's notice.

1 tbsp	vegetable oil	15 mL
2	onions, chopped	2
4	cloves garlic, minced	4
2 cups	cubed peeled potatoes	500 mL
1 tsp	dried mint	5 mL
½ tsp	each salt and pepper	2 mL
5 cups	chicken or vegetable stock	1.25 L
4 cups	frozen peas	1 L
½ cup	light sour cream	125 mL
Half	sweet red pepper, finely diced	Half

• In large saucepan, heat oil over medium heat; fry onions, garlic, potatoes, mint, salt and pepper, stirring occasionally, until onions are softened, about 8 minutes.
• Add stock and peas; bring to boil. Reduce heat to medium-low; cover and simmer until potatoes are tender, about 10 minutes.
• In blender in batches, or using immersion blender, purée until smooth. Strain if desired. *(Make-ahead: Let cool for 30 minutes; refrigerate, uncovered, in airtight container until cold. Cover and refrigerate for up to 24 hours.)*
• Return to saucepan; heat until hot. Ladle into warmed soup bowls. Spoon sour cream into small plastic bag with 1 corner snipped off; pipe tree design over soup. Sprinkle with red pepper.

MAKES 8 SERVINGS.

PER SERVING: about 157 cal, 9 g pro, 4 g total fat (1 g sat. fat), 23 g carb, 4 g fibre, 2 mg chol, 701 mg sodium. % RDI: 6% calcium, 11% iron, 9% vit A, 42% vit C, 22% folate.

Salmon Cheesecake

Top each serving with a smoked salmon curl and crème fraîche or sour cream.

1 cup	crushed salted crackers	250 mL
⅓ cup	butter, melted	75 mL
2 tbsp	cornmeal	25 mL
2	pkg (each 8 oz/250 g) cream cheese, softened	2
3	eggs	3
3 tbsp	milk	50 mL
1 tbsp	lemon juice	15 mL
½ tsp	pepper	2 mL
4 oz	smoked salmon, chopped	125 g
⅓ cup	minced green onion	75 mL
2 tbsp	minced fresh parsley	25 mL

• Grease bottom of 9-inch (2.5 L) springform pan; line side with parchment paper. Set on square of heavy-duty foil; press up side.
• In bowl, stir crumbs, butter and cornmeal until moistened; press into prepared pan. Bake in centre of 350°F (180°C) oven until golden, about 10 minutes. Let cool on rack.
• In large bowl, beat cream cheese until fluffy; beat in eggs, 1 at a time. Beat in milk, lemon juice and pepper; stir in salmon, green onion and parsley. Pour over crust.
• Set pan in larger pan; pour enough hot water into larger pan to come 1 inch (2.5 cm) up sides. Bake in centre of 325°F (160°C) oven until edge is set but centre still jiggles slightly, about 35 minutes. Remove from water; transfer to rack. Remove foil; let cool. Cover and refrigerate until set, 2 hours. *(Make-ahead: Refrigerate for up to 2 days.)*

MAKES 16 TO 20 SERVINGS.

PER EACH OF 20 SERVINGS: about 154 cal, 4 g pro, 13 g total fat (8 g sat. fat), 5 g carb, 19 g fibre, 68 mg chol, 205 mg sodium. % RDI: 3% calcium, 5% iron, 14% vit A, 2% vit C, 5% folate.

Crab Cakes with Citrus Mayo

Chipotle hot pepper sauce gives this sit-down appetizer the nicest hint of smoke and fire.

1 tbsp	butter	15 mL
2	cloves garlic, minced	2
½ tsp	dried thyme	2 mL
½ cup	fresh bread crumbs	125 mL
2	pkg (each 7 oz/200 g) frozen crabmeat, thawed	2
¼ cup	minced fresh chives or green onion	50 mL
1	egg	1
1 tsp	Dijon mustard	5 mL
¼ tsp	pepper	1 mL

CITRUS MAYO:

⅔ cup	light mayonnaise	150 mL
1½ tsp	each grated lemon and orange rind	7 mL
1½ tsp	each lemon and orange juice	7 mL
½ tsp	chipotle hot pepper sauce or hot pepper sauce	2 mL

WATERCRESS SALAD:

4 cups	watercress leaves and tender stems only (about 2 bunches)	1 L
4	radishes, thinly sliced	4
1	Belgian endive, sliced	1
1 tbsp	vegetable oil	15 mL
1 tbsp	extra-virgin olive oil	15 mL
1 tbsp	each lemon and orange juice	15 mL
½ tsp	Dijon mustard	2 mL
Pinch	each salt and pepper	Pinch

● CITRUS MAYO: In small bowl, whisk together mayonnaise, lemon and orange rinds and juice, and hot pepper sauce. Transfer 3 tbsp (50 mL) to large bowl for crab cakes. Cover and refrigerate remainder for garnish.

● In skillet, melt butter over medium heat; fry garlic and thyme until fragrant, about 1 minute. Add bread crumbs; cook, stirring often, until golden, about 6 minutes. Transfer to shallow dish.

● In sieve, pick through crabmeat to remove any cartilage; press to remove liquid. Add to Citrus Mayo. Add chives, egg, mustard and pepper; stir until combined. Press by heaping 1 tbsp (15 mL) into ½-inch (1 cm) thick patties; press lightly into bread crumb mixture to coat both sides. *(Make-ahead: Freeze on baking sheet until firm, about 2 hours. Layer between waxed paper in airtight container and freeze for up to 2 weeks. Thaw in refrigerator.)*

● Arrange crab cakes on parchment paper–lined rimmed baking sheet; bake in 425°F (220°C) oven, turning once, until crisp and golden, about 14 minutes.

● WATERCRESS SALAD: Meanwhile, in large bowl, combine watercress, radishes and endive. In small bowl, whisk together vegetable and olive oils, lemon and orange juices, mustard, salt and pepper; add to watercress mixture and toss to coat. Divide among plates. Top each with 2 crab cakes and spoonful of reserved Citrus Mayo.

MAKES 8 SERVINGS.

PER SERVING: about 129 cal, 14 g pro, 7 g total fat (2 g sat. fat), 3 g carb, 1 g fibre, 63 mg chol, 406 mg sodium. % RDI: 5% calcium, 13% iron, 14% vit A, 28% vit C, 16% folate.

❯ *Dress Up the Dining Table*

Add instant holiday glamour with three all-out gorgeous place settings.

Pleasant Under Glass

Sunny yellow orchids brighten this lovely holiday luncheon table dressed with an Irish damask tablecloth woven with a stylized floral pattern. Personalized with a handwritten place card, a single orchid with sprigs of boxwood and berries is set beneath an upended shrimp bowl at each placesetting.

Stylish and Sophisticated

Crisscrossed over the tabletop, runners of shimmery chocolate silk contrast beautifully with the spotless linens and shining silver and crystal. Gold spray paint lends a luxurious look to inexpensive gift boxes, which hold handblown ornaments, nestled in gold tissue and adorned with sweet little satin bows, for the guests to take home.

Seasonal Hues

Red jacquard place mats and napkins are layered with gilt-rimmed chargers and pretty plates. On top, gleaming organza bags offer sugarplums (foil-covered chocolates and rosy tree balls). Simple white votive candles, in clear glass containers edged with gold, add a flickering glow. In the centrepiece, plump cream-colour roses, paired with matching mini-ornaments, boost the Christmas colour.

81

Honey Balsamic Ham

With all the fussing that's part of large festive meals, it's a relief to simply put a ham in the oven to serve with the Curried Pears, recipe this page. Ham is as delicious hot as it is cold, and the big bonuses are the smoky leftovers for sandwiches and salads and, as the feasting season ends, the bone that enriches a bean soup.

15 lb	fully cooked bone-in smoked ham	6.75 kg
2 tbsp	liquid honey	25 mL
2 tbsp	Dijon mustard	25 mL
2 tbsp	balsamic vinegar	25 mL

• Remove skin and all but ¼ inch (5 mm) fat on ham. Score diagonally through fat but not into meat to form diamond pattern. Place, scored side up, on rack in roasting pan; roast in 325°F (160°C) oven for 2 hours.

• Stir together honey, mustard and vinegar; brush about one-third over ham. Roast, brushing twice with remaining honey mixture, until meat thermometer registers 140°F (60°C), about 1 hour. *(Make-ahead: Let cool, wrap and refrigerate for up to 3 days.)* Transfer to cutting board. Tent with foil and let stand for 20 minutes before carving.

MAKES 16 TO 20 SERVINGS.

PER EACH OF 20 SERVINGS: about 229 cal, 29 g pro, 10 g total fat (4 g sat. fat), 3 g carb, 0 g fibre, 76 mg chol, 1,867 mg sodium. % RDI: 1% calcium, 14% iron, 2% folate.

Curried Pears

Small Forelle pears are just the right size to serve with ham.

1 tbsp	butter	15 mL
1	shallot or small onion, chopped	1
2 tsp	mild curry paste	10 mL
½ cup	pear nectar	125 mL
¼ cup	packed brown sugar	50 mL
6	small pears (about 3 lb/1.5 kg)	6

• In large skillet, melt butter over medium heat; fry shallot, stirring often, for 3 minutes. Stir in curry paste; cook, stirring, for 3 minutes. Add pear nectar and sugar; bring to boil, stirring until blended. Set aside.

• Peel pears, without removing stems if possible; cut in half. Using melon baller or spoon, scoop out core. Place pears in single layer, cut side up, in shallow baking dish; pour sauce over top. Cover and bake in 325°F (160°C) oven for 30 minutes.

• Turn pears over; bake, basting occasionally, until glazed and tender but not mushy, about 30 minutes. Let cool. *(Make-ahead: Refrigerate in airtight container for up to 5 days.)*

MAKES 12 PIECES.

PER PIECE: about 88 cal, trace pro, 2 g total fat (1 g sat. fat), 20 g carb, 2 g fibre, 3 mg chol, 12 mg sodium. % RDI: 1% calcium, 3% iron, 1% vit A, 5% vit C, 2% folate.

Roast Prime Rib with Rosemary Jus Lié

Roast prime rib of beef certainly speaks of a grand celebration. The simple, flavourful sauce of slightly thickened pan juices, or jus lié, mixed with wine and stock adds a touch of sheer elegance. For a dramatic holiday presentation, choose a roast with at least three ribs.

2 tbsp	chopped fresh thyme (or 2 tsp/10 mL dried)	25 mL
3	cloves garlic, minced	3
½ tsp	salt	2 mL
¼ tsp	pepper	1 mL
Pinch	cayenne pepper	Pinch
1	prime rib premium oven roast (5 to 7 lb/2.2 to 3.15 kg)	1
2	onions, thickly sliced	2
4	sprigs fresh rosemary (or 1 tbsp/15 mL dried)	4
1 cup	dry red wine	250 mL
¾ cup	beef stock	175 mL
2 tsp	cornstarch	10 mL
2 tbsp	butter	25 mL

- On cutting board, mix thyme with garlic; sprinkle with salt. Holding knife blade at very low angle, rub many times to form smooth paste. Mix in pepper and cayenne; rub over roast. Wrap and refrigerate for 4 hours. *(Make-ahead: Refrigerate for up to 24 hours.)*
- Scatter onions and rosemary in greased roasting pan. Place roast, bone side down, on onion mixture. Roast in 325°F (160°C) oven until meat thermometer inserted in centre registers 140°F (60°C) for medium-rare, 1¾ to 2 hours, or 155°F (68°C) for medium, 2¼ to 2½ hours, or to desired doneness.
- Transfer to carving board; tent with foil and let stand for at least 10 minutes or for up to 30 minutes.
- Meanwhile, skim fat from pan juices; place pan over high heat. Add wine; cook, scraping up any brown bits, until reduced by half, about 3 minutes. In small bowl, whisk stock into cornstarch; whisk into pan and bring to boil. Boil for 1 minute; stir in butter. Strain.
- Slice bones off meat and separate each rib. Slice meat and arrange on warmed platter along with ribs. Stir accumulated juices into sauce.

MAKES 8 TO 10 SERVINGS.

PER EACH OF 10 SERVINGS: about 297 cal, 32 g pro, 15 g total fat (7 g sat. fat), 3 g carb, trace fibre, 80 mg chol, 276 mg sodium. % RDI: 2% calcium, 21% iron, 2% vit A, 2% vit C, 5% folate.

Let the Roast Rest

All large pieces of meat or poultry need to rest before carving to allow juices time to redistribute evenly, resulting in much neater slices. Without a rest, juices spill out onto the carving board leaving the meat dry.

> HERE'S HOW: Upon transferring the roast or poultry from the oven to platter, loosely tent with foil for 10 to 20 minutes for a roast, and up to 30 minutes for a turkey.

Apple and Chestnut–Stuffed Roast Goose

Although turkey has far surpassed goose as Canada's favourite Christmas bird, goose is still the traditional roast for many people of Northern, Central and Eastern European descent. For lovers of tasty dark meat, nothing quite compares. Use a firm, tart apple for the stuffing, such as Northern Spy, Gravenstein, Braeburn or Granny Smith.

10 lb	goose (with neck and giblets)	4.5 kg
2 tbsp	butter	25 mL
2 tsp	fennel seeds, lightly crushed	10 mL
1	onion, finely chopped	1
1	stalk celery, finely chopped	1
1	clove garlic, minced	1
4 cups	diced cored peeled tart apples (about 4)	1 L
½ cup	chopped fresh parsley	125 mL
1 tbsp	chopped fresh thyme (or 1 tsp/5 mL dried)	15 mL
½ tsp	each salt and pepper	2 mL
4 cups	cubed white bread	1 L
3 cups	peeled cooked or canned chestnuts	750 mL
1	egg, lightly beaten	1
½ cup	dry white vermouth, white wine or beef stock	125 mL
2 tbsp	lemon juice	25 mL
2 tbsp	brandy	25 mL
3 tbsp	all-purpose flour	50 mL
2½ cups	beef or chicken stock	625 mL

• Remove neck and giblets from cavity of goose. Pull out any loose fat from cavity. Remove wing tips; reserve for stock. Finely chop liver and reserve.

• In large skillet, heat butter over medium heat; fry fennel seeds for 30 seconds. Add onion, celery and garlic; fry, stirring often, until softened, about 5 minutes.

• Add reserved liver; fry for 1 minute. Stir in apples, parsley, thyme and ¼ tsp (1 mL) each of the salt and pepper; cook for 7 minutes. Transfer to large bowl. Mix in bread, chestnuts and egg; let cool.

• Pat goose cavities dry. Stuff neck and body cavities with apple mixture; skewer closed. Tie wings to body; tie legs together. Lightly prick all over with tip of knife. Sprinkle with remaining salt and pepper.

• Place goose on rack in roasting pan; roast in 400°F (200°C) oven for 20 minutes. Reduce heat to 350°F (180°C); roast for 20 minutes. Remove from oven; pour clear fat from pan.

• Mix vermouth with lemon juice; brush over goose. Roast, basting often, until meat thermometer inserted in thickest part of thigh registers 180°F (82°C), 1¼ to 1½ hours longer. Transfer to warmed platter and tent with foil; let stand for at least 15 minutes or for up to 30 minutes.

• Skim off all but 2 tbsp (25 mL) fat from pan, retaining all pan juices. Add brandy to pan; cook over medium heat for 1 minute, scraping up any brown bits. Sprinkle with flour; cook, stirring, until lightly browned, about 2 minutes. Gradually whisk in stock; simmer until thickened, about 6 minutes. Strain. Serve with goose.

MAKES 8 SERVINGS.

PER SERVING: about 778 cal, 68 g pro, 37 g total fat (13 g sat. fat), 38 g carb, 6 g fibre, 308 mg chol, 464 mg sodium. % RDI: 10% calcium, 86% iron, 105% vit A, 37% vit C, 61% folate.

Chestnuts

Chestnuts have to be peeled and cooked before using. They can be roasted in their shells, boiled, braised, puréed or even candied (marrons glacés). Their sweet nutty flavour combines well with game, poultry, starchy vegetables, mushrooms, chocolate, whipped cream or vanilla.

❯ To prepare fresh chestnuts for cooking, cut X on flat side of each chestnut. In saucepan of boiling water, cook chestnuts, 4 at a time, until points of cut curl, about 2 minutes; drain. With knife, pull off skins. In saucepan, cover peeled chestnuts with water and bring to boil; cook over medium heat until tender, about 5 minutes.

At the store

Fresh chestnuts have the best flavour and texture, but if you don't have a kitchen brigade at your disposal, peeling them is time consuming. Look for these alternative products at grocery and specialty stores.

❯ DRIED CHESTNUTS are the least expensive and most like fresh chestnuts in flavour and texture. Look for them in Italian and Chinese grocery stores all year round. To prepare: In bowl, soak 2 cups (500 mL) chestnuts in 6 cups (1.5 L) boiling water for at least 2 hours or overnight; drain. In saucepan, cover chestnuts with water and bring to boil; cook over medium heat until tender, about 15 minutes. Drain and they are ready to use in a recipe.

❯ VACUUM-PACKED CHESTNUTS are softer than fresh but are ready to use interchangeably with prepared fresh or dried ones. Though more expensive than ready-to-use canned, their taste is superior. If you are chopping them for a recipe, look for less expensive chestnut pieces.

❯ CANNED CHESTNUTS are cooked and ready to use interchangeably with prepared fresh, dried and vacuum-packed ones. Rinse and drain well before using. Some are packed in syrup for use in desserts, so check the labels.

Mushroom Tourtière

This classic is made with ground pork, often with the addition of potatoes for thickening. Mushrooms are unconventional, but tourtière fans will be happy with the extra flavour.

1½ cups	cubed peeled potatoes	375 mL
2 lb	lean ground pork	1 kg
2 cups	sliced mushrooms	500 mL
¾ cup	finely chopped celery	175 mL
¾ cup	chicken stock	175 mL
2	onions, finely chopped	2
3	cloves garlic, minced	3
¾ tsp	salt	4 mL
½ tsp	each pepper, dried savory and thyme	2 mL
¼ tsp	each ground cloves and cinnamon	1 mL
1	bay leaf	1
	Really Flaky Pastry (recipe, this page)	
1	egg yolk	1

• In saucepan of boiling salted water, cover and cook potatoes until tender, about 12 minutes. Drain and mash; set aside.

• Meanwhile, in large skillet, sauté pork over medium-high heat, mashing with fork, until no longer pink, 8 minutes. Drain off fat.

• Add mushrooms, celery, stock, onions, garlic, salt, pepper, savory, thyme, cloves, cinnamon and bay leaf; bring to boil. Reduce heat, cover and simmer until almost no liquid remains, about 25 minutes. Discard bay leaf. Mix in potatoes. Let cool.

• On lightly floured surface, roll out 1 of the pastry discs to scant ¼-inch (5 mm) thickness. Fit into 9-inch (23 cm) pie plate. Spoon in filling. Roll out remaining pastry. Brush pastry rim with water; cover with top pastry and press edge to seal. Trim and flute.

• Roll out pastry scraps; cut out holiday shapes. *(Make-ahead: Wrap tourtière and shapes separately; refrigerate for up to 24 hours. Or overwrap in heavy-duty foil and freeze for up to 2 weeks; thaw in refrigerator. Add 20 to 30 minutes to baking time, covering with foil after 45 minutes; remove foil for last 10 minutes.)*

• Mix egg yolk with 2 tsp (10 mL) water; brush three-quarters over top. Arrange cutouts on top; brush with remaining egg wash. Cut steam vents in top. Bake in bottom third of 400°F (200°C) oven until hot and golden brown, about 50 minutes.

MAKES 8 SERVINGS.

PER SERVING: about 649 cal, 28 g pro, 39 g total fat (18 g sat. fat), 45 g carb, 3 g fibre, 171 mg chol, 831 mg sodium. % RDI: 5% calcium, 29% iron, 13% vit A, 8% vit C, 36% folate.

Really Flaky Pastry

3 cups	all-purpose flour	750 mL
1 tsp	salt	5 mL
½ cup	each cold butter and lard, cubed	125 mL
1	egg	1
2 tsp	vinegar	10 mL
	Ice water	

• In bowl, whisk flour with salt. Using pastry blender or 2 knives, cut in butter and lard until in coarse crumbs with a few larger pieces.

• In liquid measure, beat egg with vinegar; add enough ice water to make ⅔ cup (150 mL). Drizzle over flour mixture, tossing with fork until ragged dough forms.

• Press into 2 discs. Wrap and refrigerate until chilled, about 30 minutes. *(Make-ahead: Refrigerate for up to 3 days.)* Makes enough pastry for 1 double-crust 9-inch (23 cm) pie.

Shrimp Coulibiac

Shrimp replace salmon, the traditional seafood in coulibiac, for this supper dish.

1½ cups	diced peeled potatoes	375 mL
1 tbsp	extra-virgin olive oil	15 mL
2	leeks (white part only), sliced	2
1 lb	small raw shrimp, peeled and deveined	500 g
½ tsp	each salt and pepper	2 mL
2	eggs	2
¼ cup	sour cream	50 mL
3 tbsp	chopped fresh dill	50 mL
4	green onions, sliced	4
1	pkg (1 lb/450 g) frozen butter puff pastry, thawed and cold	1

• In saucepan of boiling salted water, cover and cook potatoes until tender, about 10 minutes. Drain and let cool.
• Meanwhile, in large skillet, heat oil over medium-high heat; sauté leeks until softened, 3 minutes. Add shrimp and ¼ tsp (1 mL) each of the salt and pepper; sauté until shrimp are pink, 5 minutes. Let cool.
• In large bowl, whisk 1 of the eggs; add sour cream, dill, onions and remaining salt and pepper. Add shrimp mixture and potatoes.
• Lay 1 sheet pastry on parchment paper–lined rimless baking sheet. Mound shrimp mixture in centre, leaving 2-inch (5 cm) border. Mix remaining egg with 1 tbsp (15 mL) water; brush over border. Top with second sheet; press and crimp edges.
• Brush with remaining eggwash; cut slashes for steam vents. Bake in bottom third of 375°F (190°C) oven until golden, 40 minutes.

MAKES 6 TO 8 SERVINGS.

PER EACH OF 8 SERVINGS: about 361 cal, 17 g pro, 18 g total fat (7 g sat. fat), 31 g carb, 3 g fibre, 158 mg chol, 529 mg sodium. % RDI: 6% calcium, 27% iron, 12% vit A, 8% vit C, 10% folate.

Seafood Salmon Roulade

Stuffed with shrimp and scallops and napped with a delicate beurre blanc sauce, this salmon roll makes an elegant dish for holiday entertaining. It's easier to skin and roll the salmon if it's very cold. You can ask the fishmonger to do the skinning.

2 lb	centre cut salmon fillet	1 kg
¼ tsp	each salt and pepper	1 mL
SEAFOOD STUFFING:		
1	egg white	1
8 oz	raw Black Tiger shrimp, peeled and deveined	250 g
8 oz	bay scallops	250 g
¾ cup	fresh bread crumbs	175 mL
⅓ cup	chopped fresh chives	75 mL
¼ cup	chopped fresh parsley	50 mL
1 tsp	grated lemon rind	5 mL
1 tsp	chopped fresh tarragon (or ¼ tsp/1 mL dried)	5 mL
¼ tsp	each salt and pepper	1 mL
LEMON TARRAGON BEURRE BLANC:		
2	shallots, minced	2
⅓ cup	white wine vinegar	75 mL
¼ cup	dry vermouth	50 mL
¾ cup	unsalted butter, cubed	175 mL
1 tbsp	chopped fresh tarragon	15 mL
1 tsp	lemon juice	5 mL
Pinch	salt	Pinch

• **SEAFOOD STUFFING:** In bowl, whisk egg white until frothy; set aside. Finely chop shrimp. Cut scallops into ½-inch (1 cm) cubes. Add seafood to egg white. Add bread crumbs, chives, parsley, lemon rind, tarragon, salt and pepper; toss to combine. Refrigerate.

- Place salmon fillet, skin side down, on cutting board. At 1 end corner, cut between flesh and skin just enough to grip skin. Holding skin with paper towel and angling knife slightly toward skin but without moving, slowly pull skin back and forth to remove. Discard skin. Trim any silver skin remaining.

- At thinnest long side and starting where salmon starts to thicken, cut in half horizontally almost but not all the way through; open like book. Sprinkle with half each of the salt and pepper. Leaving 1-inch (2.5 cm) border on both long and 1 short side, spread stuffing over salmon.

- Starting at side with stuffing, roll up. With kitchen string, tie at 1-inch (2.5 cm) intervals. Place, what was skin side down, on parchment paper–lined rimmed baking sheet. Sprinkle with remaining salt and pepper. *(Make-ahead: Cover and refrigerate for up to 2 hours.)*

- Roast in 375°F (190°C) oven until thermometer inserted into stuffing through end of roll registers 160°F (70°C), about 50 minutes. Transfer to cutting board and tent with foil; let stand for 10 minutes.

- LEMON TARRAGON BEURRE BLANC: Meanwhile, in small saucepan, boil shallots, vinegar and vermouth until reduced to 2 tbsp (25 mL), about 3 minutes. Reduce heat to low; whisk in butter, piece by piece, until smooth. Add tarragon, lemon juice and salt.

- Using chef's knife and gentle sawing motion, cut salmon crosswise into 1-inch (2.5 cm) thick portions, removing string. Serve with beurre blanc sauce.

MAKES 8 SERVINGS.

PER SERVING: about 414 cal, 31 g pro, 29 g total fat (13 g sat. fat), 5 g carb, trace fibre, 149 mg chol, 314 mg sodium. % RDI: 4% calcium, 10% iron, 21% vit A, 12% vit C, 16% folate.

Step 1: To cut salmon in half horizontally, start where it starts to thicken at thinnest long side.

Step 2: Starting at side with stuffing, roll up salmon.

❯ Snacks for Santa and His Team

Stand a fresh bunch of leaf-topped carrots (for the reindeer) in a tall wire basket set on a decorative platter, then surround with home-baked cookies (for Santa) and place on the hearth.

❯ 10-Minute Flower Arrangement

With knife, cut piece of floral foam to fit urn or deep, wide container; add enough water to thoroughly moisten. Choose flowers and berry sprigs in simple colour range, such as these red roses and hypericum berries. With secateurs, trim stems as you go and work from rim to centre, pushing stems into foam to create tightly packed arrangement that sits just above rim, then mounds slightly at centre.

Coq au Vin

This classic dish is ideal for entertaining, since you can sit and sip with guests while the dish simmers.

3 lb	boneless skinless chicken thighs and/or breasts	1.5 kg
2 tbsp	butter	25 mL
2 cups	pearl onions (one 284 g bag), peeled	500 mL
2 cups	button mushrooms (8 oz/250 g)	500 mL
1 cup	chopped onions	250 mL
2 tsp	chopped fresh thyme (or 1 tsp/5 mL dried)	10 mL
Pinch	each salt and pepper	Pinch
1	bay leaf	1
1½ cups	dry red wine	375 mL
1½ cups	chicken stock	375 mL
2 tbsp	tomato paste	25 mL
1 tbsp	Cognac or brandy (optional)	15 mL
2 tbsp	chopped fresh parsley	25 mL

PUFF PASTRY STARS:

Half	pkg (1 lb/450 g) frozen butter puff pastry, thawed and cold	Half
1	egg, beaten	1

● If using chicken breasts, cut crosswise in half. In shallow Dutch oven, heat 1 tbsp (15 mL) of the butter over medium-high heat; brown chicken, in batches, about 10 minutes. Remove to plate.

● Drain fat from pan; reduce heat to medium. Add pearl onions and mushrooms; fry until browned, about 5 minutes. Transfer to separate plate.

● Add remaining butter to pan; fry chopped onions, thyme, salt, pepper and bay leaf until onions are softened, about 8 minutes.

● Add wine, stock, tomato paste, and Cognac (if using); bring to boil over high heat, stirring and scraping up any brown bits. Return chicken and any accumulated juices to pan. Reduce heat to medium; cover and simmer, stirring occasionally, for 20 minutes.

● Return mushroom mixture to pan; simmer, covered and stirring occasionally, until reduced to consistency of maple syrup and juices run clear when chicken is pierced, about 25 minutes. Discard bay leaf. Stir in parsley. *(Make-ahead: Let cool for 30 minutes; refrigerate, uncovered, in airtight container until cold. Cover and refrigerate for up to 2 days. Reheat in 350°F/180°C oven for about 30 minutes.)*

● **PUFF PASTRY STARS:** Meanwhile, on lightly floured surface, roll out pastry to ¼-inch (5 mm) thickness. Using star-shaped cutters of various sizes, cut out stars. Place on rimmed baking sheet; brush with egg. Bake in centre of 400°F (200°C) oven until golden, about 15 minutes. Arrange over coq au vin.

MAKES 8 SERVINGS.

PER SERVING: about 402 cal, 37 g pro, 19 g total fat (7 g sat. fat), 19 g carb, 2 g fibre, 183 mg chol, 418 mg sodium. % RDI: 4% calcium, 26% iron, 10% vit A, 15% vit C, 12% folate.

Wine-Braised Veal Shanks

Veal shanks are sometimes labelled osso bucco in the store.

3 tbsp	all-purpose flour	50 mL
8	pieces veal hind shank (1½ inches/4 cm thick)	8
½ tsp	each salt and pepper	2 mL
4 tsp	extra-virgin olive oil	20 mL
1	onion, chopped	1
4	cloves garlic, minced	4
1 tsp	dried rosemary, crumbled	5 mL
¾ cup	white wine or sodium-reduced chicken stock	175 mL
¾ cup	sodium-reduced chicken stock	175 mL
1 tsp	grated lemon rind	5 mL
1 tbsp	lemon juice	15 mL
½ cup	halved pitted green olives	125 mL
1 tbsp	capers, rinsed	15 mL
2 tbsp	chopped fresh parsley	25 mL

• Spread flour on plate. Tie kitchen string around each veal shank. Sprinkle with ¼ tsp (1 mL) each of the salt and pepper; press into flour to coat. Reserve remaining flour.
• In large Dutch oven, heat 1 tbsp (15 mL) of the oil over medium-high heat; brown veal, in batches. Transfer to plate.

• Drain fat from pan; add remaining oil. Add onion, garlic, rosemary and remaining salt and pepper; fry over medium heat, stirring occasionally, until softened, about 5 minutes. Sprinkle with reserved flour; cook, stirring, for 1 minute.
• Add wine, stock and lemon rind and juice; bring to boil, stirring and scraping up brown bits. Return veal and any accumulated juices to pan; bring to simmer. Cover and braise in 325°F (160°C) oven, basting every 30 minutes, for 1¾ hours.
• Turn veal. Add olives and capers; cook, uncovered and basting twice, until veal is tender and sauce is thickened, 30 to 45 minutes. Sprinkle with parsley.

MAKES 8 SERVINGS.

PER SERVING: about 258 cal, 35 g pro, 10 g total fat (3 g sat. fat), 5 g carb, 1 g fibre, 148 mg chol, 540 mg sodium. % RDI: 4% calcium, 14% iron, 1% vit A, 5% vit C, 12% folate.

Turkey Phyllo Strudel

Phyllo pastry adds elegance to leftovers.

1 tbsp	extra-virgin olive oil (approx)	15 mL
2	Spanish onions, sliced	2
10	sheets phyllo pastry	10
⅓ cup	butter, melted	75 mL
2 cups	shredded smoked Gruyère cheese	500 mL
1	jar (13 oz/370 mL) roasted red peppers, drained and sliced	1
½ cup	fresh bread crumbs	125 mL
4 cups	coarsely chopped cooked turkey breast	1 L
½ tsp	pepper	2 mL

• In skillet, heat oil over medium-high heat; fry onions, adding more oil if necessary, until golden brown, 10 to 15 minutes. Set aside.

• Place 1 phyllo sheet, with long side closest, on waxed paper, covering remainder with damp towel to prevent drying out. Brush with butter. Repeat to make 5 layers.

• Sprinkle ½ cup (125 mL) of the cheese lengthwise in 3-inch (8 cm) wide strip 3 inches (8 cm) from closest edge, leaving 2-inch (5 cm) border at each end. Top with half each of the onions, red peppers, bread crumbs, turkey and pepper; sprinkle with ½ cup (125 mL) of the cheese.

• Fold phyllo bottom then sides over filling; roll up. Place, seam side down, on greased baking sheet. Brush with butter. Repeat to make 2 rolls. Bake in centre of 375°F (190°C) oven until golden, 25 to 30 minutes. Let stand for 5 minutes before slicing.

MAKES 8 SERVINGS.

PER SERVING: about 459 cal, 33 g pro, 23 g total fat (11 g sat. fat), 29 g carb, 2 g fibre, 100 mg chol, 450 mg sodium. % RDI: 30% calcium, 18% iron, 26% vit A, 88% vit C, 15% folate.

Fritto Misto

In keeping with Italian tradition, Ciustina Fernandes, mother of Canadian Living Test Kitchen alumna Emily Richards, serves this batter-coated deep-fried fish and seafood with lemon wedges on Christmas Eve.

1 cup	all-purpose flour	250 mL
2 tsp	baking powder	10 mL
½ tsp	each salt and grated lemon rind	2 mL
Pinch	pepper	Pinch
2 lb	cod or halibut fillets	1 kg
1 lb	small squid (calamari), cleaned	500 g
1 lb	large raw shrimp, peeled and deveined	500 g
	Vegetable oil for deep-frying	

• In bowl, whisk flour, baking powder, salt, lemon rind and pepper; whisk in 1 cup (250 mL) water until smooth; set aside.

• Cut cod into 3-inch (8 cm) chunks. Cut any tentacles off squid; discard. Pat shrimp, cod and squid dry with paper towel.

• In deep-fryer or deep heavy-bottomed pot, heat oil to 375°F (190°C) or until 1-inch (2.5 cm) cube of white bread turns golden in 30 seconds.

• Using fork, dip shrimp, cod and squid, 1 piece at a time, into batter, letting excess drip back into bowl. Fry, in batches and turning halfway through, until golden, 3 minutes. Using slotted spoon, transfer to paper towel–lined baking sheet. Keep warm in 250°F (120°C) oven for up to 30 minutes.

MAKES 8 TO 10 SERVINGS.

PER EACH OF 10 SERVINGS: about 244 cal, 31 g pro, 7 g total fat (1 g sat. fat), 12 g carb, trace fibre, 196 mg chol, 286 mg sodium. % RDI: 6% calcium, 13% iron, 3% vit A, 5% vit C, 11% folate.

Squash, Spinach and Three-Cheese Cannelloni

Hazelnuts add crunch to this soft, rich filling.

10	sheets (8- x 6-inch/20 x 15 cm) fresh lasagna noodles	10

SQUASH FILLING:

1	butternut squash (1¼ lb/625 g)	1
4	cloves garlic	4
Half	onion, cut into chunks	Half
2 tbsp	extra-virgin olive oil	25 mL
1 tsp	lemon juice	5 mL
¼ tsp	each salt and pepper	1 mL
½ cup	ricotta cheese	125 mL
⅓ cup	grated Parmesan cheese	75 mL
1 tbsp	chopped fresh sage	15 mL
¾ cup	chopped toasted hazelnuts	175 mL

SPINACH FILLING:

1	bag (1 lb/500 g) spinach	1
4	green onions, chopped	4
1 tbsp	extra-virgin olive oil	15 mL
½ tsp	each salt and pepper	2 mL

BÉCHAMEL SAUCE:

2 tbsp	butter	25 mL
3 tbsp	all-purpose flour	50 mL
2¼ cups	milk (approx)	550 mL
¼ tsp	each salt, pepper and nutmeg	1 mL
2½ cups	shredded Gruyère cheese	625 mL

● **SQUASH FILLING:** Peel and cube squash to make 4 cups (1 L). In roasting pan, roast squash, garlic, onion, oil, lemon juice, salt and pepper in 425°F (220°C) oven until tender, 40 minutes. Let cool.

● In food processor, purée squash mixture, ricotta, Parmesan and sage; scrape into bowl. *(Make-ahead: Cover and refrigerate for up to 24 hours.)* Stir in nuts. Set aside.

● **SPINACH FILLING:** Trim and rinse spinach; shake off water. In large saucepan, cover and cook spinach, with just the water clinging to leaves, over medium-high heat until wilted, about 5 minutes; drain in colander. Let cool; squeeze out liquid and chop. In bowl, mix together spinach, green onions, oil, salt and pepper; set aside.

● **BÉCHAMEL SAUCE:** In saucepan, melt butter over medium heat; whisk in flour and cook, whisking, for 2 minutes. Slowly whisk in milk; bring to boil. Reduce heat and simmer, whisking, until thickened, about 5 minutes. Whisk in salt, pepper and nutmeg. Remove from heat; whisk in 2 cups (500 mL) of the Gruyère until smooth. *(Make-ahead: Pour into airtight container; place plastic wrap directly on surface. Cover and refrigerate for up to 24 hours. Whisk in up to ¼ cup/50 mL more milk if too thick to spread.)* Spread 1 cup (250 mL) in 13- x 9-inch (3 L) glass baking dish. Set aside.

● Soak lasagna in cold water until pliable, 2 minutes. Blot dry on towel. Cut each into two 6½- x 4-inch (16 x 10 cm) rectangles.

● Spread scant 3 tbsp (50 mL) squash filling along 1 short side of each rectangle, leaving ½ inch (1 cm) uncovered at ends. Top with scant 2 tbsp (25 mL) spinach filling; roll up. Place snugly, seam side down, in dish. Pour remaining sauce over top; sprinkle with remaining Gruyère. Cover with foil. *(Make-ahead: Refrigerate for up to 2 hours.)*

● Bake on baking sheet in 375°F (190°C) oven for 25 minutes. Uncover and bake until bubbly and cheese is lightly browned, about 20 minutes. Let stand for 5 minutes.

MAKES 10 SERVINGS.

PER SERVING: about 503 cal, 22 g pro, 25 g total fat (10 g sat. fat), 49 g carb, 4 g fibre, 94 mg chol, 446 mg sodium. % RDI: 43% calcium, 26% iron, 96% vit A, 18% vit C, 74% folate.

Red Onion Flowers

Sliced and roasted, red onions open out into sweet and tender "flowers" for an unusual and colourful side dish.

6	small red onions (about 3½ lb/1.75 kg)	6
2 tbsp	extra-virgin olive oil	25 mL
1 tsp	crumbled dried sage, thyme or rosemary	5 mL
½ tsp	each salt and pepper	2 mL
2 tbsp	balsamic vinegar	25 mL

● Trim ½ inch (1 cm) off stem ends of onions. Keeping root ends intact, trim off roots; set each on root end. Slicing down to within ½ inch (1 cm) of base, cut top into 8 wedges. Set on root ends in 13- x 9-inch (3 L) glass baking dish. Drizzle with oil. Sprinkle with sage, salt and pepper.
● Cover with foil; roast in 400°F (200°C) oven until tender, about 1 hour. Uncover and roast, basting with pan liquid, until slightly crisp at tips, about 30 minutes. *(Make-ahead: Let cool for 30 minutes; refrigerate until cool. Cover and refrigerate for up to 24 hours. Reheat, covered, in 325°F/160°C oven, basting with pan liquid, about 30 minutes.)* Drizzle with vinegar.

MAKES 12 SERVINGS.

PER SERVING: about 72 cal, 2 g pro, 2 g total fat (trace sat. fat), 12 g carb, 2 g fibre, 0 mg chol, 99 mg sodium. % RDI: 2% calcium, 2% iron, 10% vit C, 8% folate.

Brussels Sprouts with Brown Butter, Lemon and Almonds

Here's a great side dish that you can start a day ahead, then simply assemble and warm on the stove before serving.

2 lb	small brussels sprouts	1 kg
¼ cup	butter	50 mL
½ cup	sliced almonds	125 mL
2 tbsp	chopped fresh parsley	25 mL
½ tsp	each salt and pepper	2 mL
2 tbsp	lemon juice	25 mL

● Trim brussels sprouts; cut shallow X in base of each. In saucepan of boiling salted water, cook brussels sprouts until tender-crisp, 7 to 9 minutes. Drain and chill under cold water; drain again. Press out excess water with towel. Cut in half and set aside. *(Make-ahead: Refrigerate in airtight container for up to 24 hours.)*
● In large Dutch oven, melt butter over medium heat; fry almonds, stirring often, until butter and almonds are golden brown, about 7 minutes.
● Add brussels sprouts, parsley, salt and pepper; cook, stirring occasionally, until coated and heated through, about 5 minutes. Toss with lemon juice.

MAKES 8 TO 10 SERVINGS.

PER EACH OF 10 SERVINGS: about 107 cal, 3 g pro, 8 g total fat (3 g sat. fat), 9 g carb, 4 g fibre, 12 mg chol, 393 mg sodium. % RDI: 4% calcium, 10% iron, 11% vit A, 93% vit C, 26% folate.

Creamy Carrot Purée

This brilliant orange dish adds colour to the holiday table.

16	carrots (about 3 lb/1.5 kg)	16
4	cloves garlic	4
1 cup	chicken stock	250 mL
½ tsp	each salt, pepper and ground ginger	2 mL
½ cup	whipping cream	125 mL
¼ cup	minced fresh parsley	50 mL

• Cut carrots into 1-inch (2.5 cm) chunks. In saucepan, bring carrots, garlic, stock, salt, pepper and ginger to boil; cover and simmer until tender, about 25 minutes. Uncover and simmer until no liquid remains, about 10 minutes.

• In food processor, purée carrot mixture with cream until smooth. Place in heatproof serving dish. *(Make-ahead: Cover and refrigerate for up to 24 hours; to serve, double heating time.)*

• Cover and heat in 400°F (200°C) oven until hot, about 15 minutes, or microwave at medium (50% power) for 4 minutes. Swirl in parsley.

MAKES 8 SERVINGS.

PER SERVING: about 124 cal, 3 g pro, 6 g total fat (3 g sat. fat), 17 g carb, 4 g fibre, 19 mg chol, 273 mg sodium. % RDI: 6% calcium, 9% iron, 369% vit A, 10% vit C, 11% folate.

Spiced Whole Cranberry Sauce

Cooking cranberries in a syrup keeps them whole and gives the sauce a chunky texture. A touch of salt balances its sweetness.

1	navel orange	1
1 cup	granulated sugar	250 mL
1 cup	dry red wine or apple cider	250 mL
1	stick cinnamon	1
2	star anise (optional)	2
¼ tsp	ground cloves	1 mL
Pinch	each salt and cayenne pepper	Pinch
1	pkg (12 oz/375 g) fresh cranberries	1

• Pare rind (not including pith) off orange; cut into very thin strips (or use zester). Set aside.

• Squeeze orange juice into saucepan; add sugar, wine, cinnamon, star anise (if using), cloves, salt and cayenne. Bring to boil over medium heat; boil until syrupy and reduced to about ¼ cup (50 mL), about 18 minutes.

• Add cranberries and orange rind; simmer, stirring often, until cranberries are softened but still whole, about 8 minutes. Let cool. *(Make-ahead: Refrigerate in airtight container for up to 1 week.)*

MAKES ABOUT 2 CUPS (500 ML).

PER 2 TBSP (25 ML): about 68 cal, trace pro, 0 g total fat (0 g sat. fat), 16 g carb, 1 g fibre, 0 mg chol, 1 mg sodium. % RDI: 1% calcium, 1% iron, 10% vit C, 1% folate.

Chapter Four

PARTY
FINALES

Earl Grey
Pots de Crème

Delicately infused with tea, this custard is cool, creamy and not too sweet.

1²⁄₃ cups	whipping cream	400 mL
1¹⁄₃ cups	milk	325 mL
½ cup	granulated sugar	125 mL
6	Earl Grey tea bags	6
1	strip orange rind	1
2	eggs	2
4	egg yolks	4
SYRUP:		
¼ cup	brewed Earl Grey tea	50 mL
¼ cup	liquid honey	50 mL
2 tbsp	lemon juice	25 mL
8	slices kumquat or orange rind	8

• In saucepan, stir together cream, milk and ⅓ cup (75 mL) of the sugar over medium-high heat until steaming. Remove from heat. Add tea bags and orange rind; cover and let steep for 30 minutes.

• Place 8 ovenproof ½-cup (125 mL) Chinese tea cups or ramekins in roasting pan. Set aside.

• In bowl, whisk together eggs, egg yolks and remaining sugar until smooth; whisk in cream mixture. Strain into pitcher; pour into tea cups. Pour enough boiling water into baking pan to come 1 inch (2.5 cm) up side. Cover pan with foil.

• Bake in 325°F (160°C) oven until tip of knife inserted in centre comes out clean, about 30 minutes. Remove cups from pan; let cool completely on rack. Refrigerate, uncovered, for 2 hours. *(Make-ahead: Cover and refrigerate for up to 24 hours.)*

• SYRUP: In small saucepan, bring tea, honey, lemon juice and kumquat to boil; reduce heat and simmer until reduced to about ⅓ cup (75 mL). Let cool to room temperature. *(Make-ahead: Cover and set aside for up to 24 hours.)* Serve over pots de crème.

MAKES 8 SERVINGS.

PER SERVING: about 319 cal, 6 g pro, 22 g total fat (13 g sat. fat), 26 g carb, trace fibre, 215 mg chol, 63 mg sodium. % RDI: 9% calcium, 4% iron, 24% vit A, 3% vit C, 17% folate.

Mini Tiramisu

Choose dry crisp ladyfingers, sometimes labelled savoiardi, rather than soft ones for this recipe.

4	egg yolks	4
⅓ cup	granulated sugar	75 mL
8 oz	mascarpone cheese	250 g
⅓ cup	whipping cream	75 mL
4 tsp	instant coffee granules	20 mL
4 tsp	marsala, brandy or water	20 mL
10	crisp ladyfinger cookies	10
1 oz	bittersweet chocolate, grated	30 g

• In large heatproof bowl over saucepan of barely simmering water, beat egg yolks with 2 tbsp (25 mL) of the sugar and 2 tbsp (25 mL) water until pale and thickened, about 2 minutes. Let cool to room temperature.

• In separate large bowl, stir mascarpone cheese until smooth and softened. Stir in one-third of the egg mixture; stir in remaining egg mixture.

• In another bowl, whip cream with 2 tbsp (25 mL) of the remaining sugar. Fold one-third into cheese mixture; fold in remaining whipped cream.

• In small bowl, stir together remaining sugar, 4 tsp (20 mL) hot water, coffee granules and marsala until sugar is dissolved. Break 2 of the ladyfingers into quarters. Set aside.

• Drop 1 tbsp (15 mL) of the cheese mixture into each of eight ½-cup (125 mL) martini glasses or ramekins.

• One at a time, dip whole ladyfingers about halfway into coffee mixture; place in martini glasses with undipped end extending above rim.

• Dip ladyfinger quarters into coffee mixture; press into cheese mixture in glasses. Sprinkle with about half of the chocolate.

• Divide remaining cheese mixture among glasses; sprinkle with remaining chocolate. Refrigerate for 3 hours. *(Make-ahead: Cover with plastic wrap; refrigerate for up to 12 hours.)*

MAKES 8 SERVINGS.

PER SERVING: about 279 cal, 5 g pro, 22 g total fat (13 g sat. fat), 16 g carb, 1 g fibre, 186 mg chol, 27 mg sodium. % RDI: 4% calcium, 6% iron, 10% vit A, 9% folate.

Lemon Semifreddo with Coffee Syrup

A layer of dark coffee syrup conceals a tangy sweet lemon base. Garnish with a curled strip of lemon rind.

2	egg yolks	2
½ cup	granulated sugar	125 mL
2 tsp	finely grated lemon rind	10 mL
¼ cup	lemon juice	50 mL
¼ cup	pasteurized egg whites	50 mL
½ cup	whipping cream	125 mL
COFFEE SYRUP:		
⅓ cup	granulated sugar	75 mL
⅓ cup	water	75 mL
2 tsp	instant coffee granules	10 mL

● In heatproof bowl over saucepan of simmering water, whisk together egg yolks, ⅓ cup (75 mL) of the sugar and lemon rind and juice; cook, whisking constantly, until mixture can mound on spoon and any foam subsides, about 3 minutes. Place plastic wrap directly on surface; refrigerate until at room temperature, about 15 minutes.

● In bowl, beat egg whites until soft peaks form; beat in remaining sugar, in two additions, until stiff peaks form. Set aside.

● In separate bowl, whip cream; fold into lemon mixture. Fold one-quarter of the egg whites into lemon mixture; fold in remaining whites. Pour into 8 espresso cups, smoothing tops. Cover with plastic wrap; freeze until solid, at least 8 hours. *(Make-ahead: Overwrap with heavy-duty foil; freeze for up to 5 days.)*

● COFFEE SYRUP: In small saucepan, bring sugar, water and coffee granules to boil, stirring; boil, stirring, until syrupy, about 2 minutes. Refrigerate until cool. *(Make-ahead: Refrigerate in airtight container for up to 5 days.)* To serve, pour 2 tsp (10 mL) over each semifreddo.

MAKES 8 SERVINGS.

PER SERVING: about 152 cal, 2 g pro, 7 g total fat (4 g sat. fat), 22 g carb, trace fibre, 70 mg chol, 20 mg sodium. % RDI: 2% calcium, 1% iron, 8% vit A, 7% vit C, 4% folate.

Tunnel of Peanuts Cake

Use natural peanut butter with no added sugar for the cake.

1 cup	butter, softened	250 mL
¾ cup	packed brown sugar	175 mL
¾ cup	granulated sugar	175 mL
1 cup	natural peanut butter	250 mL
3	eggs	3
1 tsp	vanilla	5 mL
2½ cups	all-purpose flour	625 mL
1 tsp	each baking powder and baking soda	5 mL
½ tsp	salt	2 mL
1½ cups	milk	375 mL

PEANUT STREUSEL:

1 cup	finely chopped unsalted peanuts	250 mL
⅓ cup	packed brown sugar	75 mL
2 tbsp	butter, melted	25 mL

GLAZE:

¾ cup	icing sugar	175 mL
2 tbsp	milk	25 mL
2 tbsp	chopped unsalted peanuts	25 mL

• Grease 10-cup (2.5 L) Bundt or tube pan; dust with flour. Set aside.
• **PEANUT STREUSEL:** In small bowl, mix peanuts, sugar and butter; set aside.
• In large bowl, beat butter with brown and granulated sugars until fluffy; beat in peanut butter. Beat in eggs, 1 at a time, beating well after each; beat in vanilla.
• In separate bowl, whisk together flour, baking powder, baking soda and salt; stir into butter mixture alternately with milk, making 3 additions of dry ingredients and 2 of milk.

• Spoon half of the batter into prepared pan. Using back of spoon, make tunnel about 2 inches (5 cm) wide in batter. Spoon peanut streusel into tunnel, pressing lightly. Spoon remaining batter over streusel; tap pan on counter and smooth top.
• Bake in centre of 325°F (160°C) oven until cake tester inserted in centre comes out clean, about 55 minutes. Let cool in pan on rack for 10 minutes. Remove from pan to rack; let cool completely. *(Make-ahead: Wrap in plastic wrap; store in airtight container for up to 24 hours or freeze for up to 1 month.)*
• **GLAZE:** In small bowl, whisk icing sugar with milk; drizzle over cake. Sprinkle peanuts over glaze.

MAKES 16 SERVINGS.

PER SERVING: about 471 cal, 11 g pro, 27 g total fat (10 g sat. fat), 50 g carb, 2 g fibre, 78 mg chol, 324 mg sodium. % RDI: 8% calcium, 15% iron, 15% vit A, 20% folate.

Decorative Bundt Pans

Bundt pans come in many shapes, such as flowers, stars and wreaths. Made of heavy cast aluminum, these pans are usually dark and nonstick to ensure that the intricate shapes release the cake easily.
• To prepare a Bundt for baking, liberally brush the inside with vegetable oil, making sure to coat all crevices. Sprinkle a couple of spoonfuls of flour into the pan. Rotate pan, tapping to evenly coat the inside. Tap out excess flour.
• Nordic Ware recommends not greasing their pans with commercial vegetable oil spray. Over time, the sprays can pit the finish on the inside of the pan.

> Beaded Moss Tree

A tiny mossy tree trimmed in shiny beads and foil stars adds holiday cheer to any room in the house.

• With knife, trim base of floral-foam or Styrofoam cone to fit snugly into heavy-bottomed container. Set into container, gluing, if desired, to secure.

• With glue gun, cover foam with moss (sheet moss, Spanish moss or mood moss).

• With glue gun, dab end of 16-gauge copper wire, then push into tip of tree. Loosely spiral wire down and around to bottom of tree; trim end, then secure at bottom with glue.

• Cut stars from copper tooling foil (available at craft stores); with tapestry needle, press pattern of dots into foil.

• Cut 4-to 5-inch (10 to 12.5 cm) lengths of 16-gauge copper wire, then twist 1⅝ inches (4 cm) at 1 end of each into tight, flat spiral; wind each around pencil to form loose spiral or bend into zigzag, leaving 2 inches (5 cm) straight at remaining end. Glue spiral on each to foil star or thread straight end through beads as desired; dab straight ends with glue and push into foam.

Dark Chocolate Bûche de Noël

Garnish the platter with iced snowflake Sugar Cookies (recipe, page 138).

¼ cup	milk	50 mL
2 tbsp	butter	25 mL
¾ cup	sifted cake-and-pastry flour	175 mL
1 tsp	baking powder	5 mL
¼ tsp	salt	1 mL
5	eggs	5
¾ cup	granulated sugar	175 mL
1 tbsp	icing sugar	15 mL
ICING:		
1 cup	butter, softened	250 mL
⅓ cup	whipping cream	75 mL
2 tsp	vanilla	10 mL
2 cups	icing sugar	500 mL
4 oz	unsweetened chocolate, melted and cooled	125 g
CHOCOLATE BARK:		
8 oz	bittersweet chocolate, chopped	250 g

• Line 15- x 10-inch (40 x 25 cm) rimmed baking sheet with parchment paper.

• In bowl over saucepan of simmering water, heat milk with butter until melted. Remove pan from heat, leaving bowl on top to keep warm enough that finger can remain in bowl for no longer than 10 seconds.

• In separate bowl, whisk together flour, baking powder and salt; set aside.

• Separate yolks and whites of 3 of the eggs into separate bowls. Beat egg whites until foamy; beat in ¼ cup (50 mL) of the granulated sugar, about 1 tbsp (15 mL) at a time, until soft peaks form.

• Beat egg yolks and remaining eggs and granulated sugar until thick enough that batter leaves ribbons on surface when

beaters are lifted, about 5 minutes. Fold in one-third of the whites; fold in remaining whites. Sift flour mixture over top; fold in. Pour in milk mixture; fold in just until blended. Spread in prepared pan.

• Bake in centre of 350°F (180°C) oven until golden and cake springs back when lightly touched, about 12 minutes. Loosen edges with knife; place flour-dusted tea towel over cake. Top with tray larger than pan. Invert and lift off pan. Starting at corner, peel off paper. Starting at short side, roll up cake in towel; let cool on rack. *(Make-ahead: Store in airtight container for up to 24 hours.)*

• **ICING:** In bowl and with electric beaters, beat butter until fluffy; gradually beat in cream then vanilla. Beat in sugar, 1 cup (250 mL) at a time. Beat in chocolate until fluffy and smooth.

• **CHOCOLATE BARK:** Line 15- x 10-inch (40 x 25 cm) rimmed baking sheet with parchment paper; set aside.

• In bowl over saucepan of hot (not boiling) water, melt chocolate, stirring occasionally. Pour onto prepared baking sheet, spreading to scant ⅛-inch (3 mm) thickness. Refrigerate until set, about 10 minutes. Break or tear chocolate into about 3- x 1-inch (8 x 2.5 cm) pieces. Arrange in single layer on tray; cover loosely with plastic wrap and refrigerate until firm. *(Make-ahead: Refrigerate for up to 48 hours.)*

• Unroll cake; spread with 1½ cups (375 mL) of the icing. Reroll without towel; place, seam side down, on flat serving platter. Spread remaining icing all over log. Arrange Chocolate Bark over log. Refrigerate until cold. Dust bark with icing sugar.

MAKES 12 SERVINGS.

PER SERVING: about 499 cal, 7 g pro, 37 g total fat (22 g sat. fat), 45 g carb, 4 g fibre, 141 mg chol, 280 mg sodium. % RDI: 5% calcium, 19% iron, 23% vit A, 9% folate.

Chocolate Caramel Pecan Torte

Warning: This cake is for serious chocolate and caramel lovers.

4 oz	unsweetened chocolate, coarsely chopped	125 g
2¼ cups	all-purpose flour	550 mL
2¼ cups	packed brown sugar	550 mL
1 tsp	baking soda	5 mL
½ tsp	baking powder	2 mL
¼ tsp	salt	1 mL
1 cup	sour cream	250 mL
½ cup	butter, softened	125 mL
3	eggs	3
1 tsp	vanilla	5 mL
2 cups	pecan pieces	500 mL
CARAMEL:		
1½ cups	granulated sugar	375 mL
⅔ cup	whipping cream	150 mL
¼ cup	butter	50 mL
TOPPING:		
2½ cups	whipping cream	625 mL
¾ cup	Chocolate Shards (recipe follows)	175 mL
⅓ cup	pecan halves, toasted	75 mL

• Grease three 9-inch (1.5 L) round metal cake pans; line bottoms with parchment paper. Set aside.

• In bowl over saucepan of hot (not boiling) water, melt chocolate; let cool slightly.

• In large bowl, whisk flour, brown sugar, baking soda, baking powder and salt. Beat in sour cream and butter; beat in eggs, 1 at a time, beating well after each. Beat in chocolate and vanilla; beat for 2 minutes. Gradually stir in 1 cup (250 mL) water.

• Divide among prepared pans; sprinkle pecans over tops. Bake in centre of 350°F

(180°C) oven until cake tester inserted in centre comes out clean, 30 to 35 minutes. Let cool in pans on racks for 15 minutes. Turn out onto racks and peel off paper; let cool completely. *(Make-ahead: Wrap in plastic wrap and store for up to 24 hours.)*

• **CARAMEL:** In heavy saucepan, stir sugar with ⅓ cup (75 mL) water over medium heat until dissolved, brushing down side of pan with pastry brush dipped in cold water. Bring to boil; boil vigorously, without stirring but brushing down side of pan, until dark amber, about 10 minutes.

• Standing back and averting face, add cream; whisk until smooth. Whisk in butter; let cool. *(Make-ahead: Refrigerate in airtight container for up to 3 days. Reheat to use.)*

• **TOPPING:** Whip cream. Place 1 cake layer, pecan side up, on cake plate. Drizzle with 2 tbsp (25 mL) caramel. Spread with 1 cup (250 mL) whipped cream. Drizzle with 2 tbsp (25 mL) caramel, being careful not to let any drip down side. Repeat layers once.

• Top with remaining cake layer. Spread remaining whipped cream over top and side. Drizzle 2 tbsp (25 mL) caramel over top. Garnish with chocolate shards and pecans. Serve with remaining caramel.

MAKES 12 TO 16 SERVINGS.

PER EACH OF 16 SERVINGS: about 685 cal, 7 g pro, 45 g total fat (21 g sat. fat), 71 g carb, 3 g fibre, 124 mg chol, 251 mg sodium. % RDI: 9% calcium, 18% iron, 27% vit A, 2% vit C, 15% folate.

Chocolate Shards

• In heatproof bowl over saucepan of hot (not boiling) water, melt 4 oz (125 g) semisweet chocolate. Spread on rimless baking sheet; refrigerate until firm, about 15 minutes.

• Place pan on damp towel; let stand for 3 minutes. Bracing pan against body, scrape metal spatula through chocolate toward body to make shards, refrigerating for 3 to 4 minutes if chocolate softens. **Makes 1½ cups (375 mL).**

❯ Chocolate Curlicues

● On parchment or waxed paper, draw patterns to be piped (such as holly leaves, curlicues, stars or spirals. Turn over and place on rimmed baking sheet.

● In heatproof bowl over saucepan of hot (not boiling) water, melt 4 oz (125 g) white or dark chocolate. Spoon into small plastic bag; press out air and seal. Snip off 1 corner to make small opening.

● Squeezing gently, trace chocolate over designs. Refrigerate until set, about 15 minutes.

❯ Chocolate Leaves

● Rose, lemon, orange and basil leaves all make attractive moulds for chocolate garnishes.

● Swish leaves in soapy water; rinse and blot dry. Or cut leaf shapes from cabbage leaves using X-acto knife.

● In heatproof bowl over saucepan of hot (not boiling) water, melt 3 oz (90 g) dark or white chocolate.

● Holding stem end of leaf between thumb and forefinger and supporting leaf with palm, brush chocolate over back of leaf. Place on waxed paper–lined rimmed baking sheet. Refrigerate until firm, about 15 minutes. Repeat if using white chocolate.

● Starting at stem end, gently peel away leaf; discard.
(Make-ahead: Refrigerate in single layer in airtight containers for up to 1 week.)

> Dusting with Templates

• On construction paper, trace serving plate. Draw pattern desired around inside edge of circle no deeper than rim of plate.
• With X-acto knife, cut out pattern. Leaving 1-inch (2.5 cm) border beyond edge of circle, cut out template.
• Place template over dessert plate. Spoon icing sugar or cocoa powder into small fine sieve. Gently shake sieve over template until all surfaces of plate visible through cutouts are lightly dusted. Carefully lift template straight up to remove.
• Alternatively, cut stars or other shapes from construction paper. Lay cutouts over plate and dust icing sugar around edges. Slip edge of knife under cutouts and lift straight up from plate.

> Candied Citrus Rind

• Using channelling knife, cut 6- to 12-inch (15 to 30 cm) long strips of orange, lemon or grapefruit rind.
• In small saucepan, bring 1 cup (250 mL) granulated sugar and ¾ cup (175 mL) water to boil; boil for 1 minute. Reduce heat to simmer. Immerse strips, 3 at a time, in syrup; simmer for 2 minutes. Remove with tongs. Drain in sieve, shaking to remove excess.
• Place 1 cup (250 mL) granulated sugar in bowl; add rind, rolling with fork to coat. Roll pieces around handle of wooden spoon; refrigerate until spirals hold, 30 minutes. Gently pull out spoon. *(Make-ahead: Cover with sugar; store for up to 2 days.)*
• **For confetti:** Cut strips of rind from fruit. Using small end of metal piping tip, punch out circles in rind. Immerse in simmering syrup for 1 minute before coating in sugar.

Golden Brazil Nut Fruitcake

This traditional cake pleases even people with fruitcake prejudices. Make it at least a month ahead to let it mellow before icing.

2 cups	candied mixed peel	500 mL
1½ cups	each coarsely chopped dried apricots and dried pears	375 mL
1½ cups	coarsely chopped candied pineapple	375 mL
¼ cup	chopped crystallized ginger	50 mL
½ cup	amber rum or brandy	125 mL
2¼ cups	all-purpose flour	550 mL
1½ tsp	ground mace	7 mL
1 tsp	each cinnamon and ground allspice	5 mL
½ tsp	salt	2 mL
¼ tsp	baking soda	1 mL
1 cup	butter, softened	250 mL
1 cup	packed light brown sugar	250 mL
¼ cup	liquid honey	50 mL
1 tsp	vanilla	5 mL
6	eggs	6
1½ cups	coarsely chopped Brazil nuts	375 mL
¼ cup	apricot jam, melted and strained	50 mL
2	pkg (each 200 g) marzipan	2
8 oz	fondant	250 g
	Pearl dragées	

• In large bowl, toss together mixed peel, apricots, pears, pineapple, ginger and rum. Cover and let stand for 24 hours, stirring occasionally.

• Line 9-inch (2.5 L) springform pan with parchment paper; set aside.

• In bowl, whisk together flour, mace, cinnamon, allspice, salt and baking soda; remove 1 cup (250 mL) and toss with fruit mixture.

• In separate bowl, beat together butter, brown sugar and honey until fluffy; beat in vanilla. Beat in eggs, 1 at a time. Stir in flour mixture just until incorporated. Add fruit mixture and Brazil nuts; stir to combine. Scrape into prepared pan, smoothing top.

• Set shallow pan on bottom rack of 250°F (120°C) oven; pour in enough hot water to come halfway up side. Bake cake on centre rack until cake tester inserted in centre comes out clean, 4½ to 5 hours. Let cool in pan on rack.

• Remove cake from pan; peel off paper. Cut double-thickness square of cheesecloth large enough to wrap cake; soak in rum. Wrap around cake; wrap in plastic wrap then foil. Refrigerate for 1 month. *(Make-ahead: Refrigerate for up to 3 months.)*

• Brush jam over top and side of cake. On icing sugar–dusted surface, place the 2 pieces of marzipan on top of each other; roll out to 15-inch (38 cm) circle. Roll up around rolling pin; unroll over cake, letting marzipan drape down side. Smooth over top and side, pressing gently. Trim bottom. Let dry at room temperature for 24 hours.

• On icing sugar–dusted surface, roll out fondant to ½-inch (1 cm) thickness. Using cutters, cut out snowflakes; brush backs with water and press onto cake. Decorate with dragées. *(Make-ahead: Refrigerate in airtight container for up to 1 week.)*

MAKES 60 SERVINGS.

PER SERVING: about 199 cal, 3 g pro, 8 g total fat (3 g sat. fat), 31 g carb, 2 g fibre, 28 mg chol, 79 mg sodium. % RDI: 3% calcium, 9% iron, 6% vit A, 8% vit C, 6% folate.

Plum and Carrot Pudding

This heritage pudding is loosely based on the family recipe of the late Madame Benoit.

1 cup	currants	250 mL
½ cup	lexia or muscat raisins	125 mL
½ cup	each golden raisins and candied mixed peel	125 mL
½ cup	brandy	125 mL
3 cups	fine fresh bread crumbs	750 mL
½ cup	sliced almonds	125 mL
½ cup	grated carrots	125 mL
2 tbsp	all-purpose flour	25 mL
1 tsp	allspice	5 mL
½ tsp	ground nutmeg	2 mL
4	eggs, separated	4
⅔ cup	granulated sugar	150 mL
¾ cup	butter, softened	175 mL
	Butterscotch Brandy Sauce (recipe follows)	

• Grease 8-cup (2 L) pudding mould or bowl; set aside.

• In large bowl, mix currants, lexia and golden raisins, peel and brandy. Cover and let stand for 24 hours. (Or heat to steaming in microwave oven; let stand for 1 hour.)

• Stir in bread crumbs, almonds, carrots, flour, allspice and nutmeg; set aside.

• In bowl, beat egg whites until soft peaks form; gradually beat in half of the sugar until stiff glossy peaks form.

• In separate bowl, beat butter with remaining sugar until fluffy; beat in egg yolks, 1 at a time. Scrape over fruit mixture; stir to combine. Stir in about one-quarter of the egg white mixture; fold in remainder. Pack into prepared mould. Cover with waxed paper cut to fit over batter. Cover mould with foil; tie about 1 inch (2.5 cm) from top edge. Press foil up over string.

• Place on rack in deep pot; pour in enough boiling water to come halfway up side of mould. Cover and bring to boil; reduce heat and simmer, maintaining water level, until skewer inserted in centre comes out clean, 2½ to 3 hours. Let cool on rack. Unmould, wrap and refrigerate for 3 weeks. *(Make-ahead: Refrigerate for up to 2 months or freeze for up to 1 year.)*

• To serve, steam as above until piping hot, about 1 hour.

MAKES 12 SERVINGS.

PER SERVING (WITHOUT SAUCE): about 461 cal, 5 g pro, 18 g total fat (9 g sat. fat), 73 g carb, 3 g fibre, 98 mg chol, 200 mg sodium. % RDI: 7% calcium, 14% iron, 21% vit A, 2% vit C, 11% folate.

Butterscotch Brandy Sauce

1½ cups	packed brown sugar	375 mL
2 cups	boiling water	500 mL
¼ cup	cornstarch	50 mL
2 tbsp	each butter and brandy	25 mL
1 tsp	vanilla	5 mL
½ tsp	ground nutmeg	2 mL

• In heavy saucepan, melt sugar with ⅓ cup (75 mL) of the boiling water over medium heat until slightly darkened. Gradually stir in remaining boiling water; cook until smooth and sugar is dissolved.

• In bowl, stir cornstarch with 3 tbsp (50 mL) cold water until smooth. Stir in a little of the hot liquid; whisk back into pan and cook, whisking, until clear, 3 minutes. *(Make-ahead: Let cool; refrigerate in airtight container for up to 24 hours. Rewarm.)* Stir in butter, brandy, vanilla and nutmeg.

MAKES ABOUT 3 CUPS (750 ML).

PER ¼ CUP (50 ML): about 137 cal, 0 g pro, 2 g total fat (1 g sat. fat), 29 g carb, 0 g fibre, 5 mg chol, 25 mg sodium. % RDI: 2% calcium, 4% iron, 2% vit A.

Cranberry Apple Mincemeat Tarts

Mincemeat without meat or suet? Yes! And this one has all the rich, fruity spiciness that has made mincemeat a traditional holiday treat. Because mincemeat stores so well, you can use it all at once or just as you need it.

1	navel or seedless orange (unpeeled), coarsely chopped	1
4 cups	cranberries	1 L
4 cups	chopped cored peeled apples	1 L
2¾ cups	granulated sugar	675 mL
1½ cups	golden raisins	375 mL
1½ cups	chopped dried apricots	375 mL
¾ cup	apple juice	175 mL
½ cup	mixed candied fruit	125 mL
¼ cup	marmalade	50 mL
¼ cup	butter, cubed	50 mL
1 tsp	ground ginger	5 mL
¾ tsp	each ground cinnamon, nutmeg and allspice	4 mL
¼ cup	brandy	50 mL

PASTRY:

6 cups	all-purpose flour	1.5 L
¼ cup	granulated sugar	50 mL
1 tsp	salt	5 mL
3 cups	butter, cubed	750 mL
4 tsp	grated lemon rind	20 mL
1⅓ cups	ice water (approx)	325 mL

• In food processor and using pulsing motion, chop orange chunks to size of currants; place in large saucepan. Add cranberries, apples, sugar, raisins, apricots, apple juice, candied fruit, marmalade, butter, ginger, cinnamon, nutmeg and allspice; bring to boil over medium heat. Reduce heat and simmer, stirring occasionally, until very little liquid remains, about 45 minutes.

• Add brandy; simmer until spoon dragged through leaves hollow that fills in slowly, about 5 minutes. *(Make-ahead: Let cool; refrigerate in airtight container for up to 3 weeks or freeze for up to 3 months.)*

• **PASTRY:** In large bowl, whisk flour, sugar and salt. Using pastry blender, cut in butter until in fine crumbs. Stir in rind. Stirring briskly with fork, gradually sprinkle with water, adding up to 3 tbsp (50 mL) more if necessary for pastry to hold together.

• Divide pastry into quarters; press into discs. Wrap separately and refrigerate for 1 hour. *(Make-ahead: Refrigerate for up to 3 days; let stand for 15 minutes before rolling. Or freeze in airtight container for up to 3 months.)*

• On lightly floured surface, roll out each disc to ⅛-inch (3 mm) thickness. Using 3½-inch (9 cm) round cookie cutter, cut out 60 circles. Using smaller decorative cutter, cut out 60 stars or other shapes from remaining pastry, rerolling scraps.

• Fit pastry circles into 2¼-inch (5.5 cm) tart cups; fill each with about 2 tbsp (25 mL) mincemeat. Top each with small pastry cutout. Refrigerate for 30 minutes. Bake in centre of 400°F (200°C) oven until pastry is golden, about 20 minutes.

MAKES 60 TARTS.

PER TART: about 210 cal, 2 g pro, 10 g total fat (6 g sat. fat), 29 g carb, 1 g fibre, 26 mg chol, 111 mg sodium. % RDI: 1% calcium, 6% iron, 10% vit A, 7% vit C, 12% folate.

Candy Cane Cheesecake

To add restaurant pizzazz, drizzle chocolate sauce onto each plate before adding a wedge of the cheesecake.

2	pkg (each 8 oz/250 g) cream cheese, softened	2
¾ cup	granulated sugar	175 mL
3	eggs	3
2 cups	sour cream	500 mL
1 tbsp	lemon juice	15 mL
1 tsp	peppermint extract	5 mL
CRUST:		
1½ cups	chocolate wafer crumbs	375 mL
¼ cup	butter, melted	50 mL
TOPPING:		
1 cup	sour cream	250 mL
2 tbsp	granulated sugar	25 mL
½ tsp	vanilla	2 mL
2 tbsp	coarsely crushed candy canes	25 mL

● Grease bottom of 9-inch (2.5 L) springform pan; line side with parchment paper. Set pan on large square of heavy-duty foil; press foil up side of pan. Set aside.

● **CRUST:** In bowl, stir crumbs with butter until moistened; press into prepared pan. Bake in centre of 350°F (180°C) oven until set, about 10 minutes. Let cool on rack.

● Meanwhile, in large bowl, beat cream cheese until fluffy. Beat in sugar until smooth; beat in eggs, 1 at a time, just until combined. Beat in sour cream, lemon juice and peppermint extract. Pour over crust.

● Set springform pan in larger pan; pour enough hot water into larger pan to come 1 inch (2.5 cm) up sides. Bake in centre of 325°F (160°C) oven until shine disappears and edge is set yet centre still jiggles slightly, about 1 hour.

● **TOPPING:** Combine sour cream, sugar and vanilla; spread over cheesecake. Bake for 10 minutes. Turn off oven. Let cool in oven for 1 hour.

● Remove from water and transfer to rack; remove foil and let cool. Cover and refrigerate until set, about 2 hours. *(Make-ahead: Refrigerate for up to 2 days. Or overwrap in heavy-duty foil and freeze for up to 2 weeks.)*

● To serve, sift candy to remove powder; sprinkle pieces around edge.

MAKES 16 TO 20 SERVINGS.

PER EACH OF 20 SERVINGS: about 247 cal, 4 g pro, 18 g total fat (11 g sat. fat), 18 g carb, trace fibre, 76 mg chol, 171 mg sodium. % RDI: 6% calcium, 7% iron, 17% vit A, 6% folate.

TIP

❯ You can vary the cheesecake according to the season and your taste. For example, replace the peppermint extract with 2 tsp (10 mL) vanilla and top with an abundance of berries instead of the candy canes.

> Gilded Candles

Dust chunky candles with gold to double their glisten and shine. Choose pillar candles in several different sizes.

• Sprinkle gold-leaf flakes onto large, clean Styrofoam meat tray.

• Working on 1 candle at a time, apply spray adhesive to side, then wait for about 2 minutes until tacky.

• Wearing rubber gloves, pick up candle and roll in flakes. With soft-bristle artist's paintbrush, gently press flakes into adhesive, then brush off excess.

> Mirrored Glow

Help holiday candles shine their brightest. Turn pretty glassware on its head and set on a mirrored tray, then top each with a votive candle.

Whisky Chocolate Mousse

Demitasse cups or small chocolate dessert cups hold just enough mousse for a wonderful chocolate indulgence. Decorate each cup with a dollop of whipped cream and chocolate shavings.

1⅔ cups	whipping cream	400 mL
4	egg yolks	4
¼ cup	granulated sugar	50 mL
Pinch	salt	Pinch
4 oz	bittersweet chocolate, melted	125 g
2 oz	milk chocolate, melted	60 g
2 tbsp	whisky	25 mL
1 tsp	vanilla	5 mL

• In small saucepan, heat ⅔ cup (150 mL) of the cream over medium-high heat just until tiny bubbles form around edge of pan.

• Meanwhile, in heatproof bowl, whisk together egg yolks, sugar and salt; slowly whisk in cream. Place bowl over saucepan of simmering water; cook, stirring, until custard is 160°F (70°C) and thick enough to coat back of spoon, about 8 minutes. Remove from heat.

• Whisk bittersweet and milk chocolates, whisky and vanilla into custard. Place plastic wrap directly on surface; let cool.

• In separate bowl, whip remaining cream; fold one-quarter into chocolate mixture. Fold in remaining cream. Cover and refrigerate until firm, about 6 hours. *(Make-ahead: Refrigerate for up to 4 hours.)* Pipe or spoon into dessert cups.

MAKES 8 SERVINGS.

PER SERVING: about 341 cal, 4 g pro, 27 g total fat (16 g sat. fat), 20 g carb, 1 g fibre, 167 mg chol, 27 mg sodium. % RDI: 6% calcium, 7% iron, 23% vit A, 7% folate.

White Chocolate Margarita Mousse

This light, tangy dessert flavoured with tequila and lime makes a refreshingly special finish to any festive meal. For that extra flourish, serve in sugared margarita or martini glasses garnished with finely grated lime rind.

2	eggs	2
2	egg yolks	2
⅔ cup	granulated sugar	150 mL
1 tbsp	finely grated lime rind	15 mL
½ cup	lime juice	125 mL
2 tbsp	tequila	25 mL
3 oz	white chocolate, chopped	90 g
¾ cup	whipping cream	175 mL

• In heatproof bowl over saucepan of hot (not boiling) water, whisk together eggs, egg yolks, sugar, lime rind and juice and tequila; cook, whisking often, until thickened and mixture falls in ribbons when whisk is lifted, 4 to 8 minutes. Remove from heat.

• Add white chocolate; stir until melted. Pour into clean bowl; place plastic wrap directly on surface. Refrigerate until chilled, about 1 hour. *(Make-ahead: Refrigerate for up to 3 days.)*

• In bowl, whip cream; fold half into lime mixture. Fold in remaining whipped cream just until combined. Spoon into glasses or dessert dishes. *(Make-ahead: Cover and refrigerate for up to 2 days.)*

MAKES 6 SERVINGS.

PER SERVING: about 314 cal, 5 g pro, 18 g total fat (10 g sat. fat), 34 g carb, trace fibre, 183 mg chol, 47 mg sodium. % RDI: 6% calcium, 4% iron, 18% vit A, 10% vit C, 7% folate.

Ice-Cream Christmas Pudding

Combine classic Christmas pudding flavours with ice cream, et voilà — an updated, simple-to-prepare dessert. The best part? You can make it up to five days ahead.

1 cup	candied pineapple or candied mixed peel	250 mL
½ cup	each halved candied red and green cherries	125 mL
½ cup	golden raisins	125 mL
¼ cup	brandy or rum	50 mL
1	carton (4 cups/1 L) vanilla ice cream	1
1 cup	chopped pecans, toasted	250 mL
½ cup	slivered almonds, toasted	125 mL
	Chocolate Orange Sauce (recipe follows)	

● Line 6- to 8-cup (1.5 to 2 L) pudding mould or 9- x 5-inch (2 L) loaf pan with plastic wrap, leaving enough overhang to cover top; set aside.

● In large microwaveable bowl, combine pineapple, red and green cherries, raisins and brandy; microwave at high for 2 minutes, stirring twice. Let cool completely. (Or cover and soak at room temperature for 8 hours or overnight.)

● Soften ice cream in refrigerator for 30 minutes. Stir pecans and almonds into fruit mixture; stir in ice cream. Pack into prepared mould, smoothing top. Cover with overhang and freeze until solid, about 12 hours. *(Make-ahead: Overwrap with heavy-duty foil; freeze for up to 5 days.)*

● To serve, let pudding stand in refrigerator for 15 minutes. Using overhang, remove from pan. Invert onto chilled serving plate; remove plastic wrap. Dip sharp knife in hot water and wipe dry; slice pudding. Serve with sauce.

MAKES 12 SERVINGS.

PER SERVING: about 390 cal, 5 g pro, 22 g total fat (8 g sat. fat), 48 g carb, 3 g fibre, 32 mg chol, 45 mg sodium. % RDI: 10% calcium, 10% iron, 9% vit A, 25% vit C, 5% folate.

Chocolate Orange Sauce

½ cup	whipping cream	125 mL
1 tbsp	corn syrup	15 mL
3 oz	bittersweet chocolate, chopped	90 g
1 tbsp	orange liqueur	15 mL
1 tsp	grated orange rind	5 mL

● In small saucepan, bring cream and corn syrup to boil; add chocolate, liqueur and orange rind, whisking until smooth. Let stand until thickened, about 15 minutes. *(Make-ahead: Transfer to airtight container. Place plastic wrap directly on surface; cover and refrigerate for up to 5 days. Warm before serving.)*

MAKES ABOUT ¾ CUP (175 mL), ENOUGH FOR 12 SERVINGS.

PER SERVING: about 79 cal, 1 g pro, 7 g total fat (4 g sat. fat), 4 g carb, 1 g fibre, 13 mg chol, 7 mg sodium. % RDI: 1% calcium, 4% iron, 3% vit A.

Fresh Orange Compote

Sliced oranges make a delightful dessert.

4	oranges	4
2 tbsp	chopped fresh mint	25 mL
ORANGE GRAND MARNIER SAUCE:		
½ cup	granulated sugar	125 mL
1 tbsp	finely grated orange rind	15 mL
1	cinnamon stick	1
2	whole cloves	2
2 tsp	Grand Marnier or other orange-flavoured liqueur	10 mL

• **ORANGE GRAND MARNIER SAUCE:** In saucepan, bring sugar, ⅓ cup (75 mL) water, orange rind, cinnamon and cloves to boil; reduce heat and simmer for 5 minutes. Strain into bowl; add liqueur. Refrigerate until chilled, about 15 minutes.
• Cut skin and white pith from oranges. Slice ¼-inch (5 mm) thick; arrange on platter. *(Make-ahead: Cover and refrigerate sauce and oranges separately for up to 24 hours.)* Drizzle with sauce; sprinkle with mint.

MAKES 4 TO 6 SERVINGS.

PER EACH OF 6 SERVINGS: about 112 cal, 1 g pro, trace total fat (trace sat. fat), 28 g carb, 2 g fibre, 0 mg chol, 1 mg sodium. % RDI: 3% calcium, 1% iron, 2% vit A, 78% vit C, 12% folate.

Fresh Pineapple with Vanilla Wine Syrup

Fresh pineapple is a luxurious and light finish to any holiday meal. To make it even more special, this dessert is topped with a syrup made from a fruity dry white wine, such as Riesling, and a vanilla bean.

Half	vanilla bean	Half
1	bottle (750 mL) fruity dry white wine	1
¾ cup	granulated sugar	175 mL
2	strips (3 inches/8 cm) orange rind	2
2	golden pineapples	2
1	container (500 mL) vanilla ice cream	1

• Slit vanilla bean lengthwise; scrape out seeds. In saucepan, bring vanilla bean and seeds, wine, sugar and orange rind to boil over high heat. Reduce heat to medium; simmer until syrupy and reduced to ¾ cup (175 mL), about 40 minutes. Let cool. Remove bean. *(Make-ahead: Refrigerate in airtight container for up to 2 weeks.)*
• Meanwhile, on cutting board, cut peel off pineapples, leaving eyes. Cut out eyes, making shallow diagonal cuts. Quarter pineapples lengthwise; core and cut into bite-size pieces. *(Make-ahead: Refrigerate in airtight container for up to 2 days.)*
• To serve, spoon pineapple into dessert dishes; drizzle with syrup. Cut orange rind into fine strips; add to each dish along with scoop of ice cream.

MAKES 10 SERVINGS.

PER SERVING: about 179 cal, 1 g pro, 3 g total fat (2 g sat. fat), 34 g carb, 1 g fibre, 12 mg chol, 27 mg sodium. % RDI: 5% calcium, 4% iron, 4% vit A, 27% vit C, 5% folate.

Berry Almond Trifle

This trifle is a simple yet harmonious combination of berries, amaretto-soaked angel food cake and the classic custard.

1	angel food cake (300 g)	1
¼ cup	almond liqueur	50 mL
3½ cups	fresh strawberries, quartered	875 mL
1½ cups	fresh blueberries	375 mL
1 cup	whipping cream	250 mL
½ cup	toasted sliced almonds	125 mL

VANILLA CUSTARD:

8	egg yolks	8
4 cups	milk	1 L
¾ cup	granulated sugar	175 mL
½ cup	cornstarch	125 mL
1 tbsp	vanilla	15 mL

● **VANILLA CUSTARD:** In bowl, whisk together egg yolks, ½ cup (125 mL of the milk, the sugar and cornstarch.

● In heavy saucepan, heat remaining milk over medium heat just until bubbles form around edge; gradually whisk into yolk mixture. Return to pan and cook, stirring constantly, until thick enough to mound on spoon, 3 to 5 minutes.

● Strain through fine sieve into clean bowl; stir in vanilla. Place plastic wrap directly on surface. Refrigerate until cold, about 4 hours. *(Make-ahead: Refrigerate for up to 24 hours.)*

● Cut cake into 1-inch (2.5 cm) cubes; place in bowl. Drizzle with liqueur; toss with fork. Set aside.

● Set aside ½ cup (125 mL) of the strawberries and ¼ cup (50 mL) of the blueberries for garnish.

● Place one-third of the cake cubes in trifle bowl. Top with half of the remaining strawberries and one-third of the custard, spooning custard into gaps. Top with another third of the cake, pressing lightly, remaining blueberries and another third of the custard. Top with remaining cake, strawberries and custard. Cover and refrigerate for 12 hours. *(Make-ahead: Refrigerate for up to 2 days.)*

● In bowl, whip cream; spread over trifle. Sprinkle with almonds. Garnish with reserved berries.

MAKES 12 TO 16 SERVINGS.

PER EACH OF 16 SERVINGS: about 259 cal, 6 g pro, 11 g total fat (5 g sat. fat), 34 g carb, 2 g fibre, 125 mg chol, 183 mg sodium. % RDI: 12% calcium, 5% iron, 13% vit A, 35% vit C, 14% folate.

TIPS

❯ You can replace the almond liqueur with ¼ cup (50 mL) apple juice mixed with ¼ tsp (1 mL) almond extract.

❯ To toast nuts, bake on rimmed baking sheet in 350°F (180°C) oven until golden, about 6 minutes.

Cherry Panna Cotta

This silky spoon dessert has its inspiration in one served at the Fairmont Jasper Park Lodge in Jasper, Alta.

1 cup	milk	250 mL
4 tsp	unflavoured gelatin	20 mL
1	jar (19 oz/540 mL) sour cherries in syrup	1
2 cups	whipping cream	500 mL
½ cup	granulated sugar	125 mL
1 tsp	vanilla	5 mL
Dash	almond extract	Dash
⅔ cup	ruby Port	150 mL

● Pour ¼ cup (50 mL) of the milk into large bowl; sprinkle in gelatin and let stand for 5 minutes to soften.

● Meanwhile, reserving juice, drain cherries in sieve set over bowl, pressing lightly and shaking sieve occasionally.

● In saucepan, heat together remaining milk, cream and sugar, stirring, until steaming and sugar is dissolved. Pour into gelatin mixture, stirring until completely dissolved. Stir in vanilla and almond extract. Refrigerate or set over larger bowl of ice cubes and water until cold and thickened to consistency of raw egg whites, stirring often. Strain into large liquid measuring cup.

● Rinse eight 3-inch (125 mL) ramekins or moulds with cold water; place on tray. Arrange all but ½ cup (125 mL) of the cherries evenly in ramekins, reserving remainder for sauce. Pour in cream mixture. Refrigerate until set, about 4 hours. *(Make-ahead: Cover with plastic wrap; refrigerate for up to 24 hours.)*

● In small saucepan, bring reserved cherry juice and Port to boil over high heat; boil until syrupy and reduced to about ½ cup (125 mL), about 5 minutes. Let cool. Add reserved cherries. *(Make-ahead: Refrigerate in airtight container for up to 1 week.)*

● Unmould panna cotta into chilled shallow bowls; drizzle port syrup around each.

MAKES 8 SERVINGS.

PER SERVING: about 341 cal, 4 g pro, 22 g total fat (13 g sat. fat), 32 g carb, 1 g fibre, 79 mg chol, 43 mg sodium. % RDI: 8% calcium, 7% iron, 26% vit A, 3% vit C, 4% folate.

TIP

➤ To unmould panna cotta, dip mould into hot water for just a few seconds. Cover mould with serving bowl or plate and turn over, jerking mould and plate sharply to dislodge the panna cotta.

> *A Gala Ball*

Big ribbon rosettes cover an oversize Styrofoam ball. Hang one in a window or make several and stagger them above a buffet or staircase. For a luxurious look, use ribbons that shimmer or gleam.

• Start with 31 yards (28.30 m) 2¼-inch (56 mm) wide wire-edged chiffon ribbon and 3½ yards (3.20 m) same-width moiré ribbon. From chiffon, cut thirty-four 31½-inch (80 cm) lengths; from moiré, cut thirty-four 3½-inch (9 cm) lengths.

• Knot 1 end of each chiffon length; at opposite end, gently pull wire at 1 edge only, so ribbon gathers along wire and curls, and leave wire end untrimmed.

• Loop each moiré length so ends are even; gather ends together and wrap with floral wire.

• With all gathered (bottom) edges down and even, hold moiré loop tight against chiffon knot; wrap chiffon ribbon around knot/loop, tightly at first to form centre, then loosely to flare outside edge.

• Fold remaining end down, even with bottom edge; wrap wire end tightly around edge to secure (with glue gun, dab with glue, if desired).

• Shape petals as desired.

• Wrap sheet of matching foil wrapping paper around 8-inch (20.5 cm) diameter Styrofoam ball, trimming away excess, then fasten rosettes all over with glue or straight pins.

• Fasten 1 end of remaining chiffon length to top for hanging ribbon.

> *Hand-Painted Candle Holders*

Enjoy these at home or take along as hostess gifts.

• Wash and dry glass tea-light or votive holder(s), then, with paper towel and 1:1 mixture of vinegar and water, wipe area(s) to be painted. Dab separate small amount of each colour of acrylic enamel paint onto palette (such as clean Styrofoam meat tray); have paper towels, container of clear water and square of clean sponge on hand.

• With pencil, draw outline of simple seasonal motif – such as snowman, tree, or holly leaves and berries – onto small piece of paper; tape inside candle holder to use as guide while you paint. Letting dry after each colour, paint as follows: Dip fine-tip artist's paintbrush into water, blot excess on paper towel, dip tip into paint, then apply to glass, stroking fine lines, swirling large areas or dabbing on dots with tip. If desired, moisten sponge with water, blot excess on paper towel, then dab into paint and blot again before dabbing onto glass.

Classic Crème Anglaise

This velvety pouring custard is fantastic drizzled on pudding, apple crisp, bread pudding, crêpes, fruit or sponge cake.

1 cup	whipping or 18% cream	250 mL
1 cup	milk	250 mL
¼ cup	granulated sugar	50 mL
6	egg yolks	6
1 tsp	vanilla	5 mL

• In small saucepan, heat cream, milk and half of the sugar over medium heat until steaming and bubbles form around edge.
• Meanwhile, in bowl, whisk egg yolks with remaining sugar. Whisk in hot cream mixture in thin stream; stir back into pan. Cook, stirring constantly, until thick enough to coat spoon, about 5 minutes.
• Strain into clean bowl; stir in vanilla. Place plastic wrap directly on surface; let cool. Refrigerate until cold, at least 1 hour. *(Make-ahead: Refrigerate in airtight container for up to 3 days.)*

MAKES ABOUT 2 CUPS (500 ML).

PER 2 TBSP (25 ML): about 91 cal, 2 g pro, 8 g total fat (4 g sat. fat), 4 g carb, 0 g fibre, 97 mg chol, 16 mg sodium. % RDI: 3% calcium, 1% iron, 9% vit A, 5% folate.

Silky Bittersweet Chocolate Sauce

This sauce is an all-time favourite, either cold or at room temperature. To serve hot, increase chocolate to 8 oz (250 g).

1¼ cups	whipping cream	300 mL
3 tbsp	corn syrup	50 mL
6 oz	bittersweet chocolate, chopped	175 g

• In saucepan, bring cream and corn syrup to boil; remove from heat. Whisk in chocolate until smooth. Let stand until thickened, about 15 minutes. *(Make-ahead: Refrigerate in airtight container for up to 5 days.)*

MAKES ABOUT 2 CUPS (500 ML).

PER 2 TBSP (25 ML): about 127 cal, 1 g pro, 12 g total fat (8 g sat. fat), 6 g carb, 2 g fibre, 24 mg chol, 13 mg sodium. % RDI: 2% calcium, 5% iron, 6% vit A.

Cranberry Red Wine Sauce

This tangy sauce is wonderful drizzled over cheesecake, ice cream or fruit.

1	bottle (750 mL) dry red wine	1
1	can (275 mL) frozen cranberry juice cocktail concentrate, thawed	1
1¼ cups	granulated sugar	300 mL
2 tsp	vanilla	10 mL

• In large saucepan, stir together wine, cranberry concentrate and sugar over medium-high heat; bring to boil. Reduce heat to medium; simmer until reduced to 2 cups (500 mL), about 45 minutes. Stir in vanilla. *(Make-ahead: Refrigerate in airtight container for up to 2 weeks.)*

MAKES ABOUT 2 CUPS (500 ML).

PER 2 TBSP (25 ML): about 113 cal, trace pro, 0 g total fat (0 g sat. fat), 27 g carb, 0 g fibre, 0 mg chol, 3 mg sodium. % RDI: 1% calcium, 2% iron, 18% vit C.

Chapter Five

COOKIES, BARS & SQUARES

Pistachio Thumbprints with White Chocolate

Chopping the pistachios by hand takes time, but you can control the fineness.

1 cup	butter, softened	250 mL
1⅔ cups	finely chopped shelled pistachios	400 mL
1 cup	granulated sugar	250 mL
2	eggs, separated	2
1½ tsp	vanilla	7 mL
2¼ cups	all-purpose flour	550 mL
¼ tsp	salt	1 mL
FILLING:		
7 oz	white chocolate, finely chopped	210 g
2 tsp	vegetable oil	10 mL

• Line 2 rimless baking sheets with parchment paper or grease; set aside.

• In large bowl, beat butter with ⅓ cup (75 mL) of the pistachios for 1 minute; beat in sugar until fluffy. Beat in egg yolks, 1 at a time, beating well after each; beat in vanilla. In separate bowl, whisk flour with salt; stir into butter mixture until combined. Roll by 1 tbsp (15 mL) into balls.

• In small bowl, whisk egg whites until frothy. Place remaining pistachios in separate bowl. Roll each ball in egg whites then in pistachios to coat. Place, 2 inches (5 cm) apart, on prepared pans. Using end of wooden spoon or thumb, make indentation in centre of each.

• Bake in centre of 350°F (180°C) oven just until browned on bottom and nuts are golden, about 12 minutes. Let cool on pan on rack for 5 minutes, reforming indentation. Transfer to racks; let cool.

• FILLING: In bowl over saucepan of hot (not boiling) water, melt chocolate with oil. Using scant 1 tsp (5 mL) each, fill indentations with white chocolate; let set, 45 minutes. *(Make-ahead: Layer between waxed paper in airtight container and store for up to 5 days or freeze for up to 3 weeks.)*

MAKES 60 COOKIES.

PER COOKIE: about 98 cal, 2 g pro, 6 g total fat (3 g sat. fat), 10 g carb, trace fibre, 17 mg chol, 46 mg sodium. % RDI: 1% calcium, 3% iron, 3% vit A, 4% folate.

VARIATION

Pistachio Thumbprints with Raspberry:
FILLING: Replace filling with ⅓ cup (75 mL) raspberry jam.

Vanilla Cookie Snowmen

Thanks to the icing sugar, this dough is quite hardy and can withstand repeated kneading and rolling. For sparkly snowmen, roll the balls in coarse sugar before baking them. Then stand the snowmen up in coarse sugar for presentation.

½ cup	butter, softened	125 mL
1 cup	unsifted icing sugar	250 mL
2 tsp	vanilla	10 mL
1	egg, beaten	1
2 cups	all-purpose flour	500 mL
½ tsp	baking soda	2 mL
¼ tsp	salt	1 mL
	Pretzels, curly and straight pasta and candies	

- Line 2 rimless baking sheets with parchment paper or grease; set aside.
- In large bowl, beat butter with sugar until fluffy; beat in vanilla. Beat in egg until smooth. In separate bowl, whisk together flour, baking soda and salt; add to butter mixture, stirring until incorporated.
- Working with small pieces of dough at a time, make 2 tsp (10 mL) ball, 1 tsp (5 mL) ball and ½ tsp (2 mL) ball. Place balls flat on prepared pans, one above the other, using smallest ball for head and largest for base. Do not try to stand balls up. Make arms and noses with broken pretzels or pasta; use candies for eyes, mouth and buttons.
- Bake in centre of 350°F (180°C) oven until firm to the touch, about 13 minutes. Let cool on pan on rack for 5 minutes; transfer to rack and let cool completely.

MAKES ABOUT 32 COOKIES.

PER COOKIE: about 69 cal, 1 g pro, 3 g total fat (2 g sat. fat), 9 g carb, trace fibre, 15 mg chol, 68 mg sodium. % RDI: 3% iron, 3% vit A, 5% folate.

High-Altitude Baking

Many of us deal with high-altitude baking, which affects baking in several ways.

1. The leavening agent (yeast, baking powder, baking soda) releases larger, more numerous gas bubbles that expand quickly and collapse easily, causing cakes to fall.

2. Moisture vaporizes at a lower temperature, causing a drier texture.

3. The internal temperature of a baking cake is much lower, so the cake will take longer to bake than the time that is specified.

Adapt recipes by following these simple guidelines:

❯ For cake batters, reduce baking powder or baking soda by ⅛ tsp (0.5 mL) for each 1 tsp (5 mL) called for.

❯ Because moisture vaporizes quickly, baked goods tend to stick more easily to pans. Line bottoms of baking pans with parchment or waxed paper, or grease well and dust with flour.

❯ Reduce amount of sugar in butter cakes if quantity given is more than one-half of the quantity of flour given. Reduce sugar by about 1 tbsp (15 mL) for each 1 cup (250 mL) called for. Excess sugar weakens the structure.

❯ Increase baking time by a few minutes for most baked goods. Do not adjust temperature.

Cardamom Butter Cookies

Clarified butter (instructions below) gives these Middle Eastern cookies a crisp texture.

1 cup	unsalted butter, cubed	250 mL
1 cup	icing sugar (approx)	250 mL
½ tsp	orange blossom water or vanilla	2 mL
1¾ cups	all-purpose flour	425 mL
½ tsp	ground cardamom	2 mL
¼ tsp	salt	1 mL
36	whole blanched almonds	36

• Line 2 rimless baking sheets with parchment paper or grease; set aside.
• In saucepan, melt butter over low heat; let cool for 5 minutes. Skim froth from surface. Strain butter through double-thickness cheesecloth into large bowl; refrigerate until clarified butter is solidified and milky liquid settles to bottom, about 2 hours.
• Discard milky liquid. With electric mixer, beat butter until light, creamy and doubled in volume. Beat in icing sugar, one-third at a time. Beat in orange blossom water.
• In separate bowl, whisk flour, cardamom and salt; stir into butter mixture to form crumbly dough. Turn out onto lightly floured surface; knead until smooth and pliable, 3 minutes. Shape into disc. Wrap; refrigerate until slightly firm, 30 minutes.
• On floured surface, roll dough by 1 tbsp (15 mL) into 3½-inch (9 cm) long logs; press ends together to form ring, overlapping slightly. Press almond onto joint. Place, 2 inches (5 cm) apart, on prepared pans.
• Bake in top and bottom thirds of 300°F (150°C) oven, rotating and switching pans halfway through, until tops are pale golden and bottoms are golden, about 15 minutes. Let cool on pans on racks for 5 minutes; transfer to racks and let cool completely.

(Make-ahead: Layer between waxed paper in airtight container and store for up to 1 week or freeze for up to 1 month.) Dust with 2 tbsp (25 mL) more icing sugar.

MAKES ABOUT 36 COOKIES.

PER COOKIE: about 87 cal, 1 g pro, 6 g total fat (3 g sat. fat), 8 g carb, trace fibre, 13 mg chol, 17 mg sodium. % RDI: 2% iron, 5% vit A, 4% folate.

Shortbread Stars

Buttery and tender — what more is needed for a perfect shortbread?

1 cup	butter, softened	250 mL
3 tbsp	cornstarch	50 mL
¼ cup	granulated sugar	50 mL
1¾ cups	all-purpose flour	425 mL

• Line 2 rimless baking sheets with parchment paper or leave ungreased; set aside.
• In large bowl, beat butter until fluffy; gradually beat in cornstarch, then sugar. With wooden spoon, beat in flour, ¼ cup (50 mL) at a time.
• On lightly floured surface, roll out to ¼-inch (5 mm) thickness. Using floured 2-inch (5 cm) star-shaped cookie cutter, cut out shapes. Place, 1 inch (2.5 cm) apart, on prepared pans; freeze until firm, 30 minutes.
• Bake in top and bottom thirds of 275°F (140°C) oven, rotating and switching pans halfway through, until firm, 40 to 50 minutes. Let cool on rack. *(Make ahead: Layer between waxed paper in airtight container and store for up to 1 week or freeze for up to 1 month.)*

MAKES 34 COOKIES.

PER COOKIE: about 80 cal, 1 g pro, 5 g total fat (3 g sat. fat), 7 g carb, trace fibre, 15 mg chol, 55 mg sodium. % RDI: 2% iron, 5% vit A, 3% folate.

Brownie Bow Ties

Although it takes time to cut and fold the dough over the filling, it's time well spent since it pays off in the raves you get.

1	pkg (4 oz/125 g) cream cheese, softened	1
½ cup	butter, softened	125 mL
1 tbsp	granulated sugar	15 mL
1 cup	all-purpose flour	250 mL
1	egg yolk	1
1 tbsp	coarse sugar	15 mL

BROWNIE FILLING:

2 tbsp	butter	25 mL
1½ oz	unsweetened chocolate, chopped	45 g
2 tbsp	granulated sugar	25 mL
½ tsp	vanilla	2 mL
1	egg yolk	1
2 tsp	all-purpose flour	10 mL
2 tbsp	chopped dried apricots, cherries or cranberries	25 mL

• Line 2 rimless baking sheets with parchment paper or grease; set aside.
• In large bowl, beat cream cheese with butter until fluffy; beat in granulated sugar. Stir in flour in 2 additions. Form into rectangle; cut in half. Wrap each and refrigerate until firm, about 1 hour. *(Make-ahead: Refrigerate for up to 24 hours.)*

• **BROWNIE FILLING:** In small saucepan, melt butter with chocolate over medium-low heat; remove from heat. Whisk in sugar and vanilla; let cool slightly. Whisk in egg yolk and flour; stir in apricots. Let cool.
• On lightly floured surface, roll out each half of dough into 10-inch (25 cm) square. Using fluted pastry wheel, trim edges; cut into twenty-five 2-inch (5 cm) squares.
• Shape scant ½ tsp (2 mL) filling into 1-inch (2.5 cm) long log; flatten slightly and place diagonally in centre of each square.
• Fold 1 corner of dough over filling and moisten corner with water. Fold opposite corner over first corner, overlapping slightly and pressing to seal. Arrange, 1 inch (2.5 cm) apart, on prepared pans.
• Whisk egg yolk with 1 tbsp (15 mL) water; brush over dough. Sprinkle with coarse sugar. Bake in centre of 325°F (160°C) oven until golden, about 13 minutes. Let cool on pan for 5 minutes; transfer to rack and let cool completely. *(Make-ahead: Layer between waxed paper in airtight container and store for up to 1 week or freeze for up to 1 month).*

MAKES 50 COOKIES.

PER COOKIE: about 50 cal, 1 g pro, 4 g total fat (2 g sat. fat), 4 g carb, trace fibre, 17 mg chol, 24 mg sodium. % RDI: 1% iron, 3% vit A, 3% folate.

Brownie Bow Ties
and Chocolate Stripe
Shortbread

Chocolate Stripe Shortbread

This buttery shortbread features three layers. The dark bottom is bittersweet chocolate, the centre is milk chocolate and the vanilla tops it off.

2 oz	bittersweet chocolate, chopped	60 g
1 oz	milk chocolate, chopped	30 g
1 cup	butter, softened	250 mL
½ cup	instant dissolving (fruit/berry) sugar	125 mL
1 tsp	vanilla	5 mL
2 cups	all-purpose flour	500 mL
Pinch	salt	Pinch

• Line 2 rimless baking sheets with parchment paper or grease; set aside.
• In bowl over saucepan of hot (not boiling) water, melt bittersweet chocolate. In separate bowl and in same way, melt milk chocolate. Let cool to room temperature.
• In bowl, beat butter with sugar until fluffy; stir in vanilla. Stir in flour and salt. Scrape half into separate bowl; stir in bittersweet chocolate. Remove one-third of the remaining vanilla dough and set aside. Stir milk chocolate into remaining two-thirds.
• On plastic wrap, shape half of the bittersweet chocolate dough into 9- x 2-inch (23 x 5 cm) rectangle. Shape half of the milk chocolate dough into 9- x 1¾-inch (23 x 4.5 cm) rectangle; place in centre of bittersweet chocolate dough.
• Roll half of the remaining vanilla dough into 9-inch (23 cm) log; place in centre of milk chocolate dough. Wrap plastic wrap around dough; press into triangle. Repeat with remaining dough. Refrigerate until firm, about 2 hours. *(Make-ahead: Freeze in airtight container for up to 3 weeks.)*

• Cut into ¼-inch (5 mm) thick slices. Arrange, 1 inch (2.5 cm) apart, on prepared pans. Bake in top and bottom thirds of 300°F (150°C) oven, rotating and switching pans halfway through, until firm to the touch and bottoms are slightly golden, about 20 minutes. Transfer to racks; let cool. *(Make-ahead: Layer between waxed paper in airtight container and store for up to 1 week or freeze for up to 1 month.)*

MAKES ABOUT 40 COOKIES.

PER COOKIE: about 84 cal, 1 g pro, 6 g total fat (4 g sat. fat), 8 g carb, trace fibre, 12 mg chol, 34 mg sodium. % RDI: 3% iron, 4% vit A, 6% folate.

Melting Chocolate

Chocolate, with its high ratio of cocoa butter, must be handled gently when melting so that it doesn't seize, scorch or lose shine.

❯ Chop finely. Place in heatproof glass or stainless-steel bowl with rim slightly larger than rim of saucepan. (If bowl is too large, it may be heated by the element, causing chocolate to burn; also bottom of bowl must not touch water.)

❯ Pour enough water into saucepan to come 1 inch (2.5 cm) up side. Place over medium heat and heat just until steaming (not boiling). Place bowl over saucepan. Let stand just until three-quarters of the chocolate is melted.

❯ Remove from heat and stir with metal spoon until remaining chocolate is melted.

❯ Do not cover: moisture droplets can accumulate on lid and drop into chocolate, causing it to seize.

Rolled Rugalachs

Rolled versions of this traditional Jewish holiday cookie are just as pretty as the crescent-shaped ones. Plus they're a little easier and quicker to make.

1	pkg (8 oz/250 g) cream cheese, softened	1
1 cup	butter, softened	250 mL
2 tbsp	granulated sugar	25 mL
2 cups	all-purpose flour	500 mL
FILLING:		
1½ cups	chopped walnut halves	375 mL
4 oz	semisweet chocolate, chopped	125 g
¼ cup	each granulated sugar and packed brown sugar	50 mL
¾ tsp	cinnamon	4 mL
¾ cup	orange marmalade	175 mL
TOPPING:		
1	egg, lightly beaten	1
2 tbsp	coarse or granulated sugar	25 mL

● Line 2 rimless baking sheets with parchment paper or grease; set aside.
● In bowl, beat cream cheese with butter until fluffy; beat in sugar. Stir in flour in 2 additions. Form into rectangle; cut into quarters and shape into rectangles. Wrap and refrigerate until firm, about 1 hour. *(Make-ahead: Refrigerate for up to 24 hours.)*

● **FILLING:** In bowl, stir together walnuts, chocolate, granulated and brown sugars and cinnamon.
● On lightly floured surface, roll out 1 of the quarters into 12- x 8-inch (30 x 20 cm) rectangle. Spread 3 tbsp (50 mL) of the marmalade evenly over top; sprinkle with one-quarter of the filling. Starting at long side, roll into tight log.
● Cut into twelve 1-inch (2.5 cm) thick slices. Arrange, standing on edge and ¼ inch (5 mm) apart, on prepared pan. Repeat with remaining dough. Refrigerate for 30 minutes.
● **TOPPING:** Brush egg over top edge of upright cookies; sprinkle with sugar. Bake in top and bottom thirds of 350°F (180°C) oven, rotating and switching pans halfway through, until golden, about 25 minutes. Let cool on pans on racks for 5 minutes; transfer to racks and let cool completely. *(Make-ahead: Layer between waxed paper in airtight container and store for up to 5 days or freeze for up to 1 month.)*

MAKES ABOUT 44 COOKIES.

PER COOKIE: about 147 cal, 2 g pro, 10 g total fat (5 g sat. fat), 14 g carb, 1 g fibre, 24 mg chol, 65 mg sodium. % RDI: 1% calcium, 4% iron, 6% vit A, 7% folate.

VARIATION

Apricot Almond Rolled Rugalachs: Replace walnuts with sliced almonds, chocolate with 1 cup (250 mL) chopped dried apricots, and marmalade with apricot jam.

Sugar Cookies

Baking cookies is the perfect way to get the family together in the kitchen. With this easy dough, it takes no time to cut the cookies into shapes, such as snowflakes, stars, trees, ornaments and even mittens, to decorate festively with the Cookie Glaze (recipe follows).

¾ cup	butter, softened	175 mL
1 cup	granulated or packed brown sugar	250 mL
1	egg	1
1 tsp	vanilla	5 mL
2½ cups	all-purpose flour	625 mL
½ tsp	baking powder	2 mL
Pinch	salt	Pinch

• Line 2 rimless baking sheets with parchment paper or grease; set aside.
• In large bowl, beat butter until fluffy; beat in sugar in 3 additions. Beat in egg and vanilla. In separate bowl, whisk together flour, baking powder and salt; stir into butter mixture in 3 additions.
• Divide dough in half; shape into discs. Wrap and refrigerate for 1 hour. *(Make-ahead: Refrigerate for up to 24 hours.)*
• On lightly floured surface, roll out each half to ¼-inch (5 mm) thickness. Using 3-inch (8 cm) cookie cutter, cut out shapes. Place, 1 inch (2.5 cm) apart, on prepared pans.

• Bake in top and bottom thirds of 375°F (190°C) oven, rotating and switching pans halfway through, until light golden on bottoms and edges, about 10 minutes. Let cool on pans on racks for 1 minute; transfer to racks and let cool completely. *(Make-ahead: Layer between waxed paper in airtight container and store for up to 1 week or freeze for up to 1 month.)*

MAKES 36 COOKIES.

PER COOKIE: about 89 cal, 1 g pro, 4 g total fat (2 g sat. fat), 12 g carb, trace fibre, 17 mg chol, 45 mg sodium. % RDI: 3% iron, 4% vit A, 5% folate.

Cookie Glaze
• In bowl, mix 2 cups (500 mL) icing sugar with 3 tbsp (50 mL) milk or water until smooth. Tint with food colouring if desired (paste food colouring gives more intense colour than liquid colouring). Add more liquid for thinner glaze. Brush tops of cooled cookies with glaze. Sprinkle with decorative candies, sugar crystals or sprinkles.

MAKES ¾ CUP (175 ML).

VARIATIONS

Sugar Cookie Mittens: Use mitten-shaped cookie cutter. Bake as directed. Decorate with Cookie Glaze (tinted as desired).

Sugar Cookie Christmas Trees, Snowmen and Snowflakes: Use Christmas tree, snowman and snowflake cookie cutters. Bake as directed. Decorate with Cookie Glaze (tinted as desired). For trees, sprinkle with coarse sugar and dot with decorator candies. For snowmen, use ribbon licorice for scarf, nose and mouth and decorator candies for buttons and eyes. For snowflakes, use white glaze and decorate with silver dragées if desired.

Glazed Almond Spritz Cookies

Spritz cookies pressed into various shapes by a cookie press are one of the season's stars. Here's a tip. The baking sheets must be cold and clean. Before starting, refrigerate the sheets and between batches immerse them in ice water and dry if you need them right away.

1 cup	butter, softened	250 mL
⅔ cup	icing sugar	150 mL
1	egg yolk	1
1½ tsp	vanilla	7 mL
¼ tsp	almond extract	1 mL
Pinch	salt	Pinch
2 cups	all-purpose flour	500 mL
½ cup	ground almonds	125 mL

ALMOND GLAZE:

1 cup	icing sugar (approx)	250 mL
¼ cup	whipping cream (approx)	50 mL
¼ tsp	almond extract	1 mL
	Silver or gold dragées or candied cherries	

• Refrigerate 2 ungreased rimless baking sheets until cold.
• In large bowl, beat butter with sugar until fluffy; beat in egg yolk, vanilla, almond extract and salt. Stir in flour, then almonds.
• In batches, pack into cookie press; press out rosettes about 1 inch (2.5 cm) in diameter onto prepared pans, about 1 inch (2.5 cm) apart.
• Bake in centre of 350°F (180°C) oven until light golden on bottom, 8 to 10 minutes. Let cool for 1 minute; transfer to racks set over waxed paper.
• **ALMOND GLAZE:** Stir together sugar, cream and almond extract, adding more sugar or cream if necessary to make pourable. Drizzle over hot cookies. Immediately press silver dragées into centre. Let cool. (*Make-ahead: Layer between waxed paper in airtight container and store for up to 1 week or freeze for up to 1 month.*)

MAKES ABOUT 90 COOKIES.

PER COOKIE: about 42 cal, 1 g pro, 3 g total fat (2 g sat. fat), 4 g carb, trace fibre, 9 mg chol, 21 mg sodium. % RDI: 1% iron, 2% vit A, 2% folate.

Speculaas

These Dutch spice cookies are traditionally moulded in carved wooden boards and unmoulded before baking. Because they reflect the design of the moulds, they got their name from the Latin word speculum *(looking glass). This recipe for an easier rolled version has the same memorable flavour.*

½ cup	butter, softened	125 mL
1 cup	packed brown sugar	250 mL
1	egg	1
1 cup	all-purpose flour	250 mL
¾ cup	whole wheat flour	175 mL
2 tsp	each cinnamon and ground ginger	10 mL
½ tsp	each baking powder and baking soda	2 mL
½ tsp	allspice	2 mL
¼ tsp	each ground cardamom, cloves and nutmeg	1 mL
¼ tsp	each salt and pepper	1 mL
1 tbsp	milk	15 mL
½ cup	sliced almonds	125 mL

- Line 2 rimless baking sheets with parchment paper or grease; set aside.
- In large bowl, beat butter with sugar until fluffy; beat in egg.
- In separate bowl, whisk together all-purpose and whole wheat flours, cinnamon, ginger, baking powder, baking soda, allspice, cardamom, cloves, nutmeg, salt and pepper; using wooden spoon, stir into butter mixture in 3 additions.
- Turn out onto lightly floured surface and gather into ball; knead 10 times. Shape into rectangle; wrap and refrigerate for 30 minutes.
- On lightly floured surface, roll out dough to ¼-inch (5 mm) thickness. Using cookie cutter, cut into 3- x 2-inch (8 x 5 cm) rectangles or other shapes; place, ½ inch (1 cm) apart, on prepared pans. Brush with milk. Press almond slices into top of each in decorative pattern.
- Bake in centre of 350°F (180°C) oven until edges darken slightly and tops are firm, 8 to 10 minutes. Let cool on pan on rack for 5 minutes; transfer to rack and let cool completely. *(Make-ahead: Layer between waxed paper in airtight container and store for up to 4 days or freeze for up to 2 weeks.)*

MAKES ABOUT 28 COOKIES.

PER COOKIE: about 101 cal, 2 g pro, 5 g total fat (2 g sat. fat), 14 g carb, 1 g fibre, 17 mg chol, 85 mg sodium. % RDI: 2% calcium, 5% iron, 3% vit A, 1% folate.

Sesame Wafers

Sesame seeds, or benne, were brought to North America by slaves from Africa. The seeds are part of many Kwanzaa festivities.

½ cup	butter, softened	125 mL
1 cup	packed brown sugar	250 mL
1	egg	1
2 tbsp	milk	25 mL
1 tsp	vanilla	5 mL
1 cup	all-purpose flour	250 mL
¼ tsp	baking powder	1 mL
⅓ cup	toasted white sesame seeds	75 mL
1 cup	pecan halves	250 mL
1 tbsp	black sesame seeds (optional)	15 mL

- Line 2 rimless baking sheets with parchment paper or grease; set aside.
- In large bowl, beat butter with sugar until fluffy; beat in egg, milk and vanilla.
- In separate bowl, whisk flour with baking powder; stir into butter mixture until smooth. Stir in all but 1 tbsp (15 mL) of the white sesame seeds. Drop by rounded 1 tsp (5 mL), about 2 inches (5 cm) apart, onto prepared pans. Press pecan half into each. Sprinkle with black sesame seeds (if using) and remaining white sesame seeds.
- Bake in top and bottom thirds of 375°F (190°C) oven, rotating and switching pans halfway through, until crisp and caramel brown, about 7 minutes. Let cool for 5 minutes; transfer to racks and let cool. *(Make-ahead: Layer between waxed paper in airtight container and store for up to 1 week or freeze for up to 1 month.)*

MAKES ABOUT 36 COOKIES.

PER COOKIE: about 90 cal, 1 g pro, 6 g total fat (2 g sat. fat), 9 g carb, trace fibre, 13 mg chol, 33 mg sodium. % RDI: 1% calcium, 4% iron, 3% vit A, 3% folate.

Lemon Pistachio Biscotti

You'll have enough biscotti for a season of guests dropping in for coffee or for some lovely gift boxes. Shelled pistachios, available at bulk food stores, save precious minutes.

1 cup	butter, softened	250 mL
2 cups	granulated sugar	500 mL
6	eggs	6
2 tbsp	grated lemon rind	25 mL
2 tsp	vanilla	10 mL
5½ cups	all-purpose flour	1.375 L
1 tbsp	baking powder	15 mL
½ tsp	salt	2 mL
2 cups	shelled salted pistachio nuts	500 mL
LEMON DRIZZLE:		
½ cup	icing sugar	125 mL
1 tbsp	lemon juice (approx)	15 mL

● Line 2 rimless baking sheets with parchment paper or grease; set aside.
● In large bowl, beat butter with sugar until fluffy; beat in eggs, 1 at a time. Beat in lemon rind and vanilla. In separate bowl, whisk together flour, baking powder and salt; stir into butter mixture. Stir in pistachio nuts.

● Divide dough into quarters; with floured hands, shape each into log about 12 inches (30 cm) long. Place 2, about 4 inches (10 cm) apart, on each prepared pan; flatten to about 3 inches (8 cm) wide, leaving slightly rounded top.
● Bake in top and bottom thirds of 325°F (160°C) oven, rotating and switching pans halfway through, until firm and just turning golden, about 30 minutes. Let cool on pan on rack for 10 minutes.
● Transfer logs to cutting board. With serrated knife, cut diagonally into ½-inch (1 cm) thick slices. Stand slices upright on same pans; bake, rotating and switching pans halfway through, until dry and crisp, 30 to 40 minutes. Transfer, cut sides up, to rack set on waxed paper; let cool.
● LEMON DRIZZLE: In small bowl, whisk icing sugar with enough of the lemon juice to create smooth liquid; drizzle over cookies. *(Make-ahead: Layer between waxed paper in airtight container and store for up to 2 weeks or freeze for up to 1 month.)*

MAKES ABOUT 80 COOKIES.

PER COOKIE: about 99 cal, 2 g pro, 4 g total fat (2 g sat. fat), 13 g carb, trace fibre, 22 mg chol, 77 mg sodium. % RDI: 1% calcium, 4% iron, 3% vit A, 2% vit C, 6% folate.

Organize the Perfect Cookie Exchange

Hosting a cookie exchange is an effortless way to collect a variety of cookies without baking them all yourself. Plus there's the added bonus of enjoying a fun visit with family, friends, neighbours and colleagues.
❯ Keep the guest list manageable. Six to eight is a good starting point. More guests will ensure a wide variety of cookies, but too many spells an excess of baked goods.
❯ Avoid duplication by asking guests to RSVP with the kind of cookie they plan to bring.
❯ Ask each guest to plan on baking one dozen cookies per guest. Suggest that guests avoid anything fragile or sticky.

Rum-Glazed Christmas Hermits

If you hanker for traditional fruitcake flavour but the time to make and age the cake has long passed, these spiced drop cookies loaded with fruit and nuts can be your last-minute satisfaction.

1 cup	butter, softened	250 mL
1 cup	packed brown sugar	250 mL
2	eggs	2
1 tsp	rum extract	5 mL
2½ cups	all-purpose flour	625 mL
1 tsp	each baking powder and cinnamon	5 mL
1 tsp	each nutmeg and ginger	5 mL
½ tsp	each baking soda and salt	2 mL
1 cup	red and/or green candied cherries, quartered	250 mL
1 cup	each raisins and candied citrus peel	250 mL
¾ cup	coarsely chopped pecans	175 mL
84	pecan halves (about 3 cups/750 mL), optional	84
RUM GLAZE:		
¾ cup	icing sugar	175 mL
2 tbsp	rum	25 mL

- Line 2 rimless baking sheets with parchment paper; set aside.
- In large bowl, beat butter with brown sugar until fluffy; beat in eggs, 1 at a time. Beat in rum extract.
- In separate bowl, whisk together flour, baking powder, cinnamon, nutmeg, ginger, baking soda and salt; stir into butter mixture in 3 additions until dough holds together. Stir in cherries, raisins, citrus peel and chopped pecans.
- Drop by level 1 tbsp (15 mL), about 2 inches (5 cm) apart, onto prepared pans. Press pecan half (if using) onto each. *(Make-ahead: Layer between waxed paper in airtight container and refrigerate for up to 24 hours or freeze for up to 1 month.)*
- Bake in top and bottom thirds of 350°F (180°C) oven, rotating and switching pans halfway through, until bottoms are golden but centres still soft, about 15 minutes. Let cool on racks.
- **RUM GLAZE:** In small bowl, stir icing sugar with rum until smooth; drizzle ½ tsp (2 mL) over each cookie. Let dry until set, about 10 minutes. *(Make-ahead: Layer between waxed paper in airtight container and store for up to 1 week or freeze for up to 1 month.)*

MAKES 84 COOKIES.

PER COOKIE: about 77 cal, 1 g pro, 3 g total fat (1 g sat. fat), 12 g carb, trace fibre, 8 mg chol, 40 mg sodium. % RDI: 1% calcium, 2% iron, 1% vit A, 3% folate.

❯ Remind guests to bring their own containers to transport cookies home. Or have guests pack their cookies in inexpensive airtight containers to avoid repacking. Have plenty of waxed paper on hand for layering and packing.
❯ Have guests bring along enough copies of their cookie recipe for everyone.
❯ Provide a decorated table to display all of the cookies.
❯ Provide beverages and snacks for guests to enjoy as they ooh and aah over the cookies.
❯ Have a good time.

❯ *O Little Town*

Your children will love this sleepy village with its tall stone church, red brick schoolhouse, barn, store and all the houses big and small (the pooch gets a cosy cabin, too). Numbered for each day of Advent, the snow-bedecked buildings are perfect places to stash special treats – and make the countdown to Christmas even more fun.

To make:

• Trim away container bottoms to create various heights (3⅛ to 6 inches/8 to 15 cm tall); push plastic spouts to inside. Set trimmed scraps aside for chimneys.

• For long low building (such as barn), glue together 2 containers of same height, triangle to triangle, then cover with walls and roof.

• For building with tall and short sections (such as church), cover 2 containers of different heights, with walls and roofs, then glue together (trim eaves on adjoining edge of small container, first).

• For each container size, make patterns:

Walls: On brown paper, lay container, triangle down; trace side edges, extending ¾ inches (2 cm) beyond bottom edge for folding allowance and drawing bottom line between them, then use ruler to draw line from each top corner to top ridge of triangle. Turn container onto next side; trace all edges, adding allowance as above. Repeat to draw all 4 sides and make pattern similar to Diagram A; cut out. Check fit by wrapping around container.

Roof: Lay container, triangle down; measure from top corner over ridge and down to other top corner on same side, then add 1 to 2 inches (2. 5 to 5 cm) overhang, for total width. Turn container to next side; measure along top edge, then add 1- to 2-inch overhang for total length. On brown paper, draw pattern piece, total width x total length; cut out.

Chimney: Trace actual-size pattern (left) onto brown paper or photocopy; cut out.

• When machine-stitching decorative details, backstitch at both ends of each seam line, then stitch again to make bolder line.

1. Walls: Using patterns, cut walls from desired colours of foam; wrap each around appropriate container, gluing 1 side at a time along container edges. Fold bottom edge of foam inside; glue.

2. Roofs: Using patterns, cut roofs from white lining (cut and glue double layer, if necessary, to prevent container edges showing). Fold each roof in half along length; centre over building. Apply glue along 1 slope at triangle edge; press roof in place. Repeat at opposite edge of same slope, then repeat with other half of roof. Carefully lift each horizontal edge, apply glue to lining; press in place.

3. Chimneys: Using pattern, cut each chimney from container scraps; fold along broken lines, then overlap and glue shaded sides. From red felt, cut 2⅛-x-1⅜-inch (5.5 x 3.5 cm) strip; wrap and glue around chimney, then fold bottom edge inside and glue. From white felt, cut 2⅛-x-¾-inch (5.5 x 2 cm) strip; wrap around top of chimney, then fold top edge inside and glue. Glue bottom edge of chimney, with short side parallel to ridge, onto roof.

4. Doors: Machine-stitch door outline of desired colour, shape and size onto felt (rectangle for house; square divided in half vertically for barn, school or store; or arch divided in half vertically for church); cut out ⅛ inch (3 mm) outside stitch line. Handstitch bead doorknobs in place, if desired. Glue door(s) onto building.

5. Windows: Machine-stitch mullion lines for each window onto felt, if desired; cut out just beyond line ends. For church, school and store, glue each onto contrasting felt, then trim, leaving ⅛- to ¼-inch (3 to 6 mm) frame. Glue onto buildings.

6. Advent-day numbers: Machine-stitch outline of 24 small rectangles or squares onto green felt; cut out ⅛ inch outside stitch line. With 2 strands of floss, backstitch number on each. Glue onto building fronts (use "24" on church).

Special Decorating Tips

• **Barn:** Cover walls with light grey or brown; with marker, draw vertical "board" edges. Cut elongated triangles for rustic metal hinges; glue across side edge of each door. Don't add windows.

• **Church:** Cover walls with dark grey. From light grey felt, cut long rectangles, then glue as "cornerstones" across and around building edges, alternating long ends. Machine-stitch, cut out and glue on cross above front doors. Use dark blue for windows or several colours for "stained glass."

• **Log cabin:** Cover walls with dark brown, then, with paint, draw thin chinking lines between "logs." Don't add window on back (north end).

• **Schoolhouse:** Cover walls with brick red, then, with paint, draw mortar lines around "bricks." If desired, machine-stitch and cut out sign, then embroider school name on it and glue above door.

• **Store:** Add large, front display windows.

• **And more...** Decorate a house to look like your house and another like your Grandma's or your best pal's. And don't forget to make a small dog house for your other best friend! Set up your village along a mantel, sideboard or window ledge, nestling the houses into quilt batting, if desired (anchor pencils in modelling clay hidden under batt, then string streetlights in between.)

You need:

• At least 26 clean, dry containers, such as cream, milk and juice cartons, for buildings

• Approx fifteen 12 x 9 inch (30.5 x 23 cm) pieces of nylon-flocked foam or felt: beige, brick red, brown, grey and pastel colours, for walls

• Felt scraps: black, light and dark blue, tan and yellow, for doors and windows

• Piece of white insulating lining, felt, low-loft batting or synthetic fleece, 59 x 29½ inches (150 x 75 cm), for snowy roofs

• Small wooden or metal beads, for doorknobs

• Embroidery floss in desired colours

• Glossy, off-white fabric paint in squeezable applicator bottle, for log chinking or brick mortar

• Permanent, medium-tip black marker, for barnboard stripes

• Glue gun

• Ruler

• Brown paper

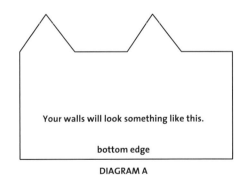

Your walls will look something like this.

bottom edge

DIAGRAM A

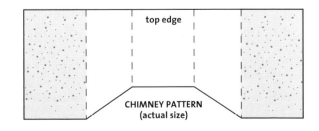

top edge

CHIMNEY PATTERN
(actual size)

Chocolate Dough

This dough and its orange variation are enough for the Two-Tone Harlequins and the Yin-Yang Cookies (recipes this page and opposite). Or make the dough and use for plain chocolate or orange cookies.

2 oz	unsweetened chocolate, chopped	60 g
½ cup	butter, softened	125 mL
¾ cup	granulated sugar	175 mL
1	egg	1
1¾ cups	all-purpose flour	425 mL
½ tsp	each salt and baking soda	2 mL

• In heatproof bowl over saucepan of hot (not boiling) water, melt chocolate, stirring occasionally. Let cool to room temperature.
• In large bowl, beat butter with sugar until fluffy; beat in egg. Stir in chocolate.
• In separate bowl, whisk together flour, salt and baking soda; stir into butter mixture in 2 additions.
• Divide dough in half; shape into rectangles. Wrap each and refrigerate until firm, about 30 minutes. *(Make-ahead: Refrigerate in airtight container for up to 3 days.)*

VARIATION

Orange Dough: Omit chocolate. Add 1 tbsp (15 mL) finely grated orange rind and ½ tsp (2 mL) vanilla along with egg.

Two-Tone Harlequins

Orange-flavoured and chocolate doughs are cut and reassembled into the diamonds of the harlequin pattern.

Half	Orange Dough (recipe, left)	Half
Half	Chocolate Dough (recipe, left)	Half
1	egg white, beaten	1

• Line 2 rimless baking sheets with parchment paper or grease; set aside.
• Divide Orange Dough in half. On lightly floured surface, form each into 7-inch (18 cm) long log. Repeat with Chocolate Dough. Wrap each and refrigerate until firm, about 30 minutes.
• With sharp knife, cut each log lengthwise into quarters; brush cut sides with egg white. Alternating orange and chocolate strips, reassemble logs. Reroll gently to seal and form 4 logs. Wrap and refrigerate until firm, about 30 minutes. *(Make-ahead: Refrigerate in airtight container for up to 3 days or freeze for up to 1 month.)*
• Cut each log into generous ¼-inch (5 mm) thick slices. Arrange, 1 inch (2.5 cm) apart, on prepared pans. Bake in centre of 350°F (180°C) oven until firm to the touch, about 10 minutes. Let cool on pan on rack for 1 minute; transfer to rack and let cool completely. *(Make-ahead: Layer between waxed paper in airtight container and store for up to 1 week or freeze for up to 2 weeks.)*

MAKES ABOUT 80 COOKIES.

PER COOKIE: about 31 cal, trace pro, 1 g total fat (1 g sat. fat), 4 g carb, trace fibre, 6 mg chol, 35 mg sodium. % RDI: 1% iron, 1% vit A, 3% folate.

Yin-Yang Cookies

Use a small plastic bag with the corner snipped off to pipe on the chocolate dots.

Half	Orange Dough (recipe, opposite)	Half
Half	Chocolate Dough (recipe, opposite)	Half
1	egg white, beaten	1
2 oz	each semisweet and white chocolate, chopped	60 g

• Line 2 rimless baking sheets with parchment paper or grease; set aside.

• On lightly floured surface, form Orange Dough into four 5-inch (12 cm) long logs. Repeat with Chocolate Dough. Wrap each and refrigerate until firm, about 15 minutes.

• With rolling pin parallel to log, press one-third of each log along edge to make lip. Brush lip with egg white. Invert 1 orange log over 1 chocolate log so lips are opposite. Reroll into log to form yin-yang design when cut. Repeat to form 4 rolls. Wrap and refrigerate until firm, 30 minutes. *(Make-ahead: Refrigerate in airtight container for up to 3 days or freeze for up to 1 month.)*

• Cut rolls into ¼-inch (5 mm) thick slices. Arrange, 1 inch (2.5 cm) apart, on pans. Bake in centre of 350°F (180°C) oven until firm to the touch, 15 minutes. Let cool on rack for 1 minute; transfer to rack and let cool.

• In bowl, melt semisweet chocolate over saucepan of hot (not boiling) water. Repeat with white chocolate. Let cool. Pipe white dot on chocolate side and chocolate dot on orange side of cookies. *(Make-ahead: Layer in waxed paper in airtight container; store for up to 1 week or freeze for up to 2 weeks.)*

MAKES ABOUT 60 COOKIES.

PER COOKIE: about 44 cal, 1 g pro, 2 g total fat (1 g sat. fat), 6 g carb, trace fibre, 8 mg chol, 47 mg sodium. % RDI: 1% iron, 2% vit A, 4% folate.

Baking Better Cookies

❯ Bring all ingredients to room temperature before starting.

❯ Make cookies the same size and shape for even baking and browning.

❯ Use rimless baking sheets with slightly slanted lips so that heat can circulate around cookies. Rimmed sheets are less suitable, but if they are all you have in your cupboard, use them. You can turn them over and use the flat bottoms. Heavy, shiny sheets are best. They bake cookies evenly, prevent bottoms from browning too quickly and do not warp.

❯ Line baking sheets with parchment paper, silicone baking liners, nonstick foil or prepare as directed in recipe.

❯ Bake one sheet at a time on rack positioned in centre of oven. However, to bake more than one sheet of cookies at a time, position racks in top and bottom thirds of oven and rotate sheets from top to bottom and from front to back halfway through baking time.

❯ If you have only one or two baking sheets, let the sheets cool completely between baking the batches. Hot baking sheets will melt cookie dough, resulting in changes to the texture and shape of cookies.

❯ Always check cookies for doneness at the earliest time called for.

❯ Let cookies cool completely on rack to prevent soggy bottoms.

❯ Store crisp and soft cookies separately in airtight containers.

Really Good Rum Balls

There are rum ball recipes galore, but none better than this one.

1 cup	icing sugar	250 mL
1 cup	ground almonds	250 mL
3 oz	bittersweet chocolate, grated	90 g
⅓ cup	dark rum	75 mL
1 tsp	vanilla	5 mL
½ cup	chocolate sprinkles	125 mL

• Line trays with waxed paper; set aside.
• In large bowl, whisk together icing sugar, almonds and bittersweet chocolate. Add ¼ cup (50 mL) of the rum and vanilla, stirring until moist; press together. Chill until firm enough to roll, about 15 minutes.
• Roll by rounded 1 tsp (5 mL) into balls, moistening and wiping hands with damp cloth as needed. Place on prepared trays.
• Pour remaining rum into shallow bowl. Pour chocolate sprinkles into separate shallow bowl. Roll balls in rum then in chocolate, pressing lightly so chocolate sticks. Let dry on tray, about 1 hour. Refrigerate until firm. *(Make-ahead: Layer between waxed paper in airtight container and refrigerate or freeze for up to 1 month.)*

MAKES ABOUT 36 BALLS.

PER BALL: about 57 cal, 1 g pro, 3 g total fat (1 g sat. fat), 6 g carb, 1 g fibre, 0 mg chol, 1 mg sodium. % RDI: 1% calcium, 2% iron, 1% folate.

Sugarless Almond Slice-and-Bake Cookies

This is an all-occasion cookie.

¾ cup	butter, softened	175 mL
1 cup	granulated sugar substitute	250 mL
1	egg	1
¾ tsp	almond extract	4 mL
2 cups	all-purpose flour	500 mL
½ tsp	baking powder	2 mL
¼ cup	sliced unblanched almonds	50 mL

• Line 2 rimless baking sheets with parchment paper or grease; set aside.
• In bowl, beat butter with sugar substitute until smooth; beat in egg then almond extract. In separate bowl, whisk flour with baking powder; stir into butter mixture in 2 additions.
• On lightly floured surface, roll dough into 2-inch (5 cm) thick log. Wrap and refrigerate until chilled, about 1 hour. *(Make-ahead: Refrigerate in airtight container for up to 3 days or freeze for up to 3 weeks.)*
• Cut log into ¼-inch (5 mm) thick slices; place on prepared pans. Press almond slice into centre of each.
• Bake in top and bottom thirds of 375°F (190°C) oven, rotating and switching pans halfway through, until golden around edges, about 10 minutes. Let cool on pans on rack for 1 minute; transfer to rack and let cool completely. *(Make-ahead: Layer between waxed paper in airtight container and store for up to 5 days or freeze for up to 1 month.)*

MAKES ABOUT 36 COOKIES.

PER COOKIE: about 68 cal, 1 g pro, 4 g total fat (2 g sat. fat), 6 g carb, trace fibre, 17 mg chol, 45 mg sodium. % RDI: 1% calcium, 3% iron, 4% vit A, 5% folate.

> Rectangular Wreath

Build a wreath around a recycled frame of any size. Or make more than one and group them together on a wall. Wind medium-gauge or floral wire in and out around picture frame, tucking sprigs of fresh or faux boxwood under wire at frame front. Create focal point inside frame by wiring stem of single fresh or faux flower or row of buds to back of frame, at bottom or top, or fasten bow or ornament at centre top.

> How to Make a Bow

You can tie a bow that looks neat and stays tied in any size you like.

1. With length of ribbon, form loop at each side of midpoint.

2. Without twisting or bunching ribbon, pass right-hand loop behind, then back up through left-hand loop.

3. Tug loops away from each other to form small, smooth knot. Adjust loops to desired shape and size, then trim V-shaped notch in each end of ribbon.

Cookie Smarts

❯ The best baking sheets are shiny and rimless with slightly curved edges to make picking up easier.

❯ To prepare baking sheets, line with parchment paper, nonstick foil or reusable silicone baking mat, or grease lightly and evenly. Occasionally, baking sheets do not need to be greased and this is noted in recipes.

❯ For bars and squares, choose shiny metal cake pans with sides at 90-degree angle.

❯ Eggs are always large and vanilla is pure vanilla extract unless otherwise noted.

❯ Butter is usually salted unless otherwise noted, but if you prefer unsalted butter, add a pinch of salt to any butter mixture.

Pignoli

These Italian macaroons, with a crisp outside and chewy heart, are named for their most important ingredient — pine nuts.

1	pkg (200 g) marzipan	1
2	egg whites	2
½ cup	granulated sugar	125 mL
2 tsp	finely chopped lemon rind	10 mL
½ cup	toasted pine nuts	125 mL

● Line 2 rimless baking sheets with parchment paper or grease; set aside.
● In food processor, coarsely chop marzipan; spread on large tray and let stand until dry, about 4 hours. (*Make-ahead: Let stand for up to 24 hours.*) Return to food processor; pulse into fine crumbs.
● In large bowl, beat egg whites until frothy; beat in sugar, 2 tbsp (25 mL) at a time, and lemon rind until soft peaks form. Fold in marzipan. Drop by 1 tbsp (15 mL), about 2 inches (5 cm) apart, onto prepared pans. Top with pine nuts; press with back of spoon.
● Bake in top and bottom thirds of 350°F (180°C) oven, rotating and switching pans halfway through, until browned, about 20 minutes. Let cool on pans on racks for 2 minutes. Transfer to racks; let cool completely. (*Make-ahead: Layer between waxed paper in airtight container and store for up to 5 days.*)

MAKES 32 COOKIES.

PER COOKIE: about 57 cal, 1 g pro, 2 g total fat (trace sat. fat), 9 g carb, 1 g fibre, 0 mg chol, 4 mg sodium. % RDI: 1% calcium, 2% iron, 1% folate.

Lemon Lime Refrigerator Cookies

Stash a few logs of dough away for when you're tempted to fill the kitchen with cookie aromas. It's practical to cut the rolls short enough that you can bake a tiny batch in a toaster oven.

1 cup	butter, softened	250 mL
1 cup	granulated sugar	250 mL
1	egg	1
1 tbsp	finely grated lemon rind	15 mL
2 tsp	finely grated lime rind	10 mL
2½ cups	all-purpose flour	625 mL
½ tsp	baking powder	2 mL
¼ tsp	salt	1 mL
4 oz	white chocolate, finely chopped (optional)	125 g
1	egg white	1
⅔ cup	finely chopped almonds	150 mL
GLAZE:		
1 cup	icing sugar	250 mL
3 tbsp	whipping cream	50 mL
1 tbsp	butter, softened	15 mL
1 tsp	finely grated lemon rind	5 mL
½ tsp	finely grated lime rind	2 mL

• Line 2 rimless baking sheets with parchment paper or grease; set aside.

• In large bowl, beat butter with sugar until fluffy; beat in egg, then lemon and lime rinds. In separate bowl, whisk together flour, baking powder and salt; stir into butter mixture, one-third at a time. Stir in white chocolate (if using).

• In small bowl, beat egg white until foamy. Sprinkle chopped almonds on waxed paper. Set aside.

• Divide dough into quarters. Place, 1 at a time, on waxed paper. Using paper as guide, roll and press into 6-inch (15 cm) long log.

• Brush with egg white; roll in one-quarter of the almonds. Wrap in plastic wrap; twist ends to seal. Refrigerate until firm, 3 hours, rerolling to keep round shape. *(Make-ahead: Refrigerate for up to 3 days or freeze in airtight container for up to 3 weeks. Let stand at room temperature for 20 minutes.)*

• With serrated knife, cut into ¼-inch (5 mm) thick slices; place, 2 inches (5 cm) apart, on prepared pans. Bake in top and bottom thirds of 375°F (190°C) oven, rotating and switching pans halfway through, until bottoms are light golden, about 10 minutes.

• GLAZE: In bowl, mix sugar, cream, butter and lemon and lime rinds until smooth; spread over hot cookies. Transfer to racks to let cool. *(Make-ahead: Layer between waxed paper in airtight container and store for up to 5 days or freeze for up to 2 weeks.)*

MAKES ABOUT 60 COOKIES.

PER COOKIE: about 77 cal, 1 g pro, 4 g total fat (2 g sat. fat), 9 g carb, trace fibre, 14 mg chol, 47 mg sodium. % RDI: 1% calcium, 2% iron, 3% vit A, 3% folate.

Cinnamon Stars

These crisp star-shaped cookies, or zimtsterne, *are a tradition in Germany. Since the dough is sticky, it takes a little more care than regular rolled cookies, but the results are well worth it.*

2½ cups	hazelnuts or walnut halves	625 mL
3	egg whites	3
Pinch	each salt and cream of tartar	Pinch
1½ cups	granulated sugar	375 mL
2 tsp	cinnamon	10 mL
½ tsp	vanilla	2 mL

• Line 2 rimless baking sheets with parchment paper or grease; set aside.
• In food processor, pulse nuts until coarsely ground; transfer to large bowl.
• In separate large bowl, beat egg whites until frothy; beat in salt and cream of tartar. Beat in 1 cup (250 mL) of the sugar, 2 tbsp (25 mL) at a time, until stiff glossy peaks form, about 5 minutes. Beat in cinnamon and vanilla.
• Remove ½ cup (125 mL) of the meringue; cover and refrigerate for topping. Stir remaining meringue into ground nuts to form sticky dough; cover and refrigerate for 2 hours. *(Make-ahead: Refrigerate for up to 6 hours.)*

• Sprinkle work surface generously with some of the remaining sugar. Working with one-third of the dough at a time, place on work surface and sprinkle generously with some of the sugar. Dampen rolling pin with moist towel.
• Roll out dough to scant ¼-inch (5 mm) thickness, remoistening pin whenever lifted. Using 2-inch (5 cm) star-shaped cookie cutter, cut out shapes; with lifter, place on prepared pans.
• With small palette knife or brush, gently spread 2 tsp (10 mL) of the reserved meringue topping over each cookie. Bake in centre of 300°F (150°C) oven until crisp, about 30 minutes. Let cool on pans for 5 minutes; transfer to racks and let cool completely. *(Make-ahead: Layer between waxed paper in airtight container and store for up to 1 week.)*

MAKES ABOUT 48 COOKIES.

PER COOKIE: about 69 cal, 1 g pro, 4 g total fat (trace sat. fat), 7 g carb, 1 g fibre, 0 mg chol, 3 mg sodium. % RDI: 1% calcium, 3% iron, 4% folate.

Church Windows

This is a Christmas no-bake classic from the kitchen of Emily Batey of London, Ont.

¾ cup	each butterscotch and chocolate chips	175 mL
½ cup	butter	125 mL
½ cup	smooth peanut butter	125 mL
2 cups	coloured miniature marshmallows	500 mL
1 cup	sweetened flaked coconut	250 mL

• In large saucepan, stir together butterscotch chips, chocolate chips, butter and peanut butter over medium-low heat until melted, 3 to 5 minutes. Let cool to room temperature, about 30 minutes.
• Stir in marshmallows and coconut. Refrigerate until firm, about 1 hour.
• Divide mixture into thirds. On 10- x 6-inch (25 x 15 cm) piece of waxed paper, roll one-third into log 6 inches (15 cm) long and 2 inches (5 cm) in diameter. Enclose in waxed paper, twisting ends to seal. Repeat with remaining mixture to make 2 more logs. Refrigerate for 1 hour. *(Make-ahead: Refrigerate for up to 2 weeks or overwrap with heavy-duty foil and freeze for up to 1 month.)* Cut logs into ½-inch (1 cm) thick slices.

MAKES 45 SLICES.

PER SLICE: about 77 cal, 1 g pro, 6 g total fat (3 g sat. fat), 6 g carb, trace fibre, 6 mg chol, 40 mg sodium. % RDI: 1% iron, 2% vit A, 1% folate.

No-Bake Cranberry Snowballs

This is your basic rice crisp cookie gone festive when rolled in coconut and studded with flecks of cranberries.

3 cups	miniature marshmallows (or 40 large)	750 mL
¼ cup	butter	50 mL
1½ tsp	vanilla	7 mL
¼ tsp	coconut extract (optional)	1 mL
3 cups	rice crisp cereal	750 mL
½ cup	chopped dried cranberries	125 mL
2 cups	sweetened flaked coconut	500 mL

• Line rimless baking sheet with waxed paper; set aside.
• In large saucepan, stir marshmallows with butter over medium-low heat until melted, 3 to 5 minutes. Remove from heat. Stir in vanilla, and coconut extract (if using).
• Add half of the cereal, stirring to coat. Stir in remaining cereal, cranberries and half of the coconut until completely coated. Let cool slightly.
• Using buttered hands, shape by heaping 1 tsp (5 mL) into balls. Place on prepared pan. Spread remaining coconut in large shallow dish; roll balls in coconut to coat. *(Make-ahead: Layer between waxed paper in airtight container and refrigerate for up to 1 week.)*

MAKES 30 BALLS.

PER BALL: about 68 cal, 1 g pro, 3 g total fat (2 g sat. fat), 10 g carb, trace fibre, 4 mg chol, 60 mg sodium. % RDI: 4% iron, 1% vit A, 1% folate.

Reverse Nanaimo Bars

Nanaimo bars are the signature Canadian bar. In this variation, reversing the colours adds a twist to tradition.

1 oz	white chocolate, chopped	30 g
¼ cup	butter	50 mL
1	egg, beaten	1
½ cup	desiccated coconut	125 mL
¼ cup	finely chopped almonds	50 mL
1½ cups	graham cracker crumbs	375 mL

FILLING:

⅓ cup	butter	75 mL
⅔ cup	cocoa powder	150 mL
1⅓ cups	icing sugar	325 mL
3 tbsp	milk	50 mL
2 tbsp	custard powder	25 mL
1 tsp	vanilla	5 mL

TOPPING:

4 tsp	vegetable oil	20 mL
4 oz	white chocolate, chopped	125 g
1 oz	bittersweet chocolate, chopped	30 g

● Line 8-inch (2 L) square metal cake pan with parchment paper, leaving 1-inch (2.5 cm) overhang for handles; set aside.

● In small heavy saucepan, melt white chocolate with butter over low heat, stirring until smooth. Stir in egg, coconut and almonds. Remove from heat; stir in cracker crumbs. Press evenly into prepared pan. Bake in centre of 350°F (180°C) oven until firm, 12 to 15 minutes. Let cool on rack.

● FILLING: In heavy saucepan, melt butter over low heat; stir in cocoa until smooth. Transfer to bowl; beat in icing sugar, milk, custard powder and vanilla until smooth. Spread over bottom layer; refrigerate until firm.

● TOPPING: Reserve ¼ tsp (1 mL) of the oil. In small heavy saucepan, melt white chocolate with remaining oil over low heat; pour over middle layer, smoothing evenly. Refrigerate until set.

● Melt bittersweet chocolate with reserved oil; drizzle over white chocolate. Refrigerate until set. *(Make-ahead: Wrap and refrigerate in airtight container for up to 3 days or freeze for up to 1 month.)* Cut into bars or squares.

MAKES ABOUT 24 BARS.

PER BAR: about 166 cal, 2 g pro, 10 g total fat (5 g sat. fat), 18 g carb, 1 g fibre, 23 mg chol, 106 mg sodium. % RDI: 2% calcium, 6% iron, 5% vit A, 4% folate.

Peanut Butter
Nanaimo Bars
and Reverse
Nanaimo Bars

Peanut Butter Nanaimo Bars

These bars tame the appetites of fans of chocolate and peanut butter.

¾ cup	butter, melted	175 mL
⅓ cup	granulated sugar	75 mL
2	eggs, beaten	2
2½ cups	graham cracker crumbs	625 mL
¾ cup	shredded sweetened coconut	175 mL
¾ cup	finely chopped roasted peanuts	175 mL
⅓ cup	cocoa powder	75 mL

FILLING:

1¼ cups	smooth peanut butter	300 mL
⅓ cup	butter	75 mL
3 cups	icing sugar	750 mL
⅓ cup	milk	75 mL

TOPPING:

8 oz	semisweet chocolate, chopped	250 g
2 tbsp	butter	25 mL
⅓ cup	finely chopped peanuts	75 mL

● Line 13- x 9-inch (3.5 L) metal cake pan with parchment paper, leaving 1-inch (2.5 cm) overhang for handles, or grease; set aside.

● In bowl, whisk together butter, sugar and eggs until smooth. Add crumbs, coconut, peanuts and cocoa powder; combine thoroughly. Press into prepared pan.

● Bake in centre of 350°F (180°C) oven until firm and no longer shiny, 12 to 15 minutes. Let cool on rack.

● **FILLING:** In saucepan, heat peanut butter with butter over medium heat, stirring until smooth. Transfer to bowl. Stir in sugar, 1 cup (250 mL) at a time. Stir in milk until smooth. Spread over base. Refrigerate until firm, about 1 hour.

● **TOPPING:** In bowl over saucepan of hot (not boiling) water, melt chocolate with butter; spread over filling. Sprinkle with nuts; refrigerate until firm, about 2 hours. *(Make-ahead: Wrap and refrigerate in airtight container for up to 1 week or freeze for up to 1 month.)* Cut into bars.

MAKES 40 BARS.

PER BAR: about 232 cal, 4 g pro, 15 g total fat (6 g sat. fat), 22 g carb, 2 g fibre, 27 mg chol, 144 mg sodium. % RDI: 1% calcium, 6% iron, 6% vit A, 9% folate.

Panpepato Bars

This Roman dolce is like chocolate fruitcake.

1 cup	whole unblanched almonds	250 mL
½ cup	each pine nuts and walnuts	125 mL
¾ cup	each raisins and candied mixed peel	175 mL
⅔ cup	all-purpose flour	150 mL
1 tsp	pepper	5 mL
¾ tsp	cinnamon	4 mL
½ tsp	ground nutmeg	2 mL
¼ tsp	ground cloves	1 mL
½ cup	liquid honey	125 mL
¼ cup	grape jelly	50 mL
3 oz	bittersweet chocolate, chopped	90 g
3 tbsp	icing sugar	50 mL

• Line 9-inch (2.5 L) square metal cake pan with parchment paper, leaving 1-inch (2.5 cm) overhang for handles; set aside.

• On rimmed baking sheet, toast almonds, pine nuts and walnuts in 350°F (180°C) oven until golden, 10 minutes. Transfer to large bowl; add raisins and mixed peel. Set aside.

• In small bowl, stir together flour, pepper, cinnamon, nutmeg and cloves; set aside.

• In saucepan, bring honey, jelly and 1 tbsp (15 mL) water to boil, stirring. Remove from heat. Stir in chocolate until melted; stir into nut mixture to coat. Stir in flour mixture until combined. Scrape into prepared pan.

• Bake in centre of 350°F (180°C) oven until set and puffed, 30 minutes. Let cool on rack. *(Make-ahead: Wrap and store in airtight container for up to 1 week or freeze for up to 1 month.)* Dust with sugar. Cut into bars.

MAKES 36 BARS.

PER BAR: about 114 cal, 2 g pro, 6 g total fat (1 g sat. fat), 16 g carb, 2 g fibre, 0 mg chol, 6 mg sodium. % RDI: 2% calcium, 6% iron, 3% folate.

Superior Bars and Squares

The secret to success is preparing the pans and cutting the sweets straight and clean. Here's how.

Preparing pans

Place cake pan on parchment paper or nonstick foil. Cut paper 3 inches (8 cm) larger on all sides. At each corner, make 3-inch (8 cm) diagonal cut toward centre. Place in pan, creasing fold all around bottom inside edge. At each corner, tuck 1 piece of paper behind the other.

Cutting Bars and Squares

Crisp bars, such as shortbread and ones rich in chocolate or with truffle icings, are easier and neater to cut while still warm. A serrated knife is recommended and after each cut, wipe blade clean with damp cloth.

Using parchment paper–liner, lift cooled bars out of pan onto cutting board. Pull paper off sides. With long knife, trim off crusty edges. Use ruler and long sharp knife to ensure evenly sized neat bars, wiping knife clean with damp cloth between cuts.

TIP

❯ You can cut into serving-size bars and layer with waxed paper in airtight container. Or you can cut whole pan into halves or quarters and wrap and store in airtight container.

Pecan Butter Tart Bars

These offer all the pleasures of butter tarts but with less fiddling with the pastry.

¼ cup	butter, softened	50 mL
¾ cup	packed brown sugar	175 mL
¼ cup	corn syrup	50 mL
2	eggs	2
2 tsp	vanilla	10 mL
2 tbsp	all-purpose flour	25 mL
Pinch	salt	Pinch

BASE:

1 cup	all-purpose flour	250 mL
¼ cup	packed brown sugar	50 mL
½ cup	cold butter, cubed	125 mL
¾ cup	chopped pecans	175 mL

• Line 9-inch (2.5 L) square metal cake pan with parchment paper, leaving 1-inch (2.5 cm) overhang for handles; set aside.
• BASE: In large bowl, mix flour with brown sugar. With pastry blender, cut in butter until mixture is moist and crumbly. Press into prepared pan.
• Bake in centre of 350°F (180°C) oven for 10 minutes. Sprinkle with pecans and press lightly; bake for 5 minutes.
• Meanwhile, in bowl, beat together butter, sugar and corn syrup until smooth; beat in eggs and vanilla. Stir in flour and salt; pour over base. Bake until darkened and slightly jiggly when shaken, about 20 minutes. Let cool on rack. *(Make-ahead: Wrap and store in airtight container for up to 1 week or freeze for up to 3 weeks.)* Cut into bars.

MAKES 36 BARS.

PER BAR: about 98 cal, 1 g pro 6 g total fat (3 g sat. fat), 11 g carb, trace fibre, 22 mg chol, 48 mg sodium. % RDI: 1% calcium, 3% iron, 4% vit A, 3% folate.

Orange Chocolate Shortbread Bars

If you're short on time, bars that you only have to pat onto a pan are the perfect solution.

2 cups	butter, softened	500 mL
1 cup	instant dissolving (fruit/berry) sugar	250 mL
1 tbsp	grated orange rind	15 mL
3¼ cups	all-purpose flour	800 mL
½ cup	rice flour	125 mL
1 cup	mini chocolate chips	250 mL

• Line 17- x 11-inch (45 x 29 cm) rimmed baking sheet with parchment paper, leaving 1-inch (2.5 cm) overhang for handles, or grease; set aside.
• In bowl, beat butter until fluffy; beat in sugar until smooth. Stir in orange rind. In separate bowl, whisk together all-purpose and rice flours; stir into butter mixture in 2 additions. Stir in chocolate chips. Pat into prepared pan.
• Bake in bottom third of 325°F (160°C) oven until lightly browned, 30 to 35 minutes. Let cool on pan on rack. *(Make-ahead: Wrap and store in airtight container for up to 1 week or freeze for up to 1 month.)* Cut into bars.

MAKES 72 BARS.

PER BAR: about 92 cal, 1 g pro, 6 g total fat (4 g sat. fat), 9 g carb, trace fibre, 14 mg chol, 53 mg sodium. % RDI: 2% iron, 5% vit A, 3% folate.

TIP

❯ To dress up the bars, dip the corners into melted semisweet chocolate then let set on rack.

Chocolate Toffee Squares

This sinful little square sports a cookie crumb base, an irresistible toffee centre and a ganache topping.

2 cups	vanilla wafer crumbs (about 60 cookies)	500 mL
2 tbsp	granulated sugar	25 mL
1/3 cup	butter, melted	75 mL
1	egg	1
TOFFEE FILLING:		
1 cup	butter	250 mL
1 cup	packed dark brown sugar	250 mL
1	can (300 mL) sweetened condensed milk	1
1/4 cup	corn syrup	50 mL
GANACHE TOPPING:		
6 oz	bittersweet chocolate, chopped	175 g
2/3 cup	whipping cream	150 mL

● Line 13- x 9-inch (3.5 L) metal cake pan with parchment paper, leaving 1-inch (2.5 cm) overhang for handles; set aside.
● In bowl, combine crumbs with sugar. Whisk butter with egg; stir into crumb mixture until moistened. Press into prepared pan; bake in centre of 350°F (180°C) oven until golden and firm to the touch, about 10 minutes. Let cool on rack.

● **TOFFEE FILLING:** In saucepan, melt together butter, sugar, condensed milk and corn syrup over medium heat until simmering, stirring constantly. Reduce heat to medium-low; simmer, stirring constantly, until candy thermometer reaches thread stage (230° to 234°F/110° to 112°C), 12 to 15 minutes. Pour over base. Refrigerate until cold, about 1 hour.
● **GANACHE TOPPING:** Place chocolate in bowl. In microwave oven or on stove, bring cream to boil; pour over chocolate, whisking until smooth. Let cool to room temperature. Pour over toffee layer; refrigerate until set, about 1 hour. *(Make-ahead: Wrap and refrigerate in airtight container for up to 1 week or freeze for up to 2 weeks.)* Wiping knife with damp cloth between cuts, cut into 1-inch (2.5 cm) squares.

MAKES ABOUT 96 SQUARES.

PER SQUARE: about 70 cal, 1 g pro, 5 g total fat (3 g sat. fat), 7 g carb, trace fibre, 13 mg chol, 32 mg sodium. % RDI: 2% calcium, 1% iron, 3% vit A, 1% folate.

Freezing Tips for Baked Goods

❯ The goal in packaging items for the freezer is to keep the right amount of moisture in the product and the freezer's dry air, odours and flavours out. Use plastic wrap and resealable plastic bags that are specially designed for freezing.

❯ Heavy-duty foil provides the best seal when it is wrapped over plastic wrap and edges are double-folded.

❯ Cool all baked goods completely before packaging them for the freezer in order to avoid excess moisture in the package.

❯ Good-quality rigid airtight plastic containers with tight-fitting lids provide protection from freezer burn and crushing.

❯ Freeze pie shells in pie plates until firm. Transfer to rigid airtight containers and return to the freezer. Before thawing, return frozen shells to their original pie plates and proceed with the recipe.

❯ Cookies, bars, squares and small cakes can be wrapped individually or as quarters, halves or a whole making in plastic wrap. Then overwrap in foil and enclose in airtight container or resealable plastic bag for maximum protection.

❯ Before freezing, label products with masking tape or adhesive labels. Include the contents, the date and thawing and baking instructions for easy reference.

❯ Be sure to check the recipe before thawing a product. Some, such as pies, phyllo products and tart shells, are better when baked right from the freezer.

Marzipan Blondie Bars

Almond lovers will enjoy these dense bars.

¼ cup	rum or brandy	50 mL
1 cup	dried cranberries	250 mL
1 cup	butter, softened	250 mL
2 cups	granulated sugar	500 mL
4	eggs	4
1 tbsp	vanilla	15 mL
½ tsp	almond extract	2 mL
2½ cups	all-purpose flour	625 mL
½ cup	ground almonds	125 mL
2 tsp	baking powder	10 mL
¼ tsp	salt	1 mL
1 cup	sliced almonds	250 mL
1	pkg (200 g) marzipan, diced	1
1 tbsp	icing sugar	15 mL

● Line 13- x 9-inch (3.5 L) metal cake pan with parchment paper, leaving 1-inch (2.5 cm) overhang, or grease; set aside.
● In saucepan, bring rum to boil; stir in cranberries. Let cool.
● In bowl, beat butter with sugar until fluffy; beat in eggs, 1 at a time. Beat in vanilla and almond extract. In separate bowl, whisk flour, ground almonds, baking powder and salt; stir into butter mixture. Mix in sliced almonds, cranberry mixture and marzipan. Scrape into pan.
● Bake in centre of 350°F (180°C) oven until tester comes out clean, 45 minutes. Let cool. *(Make-ahead: Wrap and store in airtight container for up to 4 days or freeze for up to 1 month.)* Dust with sugar. Cut into bars.

MAKES 40 BARS.

PER BAR: about 170 cal, 3 g pro, 9 g total fat (3 g sat.fat), 22 g carb, 1 g fibre, 34 mg chol, 82 mg sodium. % RDI: 2% calcium, 5% iron, 5% vit A, 2% vit C, 6% folate.

Gluten-Free Sticky Toffee Squares

Whether you're on a special diet or not, these will be a hit. Rice flour is available in the baking section of supermarkets. Xanthan gum gives strength to gluten-free baked goods; look for it in health and bulk food stores.

1¾ cups	rice flour	425 mL
1 cup	packed brown sugar	250 mL
½ cup	tapioca flour	125 mL
2 tsp	xanthan gum	10 mL
¾ cup	cold butter, cut in ½-inch (1 cm) pieces	175 mL

FILLING:

⅔ cup	butter	150 mL
½ cup	packed brown sugar	125 mL
½ cup	whipping cream	125 mL
¼ cup	corn syrup	50 mL
1 cup	chopped macadamia nuts or pecans	250 mL
½ cup	candied orange peel	125 mL

GARNISH:

4 oz	semisweet chocolate, melted	125 g

- Line 13- x 9-inch (3.5 L) metal cake pan with parchment paper, leaving 1-inch (2.5 cm) overhang for handles; set aside.
- In food processor fitted with metal blade, pulse together flour, sugar, tapioca and xanthan gum. Add butter; pulse until in tiny bits and mixture is crumbly and coming together slightly. Press into prepared pan. Bake in centre of 325°F (160°C) oven until golden and slightly puffed, about 25 minutes. Let cool on rack.
- **FILLING:** In saucepan, bring butter, sugar, cream and corn syrup to boil, stirring constantly; cook for 3 minutes. Remove from heat; stir in nuts and candied peel. Pour over base, distributing nuts evenly. Bake in centre of 325°F (160°C) oven until bubbly at edges, about 35 minutes. Let cool on wire rack.
- **GARNISH:** Drizzle chocolate in zigzag pattern over top. Refrigerate until set. *(Make-ahead: Wrap and refrigerate in airtight container for up to 5 days or freeze for up to 1 month.)* Cut into bars.

MAKES 40 SQUARES.

PER SQUARE: about 181 cal, 1 g pro, 11 g total fat (6 g sat. fat), 21 g carb, 1 g fibre, 24 mg chol, 78 mg sodium. % RDI: 1% calcium, 2% iron, 7% vit A, 1% folate.

Chocolate Hazelnut Tassies

These tiny tarts feature pastry and rich chocolate filling — more candy than cookie!

½ cup	butter, softened	125 mL
4 oz	cream cheese, softened	125 g
1¼ cups	all-purpose flour	300 mL
½ cup	finely chopped hazelnuts	125 mL
GANACHE FILLING:		
4 oz	semisweet or bittersweet chocolate, chopped	125 g
½ cup	whipping cream	125 mL
2 tsp	hazelnut liqueur (optional)	10 mL
12	whole hazelnuts (approx)	12

• Grease 24 mini-muffin cups; set aside.

• In large bowl, beat butter with cheese; stir in flour and hazelnuts until combined. Place 1 tbsp (15 mL) into each prepared cup; press evenly over bottom and up side. Freeze until solid, about 1 hour. *(Make-ahead: Wrap in heavy-duty foil and freeze for up to 2 weeks.)*

• Bake in centre of 325°F (160°C) oven until golden, about 30 minutes. Let cool in pan on rack.

• GANACHE FILLING: Meanwhile, place chocolate in bowl. In small saucepan, bring cream, and liqueur (if using) to boil; pour over chocolate and whisk until smooth. Pour into shells.

• Cut each hazelnut in half; place in centre of each tart. Let stand until ganache is firm, about 30 minutes. *(Make-ahead: Refrigerate in single layer in airtight container for up to 5 days.)*

MAKES 24 TARTS.

PER TART: about 135 cal, 2 g pro, 11 g total fat (6 g sat. fat), 8 g carb, 1 g fibre, 22 mg chol, 56 mg sodium. % RDI: 2% calcium, 4% iron, 7% vit A, 5% folate.

Baking Basics

Measuring

Follow either the metric or the imperial measures throughout a recipe, not a combination. There are two types of measuring cups — one for dry ingredients and one for wet.

❯ Dry ingredient measures come in sets of different sizes: ¼ cup (50 mL), ⅓ cup (75 mL), ½ cup (125 mL) and 1 cup (250 mL).

❯ Liquid ingredient glass measuring cups are marked on the outside.

❯ Measuring spoons are used for both dry and liquid ingredients: ¼ tsp (1 mL), ½ tsp (2 mL), 1 tsp (5 mL) and 1 tbsp (15 mL).

Dry Ingredients

❯ Lightly spoon dry ingredients, such as all-purpose flour and granulated sugar, into dry measure.

❯ Do not pack down or tap measure on counter (except for brown sugar, which should be packed enough to keep cup shape when dumped out).

❯ Fill measure until heaping. Then, working over canister, push straight edge of knife across top of measure.

Liquid ingredients

❯ Place liquid measuring cup on counter. Pour in liquid to desired level, then bend down to check measurement at eye level.

❯ If liquid doesn't come exactly to desired mark on outside, pour off a little or add a little as needed.

Sifting

❯ All-purpose flour does not require sifting.

❯ Sift cake-and-pastry flour before measuring. Spoon and sweep as above.

❯ Sift cocoa powder and icing sugar after measuring to eliminate lumps.

Chapter Six

SWEET & SAVOURY BREADS

Apricot Almond Crescent Wreath

Baked into a wreath, crescent rolls make a gorgeous presentation.

1	pkg (200 g) marzipan	1
	Sweet Dough (recipe follows)	
¾ cup	apricot jam	175 mL
⅔ cup	icing sugar	150 mL
⅓ cup	sliced almonds, toasted	75 mL
2 tsp	sifted icing sugar	10 mL

• Line 12-inch (30 cm) round pizza pan with parchment paper or grease; set aside.
• Divide marzipan into thirds. Roll each into 8-inch (20 cm) rope; cut into quarters to make 12 pieces total. Set aside.
• Punch down dough; turn out onto lightly floured surface. Roll out into 14-inch (35 cm) circle; spread with ½ cup (125 mL) of the jam. Using pizza cutter, cut into quarters; cut each into 3 triangles to make 12 triangles.
• Place 1 piece of marzipan 1 inch (2.5 cm) from wide end of each triangle; starting at wide end, roll up. Arrange crescents, ¼ inch (5 mm) apart, in circle on prepared pan. Cover with plastic wrap; let rise in warm place until doubled in bulk, about 45 minutes.
• Place foil-lined rimmed baking sheet on bottom rack of oven to catch any drips. Bake crescents in centre of 375°F (190°C) oven until golden, about 28 minutes. Transfer to rack to let cool. *(Make-ahead: Wrap in plastic wrap and set aside for up to 24 hours or overwrap in heavy-duty foil and freeze for up to 2 weeks.)*
• In microwaveable bowl, microwave remaining jam for about 20 seconds on medium until melted. Strain through fine sieve into bowl. Stir in ⅔ cup (150 mL) icing sugar and 1 tbsp (15 mL) water until smooth; brush over wreath.
• Sprinkle wreath with almonds; dust with sifted icing sugar.

MAKES 12 PIECES.

PER PIECE: about 399 cal, 9 g pro, 12 g total fat (3 g sat. fat), 66 g carb, 3 g fibre, 44 mg chol, 260 mg sodium. % RDI: 6% calcium, 20% iron, 6% vit A, 38% folate.

Sweet Dough

¼ cup	granulated sugar	50 mL
1	pkg active dry yeast (or 2¼ tsp/11 mL)	1
¾ cup	milk	175 mL
¼ cup	butter	50 mL
1 tsp	salt	5 mL
2	eggs	2
4 cups	all-purpose flour (approx)	1 L

• Remove 2 tsp (10 mL) of the sugar to large bowl. Add ¼ cup (50 mL) warm water; stir to dissolve sugar. Sprinkle in yeast; let stand until frothy, about 10 minutes.
• Meanwhile, in small saucepan, heat milk, remaining sugar, butter and salt until butter is melted; let cool to lukewarm. Stir into yeast mixture. Beat in eggs. Stir in enough of the flour, 1 cup (250 mL) at a time, to form shaggy dough.
• Turn out onto lightly floured surface; knead, adding enough of the remaining flour as necessary, until smooth and elastic, about 10 minutes.
• Place in greased bowl, turning to grease all over. Cover with plastic wrap; let rise in warm place until doubled in bulk, about 1½ hours.

MAKES 2 LB (1 KG).

Panettone

Literally meaning "big bread," panettone is a tall Italian Christmas loaf that originated in Milan, Italy.

¼ cup	brandy or rum	50 mL
½ cup	golden raisins	125 mL
4	egg yolks	4
2	eggs	2
⅔ cup	granulated sugar	150 mL
1 tbsp	each grated orange rind and lemon rind	15 mL
1 tbsp	vanilla	15 mL
1½ tsp	salt	7 mL
¾ cup	butter, softened	175 mL
4 cups	all-purpose flour (approx)	1 L
½ cup	chopped mixed candied peel	125 mL

SPONGE:

1	pkg active dry yeast (or 2¼ tsp/11 mL)	1
⅔ cup	warm milk	150 mL
1 cup	all-purpose flour	250 mL

TOPPING:

2 tsp	butter, melted	10 mL

• Grease panettone mould or 2 lb (1 kg) coffee can. Line bottom and side with parchment paper to extend 1 inch (2.5 cm) above rim. Or set out paper panettone mould of same capacity.

• SPONGE: In large bowl, sprinkle yeast over milk; cover and let stand until yeast starts to rise to surface, about 10 minutes. Stir in flour to make sticky dough. Cover with greased plastic wrap; let rise in warm place until bubbly and doubled in bulk, about 1½ hours.

• In glass measuring cup, microwave brandy at high for about 20 seconds or until hot. Add raisins; cover and let stand until plump, about 1 hour. Reserving liquid, drain, pressing raisins to release any liquid. Set aside separately.

• In large bowl, beat together egg yolks, eggs, sugar, orange and lemon rinds, vanilla, salt and reserved soaking liquid until light and thickened. Beat in butter, 1 tbsp (15 mL) at a time, to form curdled-looking mixture.

• Add Sponge and 3 cups (750 mL) of the flour; mix by hand until sticky dough forms. Transfer to well-floured surface; knead until smooth and rather buttery, adding as much of the remaining flour as necessary, about 8 minutes. Let rest for 5 minutes.

• Press down dough. Sprinkle with raisins and peel; fold over and knead in fruit. Place in greased bowl. Cover with greased plastic wrap; let rise in warm place until doubled in bulk, about 2 hours. Punch down dough. Turn out onto floured surface; form into ball, pinching bottom to make top smooth.

• Place dough, seam side down, in mould. Cover and let rise in warm place for about 2 hours, or in refrigerator for up to 12 hours, or until doubled in bulk; remove from refrigerator 1 hour before baking.

• TOPPING: Cut ¼-inch (5 mm) deep X in loaf. Brush top with butter. Bake in bottom third of 350°F (180°C) oven until tester inserted in centre comes out clean, 1½ to 1¾ hours, covering with foil after 40 minutes if darker than milk chocolate. Let cool on rack for 1 hour. Pull paper to remove from can. *(Make-ahead: Wrap in plastic wrap and set aside for up to 24 hours or overwrap in heavy-duty foil and freeze for up to 2 weeks.)*

MAKES 1 LOAF, OR 12 SLICES.

PER SLICE: about 426 cal, 8 g pro, 16 g total fat (9 g sat. fat), 63 g carb, 2 g fibre, 132 mg chol, 402 mg sodium. % RDI: 4% calcium, 21% iron, 15% vit A, 2% vit C, 62% folate.

Swedish Saffron Bread

Swedish-born Anna Buchnea of Toronto says Christmas wouldn't feel right without this fragrant golden bread from her mother's cookbook. Anna makes the recipe into buns for St. Lucia Day, the start of Christmas festivities. For the rest of the holiday season, the recipe is made into this braided loaf.

1 tsp	saffron threads	5 mL
⅔ cup	granulated sugar	150 mL
1 cup	milk	250 mL
1 tbsp	active dry yeast	15 mL
1	egg, beaten	1
⅓ cup	butter, melted	75 mL
¼ tsp	salt	1 mL
4 cups	all-purpose flour	1 L
⅓ cup	chopped blanched almonds	75 mL
⅓ cup	raisins	75 mL
GLAZE:		
1	egg, beaten	1
1 tbsp	pearl sugar or coarse sugar	15 mL

● Line large rimmed baking sheet with parchment paper or grease; set aside.
● With mortar and pestle, mash saffron threads with 1 tbsp (15 mL) of the sugar until very fine; set aside.
● In small saucepan, heat milk until warm (100 to 110°F/38 to 43°C). In large bowl, combine yeast, 1 tbsp (15 mL) of the remaining sugar and ½ cup (125 mL) of the warm milk; let stand until frothy. Stir in egg, butter, remaining sugar and milk, salt and saffron mixture.

● With electric mixer, beat in 2 cups (500 mL) of the flour. With wooden spoon, stir in remaining flour along with almonds and raisins, working with hands if necessary to incorporate all flour.
● Turn out onto lightly floured surface; knead until smooth and elastic, about 5 minutes. Place in greased bowl, turning to grease all over. Cover with plastic wrap; let rise in warm place until doubled in bulk, about 1½ hours.
● Punch down dough. Place on lightly floured surface; divide into thirds. Shape each third into 18-inch (45 cm) long rope.
● Arrange ropes side by side and pinch ends together at 1 end; braid to form loaf, pinching other end. Place on prepared pan; cover and let rise in warm place until 1½ times larger in bulk, about 1 hour.
● GLAZE: Brush top of loaf with egg; sprinkle with sugar. Bake in centre of 375°F (190°C) oven until loaf sounds hollow when tapped on bottom, about 30 minutes. *(Make-ahead: Wrap in plastic wrap and set aside for up to 24 hours or overwrap in heavy-duty foil and freeze for up to 2 weeks.)*

MAKES 1 LOAF, OR 16 SLICES.

PER SLICE: about 227 cal, 5 g pro, 6 g total fat (3 g sat. fat), 37 g carb, 1 g fibre, 38 mg chol, 92 mg sodium. % RDI: 3% calcium, 11% iron, 6% vit A, 25% folate.

Chocolate Butterscotch Babka

Baking this mega yeast bread in a tube pan gives it impressive height.

⅓ cup	granulated sugar	75 mL
½ cup	warm water	125 mL
1	pkg active dry yeast (or 2¼ tsp/11 mL)	1
¾ cup	butter, softened	175 mL
¾ cup	milk	175 mL
2	eggs	2
1 tsp	each salt and vanilla	5 mL
4 cups	all-purpose flour (approx)	1 L
CHOCOLATE BUTTERSCOTCH FILLING:		
⅔ cup	granulated sugar	150 mL
⅓ cup	cocoa powder	75 mL
¾ cup	butterscotch chips	175 mL
STREUSEL TOPPING:		
⅓ cup	icing sugar	75 mL
¼ cup	all-purpose flour	50 mL
2 tbsp	cold butter, cubed	25 mL
1	egg, beaten	1

● Grease 10-inch (4 L) tube pan with removable bottom; set aside.

● In large bowl, dissolve 1 tsp (5 mL) of the sugar in warm water. Sprinkle in yeast; let stand until frothy, about 10 minutes.

● Meanwhile, in saucepan, stir together remaining sugar, ¼ cup (50 mL) of the butter and milk; warm over medium heat until butter is melted and sugar is dissolved. Let cool to lukewarm, about 5 minutes. Whisk into yeast mixture along with eggs, salt and vanilla. Stir in enough of the flour to make soft, slightly sticky dough.

● Turn out onto lightly floured surface. Knead, adding enough of the remaining flour to prevent sticking, until smooth and elastic, about 8 minutes. Place in greased bowl, turning to grease all over. Cover with plastic wrap; let rise in warm place until doubled in bulk, about 1 hour.

● Punch down dough. Turn out onto lightly floured surface, roll out to 22- x 10-inch (55 x 25 cm) rectangle. Spread remaining butter over dough, leaving 1-inch (2.5 cm) border uncovered on 1 long side.

● **CHOCOLATE BUTTERSCOTCH FILLING:** In bowl, sift together sugar and cocoa. Sprinkle cocoa mixture, then butterscotch chips evenly over butter.

● Starting at long side without border, roll up dough jelly roll–style. Pinch bottom edge to seal. Twist ends in opposite directions 6 to 8 times; fit into prepared pan, pinching ends together to seal.

● Cover and let rise in warm place until doubled in bulk, 1 to 1½ hours. *(Make-ahead: Cover and refrigerate for up to 8 hours. Let come to room temperature, about 30 minutes.)*

● **STREUSEL TOPPING:** Meanwhile, in bowl, stir sugar with flour; using pastry cutter or 2 knives, cut in butter until crumbly. Brush egg over top of dough; sprinkle streusel over top.

● Bake in centre of 350°F (180°C) oven until golden brown, about 35 minutes. Remove outside of pan; let cool on rack. Remove pan bottom. *(Make-ahead: Wrap in plastic wrap and set aside for up to 24 hours or overwrap in heavy-duty foil and freeze for up to 2 weeks.)*

MAKES 1 BABKA, 14 TO 16 SLICES.

PER EACH OF 16 SLICES: about 332 cal, 6 g pro, 14 g total fat (9 g sat. fat), 47 g carb, 2 g fibre, 63 mg chol, 265 mg sodium. % RDI: 3% calcium, 13% iron, 11% vit A, 24% folate.

› *Branching Elegance*

Start with transparent and tall, heavy-bottomed container.

• Place 1 or more strings of mini-lights inside.

• Cut branches (go natural for rustic look; spray-paint white, silver or gold for elegant look). Arrange in container.

• If desired, fill between branches and around rim with mood moss or sheet moss.

• Decorate branches sparingly with lightweight ornaments in monochromatic colours.

› *Twig Tree*

Here's instant fun without any needles to clean up. Start with tall, heavy-bottomed container (if using lightweight pail as shown, increase stability by setting brick or stones inside, first).

• With knife, cut floral foam to fit snugly and push inside.

• Cut twigs to about 3 times the container height, then push cut ends into foam to secure (position vertically at centre, then angle out closer to container side.

• If desired, string mini-lights through twigs or encircle bottom of container.

• Decorate twigs sparingly with a selection of lightweight ornaments.

Tear-and-Share Checkerboard Rolls

These black and white rolls make a delightful presentation on the holiday buffet table.

	Savoury Dough (recipe follows)	
⅓ cup	grated Parmesan cheese	75 mL
3 tbsp	poppy seeds	50 mL
¼ cup	sesame seeds	50 mL
3 tbsp	butter, melted	50 mL

• Grease two 9-inch (2.5 L) square metal cake pans; set aside.

• Punch down dough. Turn out onto lightly floured surface; shape into log. Cut into 32 pieces; shape each into ball, stretching and pinching dough underneath to make tops smooth.

• In shallow bowl, combine half of the Parmesan cheese with poppy seeds. In separate shallow bowl, combine sesame seeds with remaining Parmesan. Place butter in another shallow bowl.

• Roll balls in butter, rewarming butter if necessary. Roll half of the balls in poppy seed mixture; roll remaining balls in sesame seed mixture. Alternately arrange 16 balls in each prepared pan. Cover and let rise in warm place until doubled in bulk, about 45 minutes.

• Bake in centre of 400°F (200°C) oven until golden and rolls sound hollow when tapped on bottom, about 22 minutes. Remove from pans; let cool on rack. *(Make-ahead: Store in airtight container for up to 24 hours or wrap and freeze in airtight container for up to 2 weeks.)*

MAKES 32 ROLLS.

PER ROLL: about 69 cal, 2 g pro, 3 g total fat (1 g sat. fat), 8 g carb, trace fibre, 4 mg chol, 142 mg sodium. % RDI: 3% calcium, 5% iron, 1% vit A, 8% folate.

Savoury Dough

2 tsp	granulated sugar	10 mL
1	pkg active dry yeast (or 2¼ tsp/11 mL)	1
3 tbsp	vegetable oil	50 mL
2½ tsp	salt	12 mL
4 cups	all-purpose flour (approx)	1 L

• In large bowl, dissolve sugar in ¼ cup (50 mL) warm water. Sprinkle in yeast; let stand until frothy, about 10 minutes.

• Stir in 1¼ cups (300 mL) warm water, oil and salt. Stir in enough of the flour, 1 cup (250 mL) at a time, to form shaggy dough.

• Turn out onto lightly floured surface; knead, adding enough of the remaining flour as necessary, until smooth and elastic, about 10 minutes.

• Transfer to large greased bowl, turning to grease all over. Cover with plastic wrap; let rise in warm place until doubled in bulk, about 1½ hours.

MAKES 2 LB (1 KG).

Stand Mixer Savoury Dough

• In mixer, prepare yeast mixture and let stand until frothy. With paddle attachment, stir in warm water, oil, salt and all but ½ cup (125 mL) of the flour, incorporating 1 cup (250 mL) at a time, to make shaggy dough.

• Switch to dough hook. Mix on low speed, scraping down bowl halfway through and adding enough of the remaining flour as necessary to make dough smooth and elastic, about 8 minutes.

Bread Machine Savoury Dough

• In pan of 1½- to 2-lb (750 g to 1 kg) bread machine, add (in order) 1½ cups (375 mL) warm water, oil, sugar, salt, flour and bread machine yeast. Choose dough setting.

Romano
Brunch Braid

There's a touch of fennel in the ricotta romano filling.

1 tbsp	packed brown sugar	15 mL
¾ cup	warm water	175 mL
1	pkg active dry or quick-rising yeast (2¼ tsp/11 mL)	1
2 tbsp	extra-virgin olive oil	25 mL
¼ cup	grated Romano cheese	50 mL
2¼ cups	all-purpose flour (approx)	550 mL
1 tsp	salt	5 mL
1	egg white, beaten	1

FILLING:

1	tub (475 g) ricotta cheese	1
1	egg	1
¼ cup	chopped fresh parsley	50 mL
1 tsp	fennel seeds, crushed	5 mL
¼ tsp	each salt and pepper	1 mL
¼ cup	grated Romano cheese	50 mL

• Line large rimmed baking sheet with parchment paper or grease; set aside.
• In large bowl, dissolve sugar in warm water. Sprinkle in yeast; let stand until frothy, about 10 minutes. Whisk in oil. Stir in Romano cheese, 1½ cups (375 mL) of the flour and salt, adding enough of the remaining flour to make soft sticky dough.
• Turn out onto lightly floured surface; knead until smooth, about 5 minutes. Place in greased bowl, turning to grease all over; cover with plastic wrap and let rise in warm place until doubled in bulk, about 1 hour.
• FILLING: Meanwhile, in sieve set over bowl, drain ricotta in refrigerator until no liquid is released when cheese is pressed, about 45 minutes.

• In separate bowl, whisk together egg, parsley, fennel seeds, salt and pepper. Whisk in ricotta and Romano cheeses until combined; set aside.
• Punch down dough; turn out onto lightly floured surface. Roll out to 15- x 10-inch (38 x 25 cm) rectangle. Place on prepared pan and reshape rectangle. Spoon filling lengthwise along centre in 4-inch (10 cm) wide strip. Using scissors and starting at 1 corner, cut dough diagonally to form strips about 1 inch (2.5 cm) wide and 2 inches (5 cm) long on both sides. Crisscross strips over filling to create braided look. Brush with egg white.
• Bake in centre of 400°F (200°C) oven until golden and loaf sounds hollow when tapped on bottom, about 30 minutes. Let cool on rack before serving. *(Make-ahead: Cover and refrigerate for up to 8 hours.)*

MAKES 6 TO 8 SERVINGS.

PER EACH OF 8 SERVINGS: about 313 cal, 14 g pro, 14 g total fat (7 g sat. fat), 31 g carb, 1 g fibre, 61 mg chol, 504 mg sodium. % RDI: 19% calcium, 17% iron, 10% vit A, 3% vit C, 49% folate.

Bread Machine
Romano Brunch Braid
(for dough only)

Into pan of bread machine, add (in order) water, oil, sugar, salt, cheese, 2 cups (500 mL) flour and bread machine yeast. Choose dough setting. (Dough springs back when rolling out, so let rest for 5 minutes before rolling out.)

Onion Fennel Seed Crackers

Break these lengthwise into long elegant pieces and serve with cheese or dip.

2½ cups	all-purpose flour	625 mL
2 tbsp	fennel seeds	25 mL
4 tsp	granulated sugar	20 mL
2 tsp	salt	10 mL
1 tsp	each baking powder and pepper	5 mL
1 cup	chopped onion	250 mL
2	eggs	2
¼ cup	extra-virgin olive oil or vegetable oil	50 mL

• Lightly grease 2 rimless baking sheets; set aside.
• In large bowl, whisk together flour, fennel seeds, sugar, salt, baking powder and pepper; set aside. In food processor, purée together onion, eggs and oil; scrape over dry ingredients and stir to form dough.
• Turn out onto lightly floured surface; knead until firm but pliable, 5 minutes. Cut into 16 pieces; shape each into ball. Cover with plastic wrap; let rest for 30 minutes.
• On lightly floured surface, roll out balls as thinly as possible into long rectangles with rounded edges. Transfer to prepared pans. Bake in top and bottom thirds of 400°F (200°C) oven, rotating and switching pans halfway through, until golden, 10 minutes.
• Reduce heat to 300°F (150°C); bake until golden brown and crisp, 8 to 10 minutes. Transfer to racks and let cool. *(Make-ahead: Store in airtight container for up to 1 week or freeze for up to 1 month.)*

MAKES 16 PIECES, OR 32 SERVINGS.

PER SERVING: about 60 cal, 2 g pro, 2 g total fat (trace sat. fat), 9 g carb, 1 g fibre, 12 mg chol, 156 mg sodium. % RDI: 1% calcium, 4% iron, 1% vit A, 10% folate.

Angel Biscuits

A touch of yeast adds heavenly lightness to brunch-friendly biscuits. You can also serve them with holiday soups and cold meats.

2 tsp	active dry yeast	10 mL
¼ cup	warm water	50 mL
2½ cups	all-purpose flour	625 mL
1 tbsp	granulated sugar	15 mL
1½ tsp	baking powder	7 mL
1 tsp	dried oregano or thyme	5 mL
½ tsp	baking soda	2 mL
½ tsp	salt	2 mL
½ cup	cold butter, cubed	125 mL
½ cup	grated hard cheese (such as Parmesan)	125 mL
1 cup	buttermilk	250 mL
1	egg yolk	1

• Line rimless baking sheet with parchment paper or dust with flour; set aside.
• In bowl, stir yeast with water; let stand until frothy, about 10 minutes.
• Meanwhile, in large bowl, whisk together flour, sugar, baking powder, oregano, baking soda and salt. With pastry blender, cut in butter until mixture is crumbly. Stir in cheese.
• Whisk buttermilk into yeast mixture; scrape over dry ingredients and toss with fork to form soft dough.
• Turn out onto lightly floured surface; knead 10 times to form smooth dough. Roll out to ¾-inch (2 cm) thickness. With floured 2-inch (5 cm) round cutter, cut out biscuits, rerolling and cutting scraps. Transfer to prepared pan; let rise for 15 minutes.
• Mix egg yolk with 1 tsp (5 mL) water; brush over biscuits.

• Bake in centre of 400°F (200°C) oven until golden, about 15 minutes. Let cool. *(Make-ahead: Store in airtight container for up to 24 hours or wrap individually and freeze in airtight container for up to 2 weeks.)*

MAKES ABOUT 28 BISCUITS.

PER BISCUIT: about 86 cal, 2 g pro, 4 g total fat (3 g sat. fat), 10 g carb, trace fibre, 19 mg chol, 152 mg sodium. % RDI: 4% calcium, 4% iron, 4% vit A, 14% folate.

Crunchy-Top Cranberry Muffins

You can make the muffin batter ahead and freeze it in the muffin cups — ready and waiting to pop frozen into the oven Christmas morning. Serve with steaming cups of café au lait or hot chocolate and a bowl of clementines for an easygoing yet festive breakfast.

2 cups	all-purpose flour	500 mL
¾ cup	granulated sugar	175 mL
1 tbsp	baking powder	15 mL
1 tsp	baking soda	5 mL
½ tsp	salt	2 mL
½ tsp	ground cardamom or cinnamon	2 mL
½ cup	plain yogurt	125 mL
¼ cup	orange juice	50 mL
¼ cup	vegetable oil	50 mL
2	eggs	2
1½ cups	whole cranberries	375 mL
TOPPING:		
¼ cup	granulated sugar	50 mL
1 tbsp	grated orange rind	15 mL

• Line 12 muffin cups with paper liners or grease; set aside.
• In large bowl, whisk together flour, sugar, baking powder, baking soda, salt and cardamom.
• In separate bowl, whisk together yogurt, orange juice, oil and eggs; pour over flour mixture. Sprinkle with cranberries. Stir just until dry ingredients are moistened. Spoon into prepared cups, filling three-quarters full.
• TOPPING: Combine sugar with orange rind; sprinkle 1 tsp (5 mL) over each muffin. *(Make-ahead: Cover with plastic wrap; freeze for up to 2 days.)*
• Bake in centre of 400°F (200°C) oven until tops are firm to the touch, 25 to 30 minutes.

MAKES 12 MUFFINS.

PER MUFFIN: about 210 cal, 4 g pro, 6 g total fat (1 g sat. fat), 36 g carb, 1 g fibre, 37 mg chol, 275 mg sodium. % RDI: 5% calcium, 7% iron, 2% vit A, 5% vit C, 13% folate.

Chapter Seven

FUN FAMILY PROJECTS

Gingerbread Dough

Use this basic dough for a variety of festive creations in this chapter.

1 cup	butter, softened	250 mL
1 cup	granulated sugar	250 mL
2	eggs	2
¾ cup	fancy molasses	175 mL
½ cup	cooking molasses	125 mL
6 cups	all-purpose flour	1.5 L
2 tsp	ground ginger	10 mL
1 tsp	each baking soda and salt	5 mL
1 tsp	each ground cloves and cinnamon	5 mL

• In large bowl, beat butter with sugar until fluffy; beat in eggs, 1 at a time. Beat in fancy molasses and cooking molasses.
• In separate bowl, whisk together flour, ginger, baking soda, salt, cloves and cinnamon; add, half at a time, to molasses mixture, mixing well and blending with hands, if necessary.
• Divide into quarters and shape into discs or rectangles; wrap each in plastic wrap. Refrigerate until firm, about 2 hours. *(Make-ahead: Refrigerate for up to 1 week or overwrap in heavy-duty foil and freeze for up to 2 weeks.)*

MAKES 1 BATCH.

Royal Icing

Meringue powder is available at bulk or cake-decorating supply stores. For decorating, set aside 2 cups (500 mL) of this icing for the Icing Paint (recipe, this page).

¼ cup	meringue powder	50 mL
4⅔ cups	icing sugar	1.15 L

• In bowl, beat meringue powder with ½ cup (125 mL) water until foamy, about 2 minutes.
• Add icing sugar; beat until stiff, about 9 minutes. Cover with damp cloth to prevent drying out.

MAKES ABOUT 2½ CUPS (625 mL).

Icing Paint

This type of icing is thin enough to cover complete surfaces like paint. After decorating gingerbread, it takes about 4 hours to dry completely.

2 tbsp	water (approx)	25 mL
2 cups	Royal Icing (recipe, this page)	500 mL

• In small bowl, whisk water into icing until smooth, adding up to 1 tbsp (15 mL) more water if necessary to make icing thin enough to paint onto cookies.

MAKES 2 CUPS (500 mL).

Gingerbread Christmas Trees and Snowmen

Deck the halls with a selection of colourful iced gingerbread cookies of any shape, from snowmen and trees to ornaments, stars, bells, people — and more. When you finish decking the halls, hang them on the tree, or use them as place cards or gift tags. You can omit outlining the cookies with Royal Icing, but this step adds a lovely neat touch, especially for novices.

Gingerbread Dough
(recipe, page 177)

Royal Icing (recipe, page 177)

Icing Paint (recipe, page 177)

Assorted candies, coloured coarse sugar, sour strips, sprinkles and silver dragées

• Working with one-quarter of the dough at a time, roll between waxed paper to scant ¼-inch (5 mm) thickness. Remove top sheet of paper. Using 3- to 4-inch (8 to 10 cm) Christmas cookie cutters, such as snowmen and trees, cut out shapes. Peel away scraps. Slide paper and dough onto rimless baking sheet; refrigerate until firm, about 30 minutes.

• Line rimless baking sheets with parchment paper. Transfer as many cutouts to prepared pans as can fit 1 inch (2.5 cm) apart. With blunt end of wooden skewer, poke hole through tops.

• Bake in top and bottom thirds of 325°F (160°C) oven, rotating and switching pans halfway through, until firm to the touch, about 18 minutes.

• While still hot, twist skewer through existing holes to enlarge. Transfer to racks; let cool completely.

• Using small piping bag fitted with small plain tip and ½ cup (125 mL) of the Royal Icing, pipe outline around edges of cookies. Let dry on rack, about 2 hours.

• Tint ½ cup (125 mL) of the Icing Paint green and ¼ cup (50 mL) red. If desired, tint 2 tsp (10 mL) of the Icing Paint yellow for brooms and 2 tsp (10 mL) black for top hats. Leave remaining Icing Paint white.

• Using small brush and working inside outline, paint snowmen with white icing paint and trees with green icing paint.

• While still wet, stick on candies for face, hat, buttons and brooms. Let dry completely on rack, about 4 hours.

• Paint toques red. Make scarves from sour strips. Let dry, about 2 hours.

• With darning needle, thread ribbon through holes.

MAKES ABOUT 100 COOKIES.

PER COOKIE (WITHOUT CANDY DECORATION): about 87 cal, 1 g pro, 2 g total fat (1 g sat. fat), 16 g carb, trace fibre, 10 mg chol, 63 mg sodium. % RDI: 2% calcium, 6% iron, 2% vit A, 5% folate.

Treescape
Candle Base

Candles in a forest of trees puts a glow on your party table. If your Christmas tree cookie cutter is smaller than called for, just make narrower rectangles for the box sides so the treetops will be higher than the box sides.

Half	Gingerbread Dough (two discs), recipe, page 177	Half
2	batches Royal Icing (recipe, page 177)	2
	Green paste food colouring	

• Working with 1 disc of dough at a time, roll between waxed paper to ¼-inch (5 mm) thickness. Remove top sheet of paper.
• Cut out one 12- x 4¼-inch (30 x 10.5 cm) rectangle, two 3½- x 2½-inch (9 x 6 cm) strips and two 12- x 2½-inch (30 x 6 cm) strips.
• Using 5¼-inch (12.5 cm) cookie cutter, cut trees out of remaining dough, rerolling scraps. Peel away scraps. Slide paper and dough onto rimless baking sheets; refrigerate until firm, about 30 minutes.

Gingerbread
Picture Frames

Frame an assortment of snapshots using these seasonally sweet do-it-yourself frames. Reroll scraps and cut out small shapes to add to frames (such as stars and trees). Hang your frame with a pretty ribbon or prop it on a small easel.

Half	Gingerbread Dough (two discs), recipe, page 177	Half
Half	Royal Icing (recipe, page 177)	Half

• In photocopier, enlarge patterns photostatically to make grid of 1-inch (2.5 cm) squares. Cut out patterns.
• Working with 1 disc of dough at a time, roll between waxed paper to 12- x 8-inch (30 x 20 cm) rectangle. Remove top paper. Using patterns and tip of knife, trace and cut out patterns. If desired, use straw to poke hole at centre of top for hanging. Peel away scraps. Make decorative cutouts from

• Line rimless baking sheets with parchment paper. Transfer as many cutouts to prepared pans as can fit 1 inch (2.5 cm) apart. Bake in top and bottom thirds of 325°F (160°C) oven, rotating and switching pans halfway through, until firm to the touch, about 18 minutes. Transfer to racks; let cool completely.

• Using icing as glue, attach short edges of strips to form rectangular box; let dry, about 2 hours. Using icing as glue, attach rectangle to base; let dry. Mix 1¼ cups (300 mL) icing with 1 tsp (5 mL) water; using palette knife, paint inside and outside of box with thinned icing. Let dry.

• Tint 1½ cups (375 mL) icing green. Using palette knife, spread over top half of back of trees; let dry. Spread over front and edges of trees, leaving trunks bare; let dry. Mix ¾ cup (175 mL) icing with ¾ tsp (4 mL) water; paint onto trees to resemble snow. Let dry. If desired, tint a little of the icing brown; pipe onto trees to resemble pine cones. With icing, attach trees to outside of box, overlapping for forest effect. Let dry completely.

MAKES 1 CANDLE BASE.

scraps as desired. Slide paper and dough onto rimless baking sheet; refrigerate until firm, about 30 minutes.

• Line rimless baking sheets with parchment paper. Transfer cutouts to prepared pans, placing 1 inch (2.5 cm) apart.

• Bake in top and bottom thirds of 325°F (160°C) oven, rotating and switching pans halfway through, until firm to the touch, about 18 minutes. Transfer to racks; let cool.

• Divide and tint icing if desired; spread or pipe decoratively onto frames and cutouts. Decorate as desired with cutouts. Cover remaining icing with plastic wrap and refrigerate. Let frames stand until completely dry, at least 8 hours.

• Trim photos slightly larger than openings in frames. Dot edges of photos with icing; place frames over photo, pressing gently to adhere. Let dry. Thread ribbon through holes and tie bow to hang if desired.

MAKES 8 FRAMES.

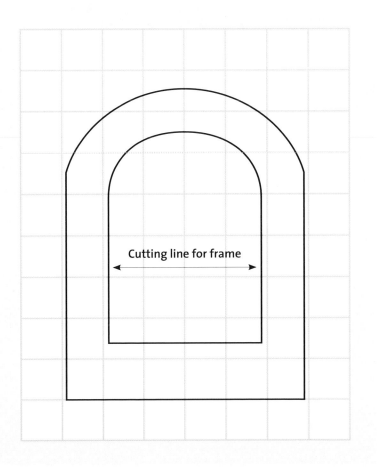

Cutting line for frame

Winter Gingerbread Village

This easy-to-work dough and icing make a charming little village of four buildings plus a clock tower, with some dough left over for steps, a bench or paving stones. Its basic pattern for a house is easily adapted to create a church, town hall, schoolhouse or shop. You can make the dough ahead, then cut and bake the pieces one day and assemble them the next.

For shrubs, secure a spiral of ribbon licorice to a gumdrop base. Make larger shrubs by wrapping the licorice around trimmed ice-cream cones. The large tree in the photo is made from fabric.

Gingerbread Dough (recipe, page 177)
Royal Icing (recipe, page 177)
Ribbon licorice, bubble-gum tape or Fruit Roll-Ups for shingles (optional)
Assorted candies

• In photocopier, enlarge pattern pieces on page 184 by 200%; cut out from parchment or waxed paper. Cut out remaining pattern pieces as follows:
• Side: 4½ x 3½ inches (11 x 9 cm)
• Roof: 5½ x 4 inches (13 x 10 cm)
• Chimney side: 1½-inch (4 cm) square
• Steeple side: 2½ x ½ inches (6 x 1 cm)
• Steeple roof: 1¾ x 1¼ inches (4.5 x 3 cm)
• Schoolhouse belfry side: ¾-inch (2 cm) square
• Schoolhouse belfry roof: 1¼-inch (3 cm) square
• Clock tower sides: 8 x 1¼ inches (20 x 3 cm)
• Clock tower roof: 1¼-inch (3 cm) square
• Draw and cut out pattern pieces for doors and windows as desired.
• From foam core or heavy cardboard, cut four 8- x 6-inch (20 x 15 cm) rectangles as bases for buildings and one 4- x 3-inch (10 x 8 cm) rectangle as base for clock tower. (Or use sturdy disposable plates.)
• Between 20-inch (50 cm) lengths of waxed or parchment paper, roll out each rectangle of dough to 14 x 12 inches (35 x 30 cm), about ¼ inch (5 mm) thick. Slide paper and dough onto rimless baking sheet; chill in freezer until firm, 15 minutes. One at a time, slide back onto work surface; peel off top paper.
• With tip of knife and using patterns, cut out dough as follows: 8 front/back pieces; 8 side pieces; 8 roof pieces. Slide dough and paper back onto baking sheet. Peel away scraps and set aside. Return to freezer; chill until firm, about 15 minutes.
• Meanwhile, press scraps together; reroll to ¼-inch (5 mm) thickness. Cut any remaining building pieces; chill as directed.
• For each steeple, schoolhouse belfry and chimney, cut as follows: 2 front/back pieces; 2 side pieces. For each steeple and belfry: 2 roof pieces.
• Cut clock tower as follows: 4 clock tower sides; 1 clock tower roof.
• Cut door and window pieces as desired. Reroll scraps; cut steps, bench and other items as desired. Chill as directed.
• Line rimless baking sheets with parchment paper. Transfer as many pieces to prepared pans as can fit 1 inch (2.5 cm) apart. Bake, 1 sheet at a time, in centre of 350°F (180°C) oven until slightly darker at edges and firm to the touch, about 22 minutes for large pieces and 15 minutes for small pieces. Let cool on pans on racks.
• Using piping bag fitted with ¼-inch (5 mm) tip (or small plastic bag with corner snipped off), pipe icing along bottom and side edges of front piece and 1 side piece. Place on base, 1 inch (2.5 cm) from edges, pressing together to form corner. Repeat with back and remaining side piece. Let dry completely, about 20 minutes, propping with heavy cans if necessary. ›

• Pipe icing along top edges of walls; attach 1 roof piece. Pipe icing along top edge of roof; attach remaining roof piece. Let dry completely, about 20 minutes.
• Assemble clock tower as for buildings.
• Meanwhile, assemble chimney, steeple or schoolhouse belfry by piping icing on back of front and back pieces along side edges. Hold front piece upright on work surface; press side pieces into icing. Add back piece, pressing icing into side pieces. Let dry for 10 minutes.

• To attach steeple and schoolhouse belfry roofs, pipe icing along top edges; attach pieces. Let dry completely, about 20 minutes. To attach, pipe icing along bottom edges; press onto peak of roof.
• Decorate with gingerbread doors, windows and candies, attaching with icing. (To cover walls with icing, coat 1 at a time and decorate with candies before continuing with remaining walls.)
• To make shingles: Cut licorice into 5½-inch (13 cm) strips. Starting at bottom edge of roof, attach horizontally with icing, overlapping layers and trimming around chimney, steeple or belfry if necessary.

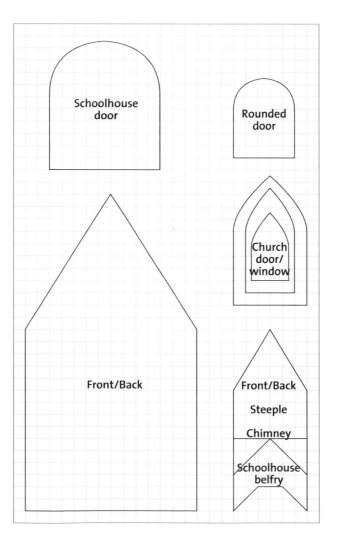

Gingerbread Boxes

Fill these small boxes with candy or tiny cookies to make the perfect present for any sweet tooth or to create a holiday decoration or dining-table centrepiece.

Half	Gingerbread Dough (two discs), recipe, page 177	Half
Half	Royal Icing (recipe, page 177)	Half

• Working with 1 disc of dough at a time, roll between waxed paper to ¼-inch (5 mm) thickness. Remove top sheet of paper. Using tip of knife, cut out four 2-inch (5 cm) square sides and one 2½-inch (6 cm) square base for each box. Peel away scraps. Slide paper and dough onto rimless baking sheets; refrigerate until firm, about 30 minutes.
• Line rimless baking sheets with parchment paper. Transfer as many cutouts to prepared pans as can fit 1 inch (2.5 cm) apart. Bake in top and bottom thirds of 325°F (160°C) oven, rotating and switching pans halfway through, until firm to the touch, about 18 minutes. Transfer to racks; let cool completely.
• Lay base flat; pipe or use palette knife or spatula to spread icing "glue" onto 3 edges of each side (don't ice top edge); place bottom edges on base to form box, propping with cans until set. Decorate as desired with icing.

MAKES 4 SMALL BOXES.

Ginger Star Wreath Centrepiece

Glowing candles surrounded by a festive wreath of gingerbread cookies makes a spectacular centrepiece.

Half	Gingerbread Dough (two discs), recipe, page 177	Half
Half	Royal Icing (recipe, page 177)	Half
	Silver dragées and silvered sugared almonds	
	Icing sugar (optional)	

• Working with 1 disc of dough at a time, roll between waxed paper to ¼-inch (5 mm) thickness. Remove top sheet of paper. Using assorted sizes of cookie cutters, cut out stars. Peel away scraps. Slide paper and dough onto rimless baking sheets; refrigerate until firm, about 30 minutes.
• Line rimless baking sheets with parchment paper. Transfer as many cutouts to prepared pans as can fit 1 inch (2.5 cm) apart. Bake in top and bottom thirds of 325°F (160°C) oven, rotating and switching pans halfway through, until firm to the touch, about 18 minutes. Transfer to racks; let cool completely.
• On heavy cardboard, trace around dinner plate; cut outer edge of wreath along traced line; cut inner edge 1 to 2½ inches (2.5 to 6 cm) inside line. Wrap with foil. Using icing as glue, attach overlapping cookies. Decorate with silver dragées and silvered sugared almonds. Dust with icing sugar if desired.

MAKES 1 WREATH CENTREPIECE.

❯ *Snowmen Ornament*

Make a cheery crowd for tree or tabletop.

• Enlarge pattern as follows: On brown paper, draw grid of horizontal and vertical lines 1-inch (2.5 cm) apart. Each square on pattern grid equals a 1-inch square on paper. Draw each pattern line onto corresponding square on paper. Transfer any markings. (Seam allowance is included.) Cut out.

• Unless otherwise indicated: Use ¼-inch (6 mm) seam allowance throughout. Backstitch at beginning and end of all seams. Use matching thread and sew with right sides together.

1. From white sweat suit fleece, cut 2 body sides and 1 body bottom; Sew 2 body sides together along centre-front/back edges; open out and, matching As, pin to body bottom and stitch, leaving open as indicated. Turn right side out and, with polyester fibrefill, stuff firmly. Turn under ¼ inch around opening; slipstitch closed. With 2 strands of black embroidery floss, embroider 3 buttons at ¼-inch intervals down centre-front seam.

2. From same fleece, cut 2 head sides and 1 head back; sew, stuff and close as for body.

3. From orange cotton fabric, cut nose; fold in half lengthwise; sew together, leaving straight edge open. Turn right side out and stuff. Turn under ⅛ inch (3 mm) around opening; slipstitch to face. With floss, satin-stitch button eyes, then outline each with backstitching; with 1 strand of floss, stitch series of tiny Xs for mouth. Hand-stitch head to top of body.

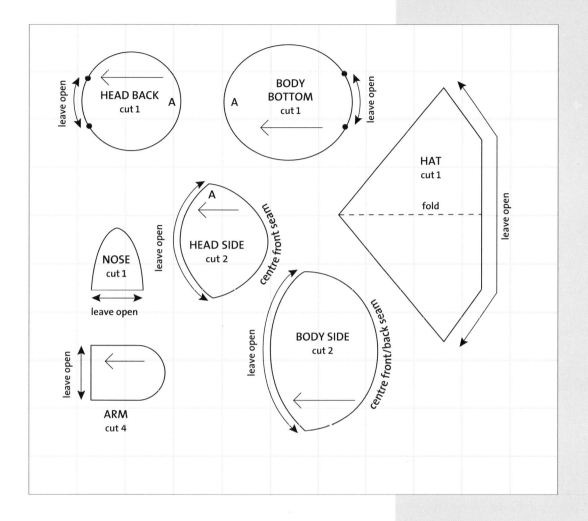

4. From white sweat suit fleece, cut 4 arms; sew together in pairs, leaving each straight edge open, then stuff in same manner as for nose. Turn under ¼ inch around each opening then slipstitch to side of body, about ¾ inch (2 cm) from centre front.

5. From blue sweat suit fleece, cut 1 hat; fold in half so angled edges are even and sew together, leaving open as indicated. Turn right side out. Turn under ¼ inch around opening; slipstitch around crown of head. Fold tip of hat down as desired; tack in place.

6. Sew twig to 1 arm.

7. For tree ornament: With clear monofilament, take tiny stitch through hat at top of head; tie ends in overhand knot to make hanging loop.

Cookie Dough Cottages

Unlike elaborate gingerbread houses, which are a major holiday project, these cute wee cottages can go from start to finish in one day. The easy pat-in dough bakes into a chewy yet crisp chocolate toffee cookie that's easily assembled into little houses — the perfect size for tiny hands to decorate.

1¼ cups	butter, softened	300 mL
1½ cups	granulated sugar	375 mL
1½ tsp	vanilla	7 mL
½ tsp	salt	2 mL
3 cups	all-purpose flour	750 mL
1 cup	chocolate chips	250 mL
1 cup	toffee bits	250 mL
	Decorations (see Cottage Decorating, page 190)	

ROYAL ICING:

3 tbsp	water	50 mL
2 tbsp	meringue powder	25 mL
2 cups	icing sugar	500 mL

• Line 17- x 11-inch (45 x 29 cm) rimmed baking sheet with parchment paper; set aside.

• In bowl, beat butter with sugar until fluffy; beat in vanilla and salt. Stir in flour, 1 cup (250 mL) at a time, to make dry crumbly dough. Stir in chocolate chips and toffee bits.

• Gently squeeze handfuls of dough just until mixture holds together; pat evenly into prepared pan. Bake in centre of 325°F (160°C) oven until firm to the touch and edges begin to turn golden, about 30 minutes. Let cool on rack until centre is firm, about 8 minutes.

• Place large cutting board on top of pan and invert cookie onto board; remove pan and peel off paper. Trim ½ inch (1 cm) from edges. With small sharp knife, cut out pieces: 2 bases, each 4½ x 3½ inches (11 x 9 cm); 4 sides, each 3 x 1¾ inches (8 x 4.5 cm); 4 roofs, each 3½ x 2½ inches (9 x 6 cm); and 4 front/back pieces (arrange pattern piece on page 190 on cookie). Transfer cutout pieces to rack; let cool completely. *(Make-ahead: Layer between waxed paper in airtight container and store for up to 5 days or freeze for up to 3 weeks.)*

• **ROYAL ICING:** Meanwhile, in large bowl, beat water with meringue powder until foamy, about 2 minutes. Beat in icing sugar, 1 cup (250 mL) at a time, until stiff peaks form when beaters are lifted, about 4 minutes. Cover with damp tea towel to prevent drying out.

• For each cottage and using wooden stir stick, coat bottom of 1 base with icing; stick to paper or china plate. Coat bottom and side edges of 1 front piece and 1 side piece with icing; join together and attach to base. Repeat with 1 back and another side piece, joining to first pieces as well. Let dry completely, about 20 minutes.

• Coat top edges of walls with icing and attach 1 roof piece; coat top edge of roof with icing, attach another roof piece and let dry, about 10 minutes. Attach decorations as desired with dabs of icing.

MAKES 2 COTTAGES.

Cottage Decorating

Use this guide for buying candy for the
Cookie Dough Cottages on page 189

➤ 3 cups (750 mL) whole unblanched
almonds, pumpkin seeds, pecan halves or
shredded-wheat squares (for roofs)

➤ 10 to 15 chocolate Kisses or Hugs

➤ 1 pkg (4 oz/113 g) cinnamon hearts or
cinnamon logs

➤ 1 pkg (300 g) chocolate or butterscotch
chips

➤ 1 cup (250 mL) jujubes or gumdrops

➤ 1 pkg (200 g) peppermints

➤ 10 multicolour jelly fruit slices

➤ 1 cup (250 mL) candy-coated chocolate
pieces

➤ 1 cup (250 L) white chocolate–covered
pretzels

➤ 2 pieces sugared ribbon licorice

➤ Red, green and black licorice

➤ 6 sugar crystal sticks (for trees)

➤ Candy-coated almonds

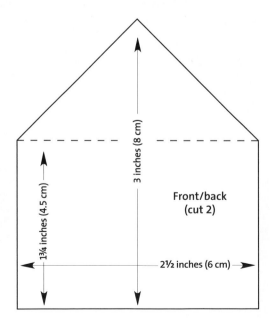

3 inches (8 cm)

1¾ inches (4.5 cm)

Front/back
(cut 2)

2½ inches (6 cm)

Mittens

*Kids can decorate these to give as gifts.
Or they can hang them along a ribbon to
garland a mantel at home or decorate a
classroom at school.*

Half	Gingerbread Dough (two discs), recipe, page 177	Half
Half	Royal Icing (recipe, page 177)	Half
	Assorted candies	

• On parchment or waxed paper, trace
mitten shape around each child's hand,
extending lines to draw 1-inch (2.5 cm) cuff
at wrist; cut out.

• Working with 1 disc of dough at a time, roll
between waxed paper to ¼-inch (5 mm)
thickness. Remove top sheet of paper. Using
patterns and tip of knife, trace and cut out
mittens. If desired, use straw to poke hole
centred along wrist edge for ribbon. Peel
away scraps. Slide paper and dough onto
rimless baking sheets; refrigerate until firm,
about 30 minutes.

• Line rimless baking sheets with parchment
paper. Transfer as many cutouts to
prepared pans as can fit 1 inch (2.5 cm)
apart. Bake in top and bottom thirds of
325°F (160°C) oven, rotating and switching
pans halfway through, until firm to the
touch, about 18 minutes. Transfer to racks;
let cool completely.

• Decorate with icing and candies. If
desired, personalize by piping name
on each.

**MAKES ABOUT EIGHT 5½-INCH (13 CM)
LONG MITTENS.**

Crispy Rice Pops

These crisp and colourful creations are the first to disappear from the bake sale table.

¼ cup	butter	50 mL
2 tsp	vanilla	10 mL
1	bag (250 g) mini-marshmallows	1
6 cups	rice crisp cereal	1.5 L
8 oz	semisweet chocolate, chopped	250 g
1 cup	candy sprinkles	250 mL

• In large saucepan, melt butter with vanilla over medium heat. Add marshmallows; cook, stirring, until melted, 8 minutes.
• Remove from heat; stir in cereal until combined. Let cool enough to handle. With greased hands, divide and shape mixture into 12 balls. Let cool completely on baking sheet.
• Meanwhile, in heatproof bowl over saucepan of hot (not boiling) water, melt chocolate. Dip half of each ball into chocolate then into sprinkles. Place on waxed paper; let dry completely.
• Insert wooden stick for holding. Wrap each in plastic wrap and tie with ribbon.

MAKES 12 POPS.

PER POP: about 310 cal, 2 g pro, 11 g total fat (6 g sat. fat), 54 g carb, 1 g fibre, 11 mg chol, 208 mg sodium. % RDI: 1% calcium, 21% iron, 4% vit A, 4% folate.

Confetti Chocolate Bark

This simple confection is easy for kids to mix up and makes a terrific gift. Candy-coated peanut butter or peanuts or other nuts work as well as the candy-coated chocolate.

1 lb	semisweet or milk chocolate, chopped	500 g
1½ cups	candy-coated chocolate pieces	375 mL

• Line rimmed baking sheet with foil; set aside.
• In heatproof bowl over saucepan of hot (not boiling) water, melt chocolate. Remove from heat; stir in candy-coated chocolate pieces.
• Pour onto prepared pan, spreading into rectangle just less than ½ inch (1 cm) thick. Refrigerate until hardened, about 1 hour. Break into pieces. *(Make-ahead: Refrigerate layered between waxed paper in airtight container for up to 1 week.)*

MAKES ABOUT 1½ LB (750 G), OR 32 PIECES.

PER PIECE: about 115 cal, 1 g pro, 7 g total fat (4 g sat. fat), 15 g carb, 1 g fibre, 1 mg chol, 10 mg sodium. % RDI: 2 calcium, 4% iron.

VARIATION

Cookies and Cream Chocolate Bark: Substitute white chocolate for semisweet. Substitute about 12 cream-filled chocolate cookies for candy-coated chocolate; chop to make 1½ cups (375 mL). Mini cookies can also be used.

Crispy Winter Wonderland

This cereal scene is a fun last-minute project, and it's easier and less expensive to create than a large gingerbread scene. Use an unopened box of rice crisp cereal. Cereal exposed to air for some time can affect the structure's stability. Also use an unopened package of marshmallows. Opened packages or bulk marshmallows may not melt evenly.

	Flaked coconut and icing sugar	

SNOW FAMILY:

5 cups	miniature marshmallows (or 40 large)	1.25 L
¼ cup	butter	50 mL
1 tsp	vanilla	5 mL
6 cups	rice crisp cereal	1.5 L
1 cup	assorted small candies	250 mL
	Gumdrops	
	Ribbon and string licorice	

CHRISTMAS TREES:

5 cups	miniature marshmallows (or 40 large)	1.25 L
¼ cup	butter	50 mL
1 tbsp	green liquid food colouring (or ⅛ tsp/0.5 mL green paste food colouring)	15 mL
6 cups	rice crisp cereal	1.5 L
30	mini-gumdrops	30
5	assorted hard candies (preferably star-shaped)	5

• **SNOW FAMILY:** In large saucepan over medium-low heat, melt marshmallows with butter, stirring constantly, until smooth, 5 minutes. Remove from heat; stir in vanilla.
• Stir in half of the cereal until combined; stir in remaining cereal to coat completely. Scrape into greased bowl; let cool slightly.

• Using greased hands, firmly press mixture into balls as follows: for adults, 4 each 2-inch (5 cm) bottoms, 1½-inch (4 cm) middles and 1-inch (2.5 cm) heads; for children, 5 each 1½-inch (4 cm) bottoms and 1-inch (2.5 cm) heads; for dogs, 2 each 1½-inch (4 cm) bodies (shape into ovals) and 1-inch (2.5 cm) heads.
• Press on assorted small candies for eyes, noses, buttons and dogs' ears and legs. Skewer gumdrops on toothpicks and insert into adults' and children's heads for hats. For scarves, wrap ribbon licorice around necks; make slit about 1 inch (2.5 cm) from 1 end of each and thread other end through to secure. Attach string licorice for dogs' tails. Refrigerate until firm, 30 minutes.
• **CHRISTMAS TREES:** Lightly grease 15- x 10-inch (40 x 25 cm) rimmed baking sheet; set aside.
• In large saucepan over medium-low heat, melt marshmallows with butter, stirring constantly, until smooth, about 5 minutes. Remove from heat; stir in food colouring until tinted evenly.
• Stir in half of the rice crisp cereal until combined; stir in remaining cereal to coat completely. Scrape onto prepared pan; let cool slightly. Using greased hands, firmly press mixture evenly over pan. Let cool for 10 minutes before cutting out shapes.
• Using graduated star-shaped cutters, cut out 10 each of 3 different-size stars.
• To assemble each tree, stack 2 of the largest stars on plate; top with 2 medium stars, angling points in between points of bottom stars. Top with 2 small stars. Decorate with mini-gumdrops; top with star-shaped hard candy.
• On large plate, arrange trees around snow family figures. Sprinkle plate with flaked coconut and dust with icing sugar.

MAKES 4 ADULT SNOW FIGURES, 5 CHILDREN, 2 DOGS AND 5 TREES.

Festive Shortbread Cookies

Get the little ones involved in making these easy cookies right from the mixing to the fun of decorating.

½ cup	butter, softened	125 mL
¼ cup	granulated sugar	50 mL
¼ tsp	vanilla	1 mL
¾ cup	all-purpose flour	175 mL
¼ cup	cornstarch	50 mL

DECORATIONS:

½ cup	milk or semisweet chocolate chips	125 mL
¼ tsp	vegetable oil	1 mL
	Candy-coated chocolate pieces, coloured sprinkles or stars	

• Line 2 rimless baking sheets with parchment paper; set aside.

• In large bowl, beat butter with sugar until fluffy; stir in vanilla. In separate bowl, whisk flour with cornstarch; stir into butter mixture, in 2 additions, until smooth.

• Turn out onto lightly floured surface. With hands, roll into two 9-inch (23 cm) logs; cut each into 9 pieces. Roll each into ball. Place, 2 inches (5 cm) apart, on prepared pans.

• Bake, 1 sheet at a time, in centre of 300°F (150°C) oven until bottoms are golden brown, 30 to 35 minutes. Let cool on pan on rack for 2 minutes; transfer to rack and let cool completely.

• **DECORATIONS:** Line rimmed baking sheet with parchment paper; set aside.

• In heatproof bowl over saucepan of hot (not boiling) water, melt chocolate chips with oil, stirring until smooth. Remove from heat.

• Dip each cookie halfway into chocolate, shaking gently over bowl to remove excess. Dip into desired candy. Set on prepared baking sheet. Refrigerate until chocolate is firm and shiny, about 30 minutes.

MAKES 18 COOKIES.

PER COOKIE (WITHOUT CANDIES): about 106 cal, trace pro, 7 g total fat (4 g sat. fat), 11 g carb, trace fibre, 15 mg chol, 40 mg sodium. % RDI: 1% calcium, 2% iron, 5% vit A, 4% folate.

❯ Paper Chain of Snow People

Scissor up a chain of snow folk, then glue on faces and colourful clothes. Drape one above a doorway or join several chains together, end to end, to wrap around a Christmas tree.

• Trace actual-size pattern onto scrap paper; cut out just outside lines.

• From large sheet of stiff white paper, cut strip 4-inch (10 cm) high and desired length (must be a multiple of 2¾ inches/7 cm). At 2¾-inch intervals, accordion-fold strip to make series of 2¾-inch wide rectangles; open out.

• With broken lines on side edges and arrow up, lay pattern on first rectangle; with pencil, trace solid lines only. Repeat, flipping pattern each time so arm heights match, to mark all rectangles. Cut along lines.

• From coloured paper, cut desired features and clothing; with glue stick, glue on.

Butterscotch Crunch Bars

Even children can contribute to the neighbourhood cookie exchange or school bake sale with these crisp and chewy bars.

28	graham crackers	28
1 cup	unsalted butter	250 mL
1 cup	packed brown sugar	250 mL
1½ cups	toasted sliced almonds	375 mL

• Lightly grease 15- x 10-inch (40 x 25 cm) rimmed baking sheet. Arrange crackers on pan; set aside.
• In saucepan, melt butter over medium heat; whisk in sugar just until combined but not boiling. Remove from heat; stir in almonds. Spread over crackers.
• Bake in centre of 375°F (190°C) oven until bubbling, about 10 minutes. Let cool in pan on rack for 10 minutes; cut into squares. *(Make-ahead: Store layered between waxed paper in airtight container for up to 3 days.)*

MAKES 28 BARS.

PER BAR: about 147 cal, 2 g pro, 10 g total fat (5 g sat. fat), 14 g carb, 1 g fibre, 18 mg chol, 50 mg sodium. % RDI: 2 calcium, 4% iron, 6% vit A, 1% folate.

Haystack Crunchies

Let the kids help make Santa's no-bake cookies the day before Christmas.

1 cup	butterscotch chips	250 mL
1 cup	peanut butter chips	250 mL
½ cup	butter	125 mL
½ cup	smooth peanut butter	125 mL
3 cups	dry chow mein noodles	750 mL
1½ cups	rice crisp cereal	375 mL
1 oz	white or semisweet chocolate, melted	30 g

• Line rimless baking sheet with waxed paper; set aside.
• In bowl over saucepan of hot (not boiling) water, melt together butterscotch and peanut butter chips, butter and peanut butter, stirring often; remove from heat. Stir in noodles and cereal to coat.
• Drop by heaping 1 tbsp (15 mL) onto prepared pan. Refrigerate or let stand until firm, 20 to 30 minutes. With fork, drizzle with chocolate. *(Make-ahead: Refrigerate layered between waxed paper in airtight container for up to 1 week or freeze for up to 3 months.)*

MAKES ABOUT 35 COOKIES.

PER COOKIE: about 123 cal, 3 g pro, 9 g total fat (4 g sat. fat), 10 g carb, trace fibre, 7 mg chol, 86 mg sodium. % RDI: 1% calcium, 4% iron, 3% vit A, 2% folate.

Chapter Eight

GIFTS FROM THE KITCHEN

Porcini Rice Mix

Porcini or morel mushrooms impart a woodsy flavour to rice. Avoid milder dried oyster and portobello mushrooms. Wrap the jar in pretty paper and include the recipe for Easy Mushroom Risotto.

2	pkg (each 14 g) dried porcini mushrooms	2
3 cups	arborio or other short-grain Italian rice	750 mL

• In bowl, mix mushrooms with rice. Spoon into decorative airtight container. *(Make-ahead: Store for up to 3 months.)*

MAKES 3 CUPS (750 ML).

Easy Mushroom Risotto

2 tbsp	butter	25 mL
1 cup	finely chopped onion	250 mL
2	cloves garlic, minced	2
1½ cups	Porcini Rice Mix (recipe, this page)	375 mL
2 cups	chicken stock	500 mL
½ cup	white wine (or chicken stock with 1 tbsp/15 mL wine vinegar)	125 mL
½ cup	grated Parmesan cheese	125 mL
2 tbsp	chopped fresh parsley	25 mL

• In large saucepan, melt 1 tbsp (15 mL) of the butter over medium heat; fry onion and garlic, stirring occasionally, until softened, about 5 minutes.
• Stir in rice mix to coat. Add 2 cups (500 mL) water, 1 cup (250 mL) of the stock and wine; bring to boil. Reduce heat to low; cover and simmer, stirring once, for 10 minutes.
• Stir rice mixture vigorously for 15 seconds. Cover and cook until just a little liquid remains and rice is still slightly firm to the bite, about 10 minutes.
• Stir in remaining stock, cheese, parsley and remaining butter; heat, stirring, until creamy and hot.

MAKES 4 SERVINGS.

PER SERVING: about 428 cal, 13 g pro, 11 g total fat (6 g sat. fat), 66 g carb, 2 g fibre, 28 mg chol, 688 mg sodium. % RDI: 18% calcium, 9% iron, 8% vit A, 7% vit C, 8% folate.

Curry Seasoning Mix

This mix is the base for a delicious dip. Use it also as a rub for chops and roasts.

½ cup	dried minced onion	125 mL
2 tbsp	curry powder	25 mL
4 tsp	each ground cumin and salt	20 mL
2 tsp	each turmeric and pepper	10 mL

• In bowl, whisk together onion, curry powder, cumin, salt, turmeric and pepper. Spoon into decorative airtight container. *(Make-ahead: Store for up to 1 month.)*

MAKES 1 CUP (250 ML).

Curry Dip

½ cup	plain yogurt	125 mL
½ cup	cream cheese, softened	125 mL
¼ cup	light mayonnaise	50 mL
1 tbsp	mango chutney	15 mL
2 tsp	Curry Seasoning Mix (recipe, this page)	10 mL
2 tbsp	chopped fresh coriander	25 mL

• In bowl, mix together yogurt, cream cheese, mayonnaise, chutney and seasoning mix. Cover and refrigerate for 2 hours. *(Make-ahead: Refrigerate for up to 3 days.)* Garnish with coriander.

MAKES 1¼ CUPS (300 ML).

PER 1 TBSP (15 ML): about 37 cal, 1 g pro, 3 g total fat (2 g sat. fat), 1 g carb, 0 g fibre, 8 mg chol, 71 mg sodium. % RDI: 1% calcium, 1% iron, 3% vit A, 1% folate.

Herb Seasoning Mix

A dried herb mix is a flavourful base for dips, rice or poultry. Visit the bulk food store and get enough for everyone on your gift list.

½ cup	dried chopped chives	125 mL
2 tbsp	dried parsley flakes	25 mL
2 tsp	each dried basil, dried thyme, garlic powder and onion powder	10 mL
1 tsp	pepper	5 mL

• In small bowl, mix together chives, parsley, basil, thyme, garlic and onion powders and pepper. Spoon into decorative container. *(Make-ahead: Store for up to 1 month.)*

MAKES 1 CUP (250 ML).

Herb Dip

½ cup	plain yogurt	125 mL
½ cup	cream cheese, softened	125 mL
¼ cup	light mayonnaise	50 mL
4 tsp	Herb Seasoning Mix (recipe, this page)	20 mL
2 tbsp	chopped fresh chives	25 mL

• In bowl, mix together yogurt, cream cheese, mayonnaise and seasoning mix. Cover and refrigerate for 2 hours. *(Make-ahead: Refrigerate for up to 3 days.)* Garnish with chives.

MAKES 1¼ CUPS (300 ML).

PER 1 TBSP (15 ML): about 35 cal, 1 g pro, 3 g total fat (2 g sat. fat), 1 g carb, 0 g fibre, 8 mg chol, 44 mg sodium. % RDI: 1% calcium, 1% iron, 3% vit A, 1% folate.

Porcini Salt

Flavoured sea salts are one of the new trends. Use them as finishing salts sprinkled on food, such as steaks, chops and fish, just before serving.

1	pkg (14 g) dried porcini mushrooms	1
¼ cup	sea salt	50 mL
Pinch	grated nutmeg	Pinch

• In clean spice or coffee grinder, pulse together mushrooms, salt and nutmeg, in 2 batches, until powdery with a few larger mushroom pieces. Spoon into decorative container. *(Make-ahead: Store for up to 1 month.)*

MAKES ABOUT ½ CUP (125 ML).

PER PINCH: about 0 cal, 0 g pro, 0 g total fat (0 g sat. fat), 0 g carb, 0 g fibre, 0 mg chol, 48 mg sodium.

Lemon Rosemary Salt

This herbed lemon finishing salt brightens up chicken, fish or vegetables.

¼ cup	fresh rosemary leaves	50 mL
¼ cup	sea salt	50 mL
2 tbsp	grated lemon rind	25 mL

• Line rimmed baking sheet with parchment paper; set aside.
• Coarsely chop rosemary. In clean spice or coffee grinder, pulse together rosemary, salt and lemon rind, in 2 batches, until combined. Spread on prepared pan.
• Bake in 225°F (110°C) oven until dry, about 10 minutes. Let cool.
• Break up dried salt. Spoon into decorative airtight container. *(Make-ahead: Store for up to 1 month.)*

MAKES ABOUT ½ CUP (125 ML).

Tandoori Spice Blend

For your foodie friends, make a jar of this blend to accompany a jar of mango chutney, a package of basmati rice, pappadams, gingerroot, garlic bulbs and the recipe for Tandoori Chicken.

⅓ cup	each cumin seeds and coriander seeds	75 mL
1	stick (3 inches/8 cm) cinnamon, broken into chunks	1
1 tbsp	whole cloves	15 mL
1 tbsp	each ground ginger, turmeric and mace	15 mL
1 tbsp	each salt and garlic powder	15 mL
1 tsp	cayenne pepper	5 mL

• In small heavy skillet, toast cumin and coriander seeds, cinnamon and cloves over medium heat, stirring, until fragrant and slightly darkened, 2 to 3 minutes; let cool.
• In clean spice or coffee grinder, grind together toasted spices, ginger, turmeric, mace, salt, garlic and cayenne pepper. Spoon into decorative airtight container. *(Make-ahead: Store for up to 1 month.)*

MAKES ¾ CUP (175 mL).

Tandoori Chicken

½ cup	plain yogurt	125 mL
1 tbsp	Tandoori Spice Blend (recipe, this page)	15 mL
1 tbsp	minced gingerroot	15 mL
2	cloves garlic, minced	2
8	chicken drumsticks, skinned, if desired	8
1 tbsp	vegetable oil	15 mL

• In large glass bowl, stir together yogurt, spice blend, ginger and garlic; add chicken, turning to coat. Cover and refrigerate for 30 minutes. *(Make-ahead: Refrigerate for up to 24 hours.)*
• Arrange chicken on greased (if skinned) foil-lined rimmed baking sheet; drizzle with oil. Bake in 400°F (200°C) oven until juices run clear when chicken is pierced, about 30 minutes. Broil until browned and crisp, about 3 minutes.

MAKES 4 SERVINGS.

PER SERVING: about 210 cal, 24 g pro, 11 g total fat (2 g sat. fat), 4 g carb, trace fibre, 84 mg chol, 248 mg sodium. % RDI: 7% calcium,14% iron, 2% vit A, 2% vit C, 1% folate.

❯ *Wine-Bottle Gift Bags*

Dress up the traditional hostess gift by stitching easy-sew bags from fancy fabric, then tie them with shiny, tasselled cord. At 12 inches (30.5 cm) tall, each bag holds a standard 750 mL wine bottle.

1. Press under ¼ inch (6 mm) along each short edge of 34½- x 7-inch (87.5 x 18 cm) rectangle of chiffon, satin or velvet, then fold in half so right sides are together and pressed ends are even. With matching thread and using ¼-inch seam allowance, stitch along each long edge (side); if desired, serge or machine-zigzag seam allowance to bind.

2. Fold pressed (top) edge down 2¾ inches (7 cm) so wrong sides are together and pin; edgestitch pressed edge, then topstitch ¾ inch (2 cm) up to form casing.

3. Lay bag flat on work surface. At each side seam, place pin 1⅜ inches (3.5 cm) from each bottom corner, then, at folded bottom edge, place pin 1⅜ inches from each bottom corner (as shown in Diagram 1.

4. Open out bag bottom, then refold, matching pins at each corner and stitch (as shown in Diagram 2); trim each corner, ¼ inch from seam. Turn right side out.

5. About ¼ inch from each side seam and parallel to it, cut small slit through outer layer of casing at each side of seam. With bodkin or large safety pin, thread 27⅝ inches (70 cm) of fine twisted cord or narrow satin ribbon into slit at left-hand side of 1 seam, clockwise around entire casing, and out slit at other side of same seam. At other side seam, repeat with second length of cord.

6. Stitch tassel to each end of cord or thread end through bead and tie in overhand knot.

DIAGRAM 1

folded bottom edge

1⅜ inches (3.5 cm)

1⅜ inches (3.5 cm)

side seams

DIAGRAM 2

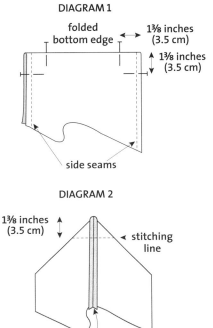

1⅜ inches (3.5 cm)

stitching line

side seam

Black Forest Brownie Mix

This mix prettily presented in layers with baking instructions written on the gift card makes a welcome present for families, teachers or colleagues.

½ cup	dried cherries or cranberries	125 mL
2 cups	semisweet chocolate chips	500 mL
¾ cup	all-purpose flour	175 mL
¼ tsp	each baking soda and salt	1 mL
¾ cup	granulated sugar	175 mL

• In 4-cup (1 L) widemouthed jar with tight-fitting lid, neatly layer cherries then half of the chocolate chips. In bowl, whisk together flour, baking soda and salt; spoon over chocolate chips.

• Cut waxed paper to fit over flour mixture and come slightly up sides. Spoon sugar onto paper; top with remaining chocolate chips. Seal jar. *(Make-ahead: Store for up to 1 month.)*

MAKES 4 CUPS (1 L).

Black Forest Brownies

	Black Forest Brownie Mix (recipe, this page)	
⅓ cup	butter	75 mL
2 tbsp	water	25 mL
2	eggs	2
1 tsp	vanilla	5 mL

• Grease 8-inch (2 L) square metal cake pan; set aside.

• In saucepan, melt together brownie mix's top layer of chocolate chips and sugar with butter and water until sugar is dissolved. Let cool for 5 minutes.

• Whisk in eggs, 1 at a time; whisk in vanilla. Stir in flour mixture, then remaining chocolate chips and cherries in brownie mix. Spread in prepared cake pan.

• Bake in centre of 350°F (180°C) oven until cake tester inserted in centre comes out with a few crumbs clinging, about 30 minutes. Cut into squares. *(Make-ahead: Store in airtight container for up to 5 days or freeze for up to 1 month.)*

MAKES 16 SQUARES.

PER SQUARE: about 217 cal, 3 g pro, 11 g total fat (6 g sat. fat), 31 g carb, 2 g fibre, 37 mg chol, 104 mg sodium. % RDI: 1% calcium, 8% iron, 5% vit A, 3% vit C, 5% folate.

Oatmeal Cookie Mix

A clear jar layered with ingredients for old-fashioned oatmeal cookies is a kind of cookie insurance for the new year when taste buds return to simpler pleasures. Attach the instructions for making the cookies.

1 cup	white chocolate chips	250 mL
1 cup	dried cranberries	250 mL
½ cup	shredded coconut	125 mL
1½ cups	large-flake rolled oats	375 mL
1 tsp	cinnamon	5 mL
1 cup	all-purpose flour	250 mL
½ tsp	each baking powder and baking soda	2 mL
¼ tsp	salt	1 mL

• In 5-cup (1.25 L) widemouthed jar with tight-fitting lid, neatly layer white chocolate chips, cranberries, coconut and rolled oats, packing down after each layer. Sprinkle cinnamon around edge.
• In bowl, whisk together flour, baking powder, baking soda and salt; spoon over cinnamon and oats. Seal jar.

MAKES ABOUT 5 CUPS (1.25 L).

Oatmeal Cookies

⅔ cup	butter, softened	150 mL
1 cup	packed light brown sugar	250 mL
1	egg	1
	Oatmeal Cookie Mix (recipe, this page)	

• Line 2 rimless baking sheets with parchment paper or grease; set aside.
• In bowl, beat butter with sugar until light; beat in egg. Add flour mixture from top of jar; stir with wooden spoon until blended. Stir in cinnamon, rolled oats, coconut, cranberries and chocolate chips, mixing well.
• Drop by 1 tbsp (15 mL), about 2 inches (5 cm) apart, onto prepared pans. Bake in centre of 350°F (180°C) oven until bottoms are golden and edges are crisp, 12 to 15 minutes. Transfer to rack; let cool. *(Make-ahead: Store in airtight container for up to 1 week or freeze for up to 3 weeks.)*

MAKES ABOUT 40 COOKIES.

PER COOKIE: about 110 cal, 1 g pro, 5 g total fat (3 g sat. fat), 15 g carb, 1 g fibre, 14 mg chol, 74 mg sodium. % RDI: 2% calcium, 4% iron, 3% vit A, 2% vit C, 2% folate.

Dark Chocolate Truffles

These rich chocolates simply melt in your mouth. Try rolling the dark chocolate truffles in cocoa powder after dipping.

8 oz	semisweet or bittersweet chocolate, finely chopped	250 g
⅔ cup	whipping cream	150 mL
¼ cup	butter, cubed	50 mL
1 tbsp	vanilla	15 mL
COATING:		
8 oz	semisweet or bittersweet chocolate, chopped	250 g

• Line 2 rimmed baking sheets with waxed paper; set aside.

• Place chocolate in heatproof bowl. In saucepan, heat cream with butter just until butter melts and bubbles form around edge of pan. Pour over chocolate; whisk until smooth. Whisk in vanilla. Cover and refrigerate until firm, about 2 hours.

• Using melon baller or teaspoon, drop by rounded 1 tsp (5 mL) onto prepared pans. Gently roll each to round off completely. Freeze until hard, about 1 hour. *(Make-ahead: Cover and freeze for up to 24 hours.)*

• COATING: In heatproof bowl over saucepan of hot (not boiling) water, melt half of the chocolate, stirring. Remove from heat; let cool slightly.

• Remove 1 pan of the truffles from freezer. Using 2 forks, dip each into chocolate, tapping forks on edge of bowl to remove excess. Return to pan. Refrigerate until coating is hardened, about 2 hours.

• In clean bowl, repeat with remaining chocolate and truffles. *(Make-ahead: Refrigerate layered between waxed paper in airtight container for up to 1 week or freeze for up to 3 months.)* Place in paper candy cups.

MAKES ABOUT 32 TRUFFLES.

PER TRUFFLE: about 93 cal, 1 g pro, 7 g total fat (4 g sat. fat), 9 g carb, 1 g fibre, 10 mg chol, 18 mg sodium. % RDI: 1% calcium, 3% iron, 3% vit A.

VARIATIONS

Cinnamon Pistachio Truffles: Add ½ tsp (2 mL) cinnamon along with vanilla. After coating truffles, roll in 1½ cups (375 mL) finely chopped toasted natural pistachios.

Hazelnut Truffles: Reduce cream to ½ cup (125 mL); replace vanilla with 3 tbsp (50 mL) hazelnut liqueur. After coating truffles, roll in 1½ cups (375 mL) finely chopped toasted skinned hazelnuts.

Pour heated cream over chocolate and whisk until smooth and chocolate is melted.

White Chocolate Coconut Truffles

Chewy toasted coconut plays off the creamy, coconut-scented white chocolate ganache filling. Like tiny snowballs, these truffles add a pretty contrast to a plate of dark chocolate truffles.

12 oz	white chocolate, finely chopped	375 g
⅓ cup	whipping cream	75 mL
¼ cup	butter, cubed	50 mL
1 tbsp	vanilla	15 mL
½ tsp	coconut extract	2 mL
COATING:		
1½ cups	sweetened shredded coconut	375 mL
8 oz	white chocolate, chopped	250 g

• Line 2 rimmed baking sheets with waxed paper; set aside.
• In large heatproof bowl over saucepan of hot (not boiling) water, heat chocolate, stirring, until half is melted. Remove from heat.
• Meanwhile, in saucepan, heat cream with butter just until butter melts and bubbles form around edge of pan. Pour over chocolate; whisk until smooth. Whisk in vanilla and coconut extract. Cover and refrigerate until firm, about 2 hours.
• Using melon baller or teaspoon, drop by rounded 1 tsp (5 mL) onto prepared pans. Gently roll each to round off completely. Freeze until hard, about 1 hour. *(Make-ahead: Cover and freeze for up to 24 hours.)*

• **COATING:** On rimmed baking sheet, toast coconut in 375°F (190°C) oven, stirring twice, until light golden, about 10 minutes. Let cool.
• In heatproof bowl over saucepan of hot (not boiling) water, melt half of the chocolate, stirring. Remove from heat; let cool slightly.
• Remove 1 pan of the truffles from freezer; using 2 forks, dip each into chocolate, tapping forks on edge of bowl to remove excess. Roll in coconut. Return to pan. Refrigerate until coating is hardened, about 2 hours.
• In clean bowl, repeat with remaining chocolate, truffles and coconut. *(Make-ahead: Refrigerate layered between waxed paper in airtight container for up to 1 week or freeze for up to 3 months.)* Place in paper candy cups.

MAKES ABOUT 32 TRUFFLES.

PER TRUFFLE: about 133 cal, 1 g pro, 9 g total fat (6 g sat. fat), 12 g carb, trace fibre, 11 mg chol, 42 mg sodium. % RDI: 3% calcium, 1% iron, 2% vit A, 1% folate.

Black Forest Fudge

This quickie fudge is so easy that the kids can help make it.

8 oz	bittersweet chocolate chopped	250 g
¾ cup	sweetened condensed milk	175 mL
1 tsp	vanilla	5 mL
1 cup	dried cherries	250 mL

• Line 8- x 4-inch (1.5 L) loaf pan with plastic wrap; set aside.
• In heatproof bowl over saucepan of hot (not boiling) water, melt chocolate with milk, stirring occasionally.
• Stir in vanilla, then cherries. Spread in prepared pan, smoothing top. Refrigerate until firm, about 3 hours.
• Remove from pan; peel off plastic wrap. Cut into small pieces. *(Make-ahead: Wrap in plastic wrap; refrigerate for up to 3 days.)*

MAKES 1¼ LB (625 G), ABOUT 32 PIECES.

PER PIECE: about 75 cal, 1 g pro, 3 g total fat (2 g sat. fat), 11 g carb, 1 g fibre, 2 mg chol, 10 mg sodium. % RDI: 2% calcium, 4% iron, 1% vit A, 1% folate.

Lemon Bark

Present this white chocolate treat dotted with bits of crunchy lemon candy in a festive cookie tin.

4 cups	pure white chocolate chips (1 lb/500 g)	1 L
1 cup	finely crushed hard lemon candies	250 mL

• Line rimmed baking sheet with parchment paper; set aside.
• In heatproof bowl over saucepan of hot (not boiling) water, melt white chocolate chips until smooth, stirring occasionally. Stir in candies. Spread to about ½-inch (1 cm) thickness on prepared pan; refrigerate until chilled and firm.
• Remove from pan; peel off paper. Break into pieces. *(Make-ahead: Store layered between waxed paper in airtight container for up to 1 week.)*

MAKES 1 LB (500 G), ABOUT 36 PIECES.

PER PIECE: about 87 cal, 1 g pro, 4 g total fat (2 g sat. fat), 13 g carb, 0 g fibre, 0 mg chol, 13 mg sodium. % RDI: 2% calcium.

Nut Brittle

Crunchy, buttery peanut brittle is a family favourite. You can make it extra special by using pine nuts or almonds instead of the peanuts. Give it in large pieces or break it up to fit any gift box or bag.

1 tbsp	vegetable oil	15 mL
4 cups	granulated sugar	1 L
½ cup	water	125 mL
⅛ tsp	cream of tartar	0.5 mL
2 cups	dry-roasted salted peanuts	500 mL
3 tbsp	butter	50 mL
1 tbsp	vanilla	15 mL

• Spread oil on rimmed baking sheet; set aside.

• In large heavy saucepan, stir together sugar, water and cream of tartar; bring to boil over medium-high heat. Boil, without stirring but brushing down side of pan occasionally with brush dipped in water, until candy thermometer registers hard-crack stage of 310°F (155°C) and small amount dropped into very cold water separates into hard brittle threads. Remove from heat.

• Quickly stir in peanuts, butter and vanilla until peanuts are coated. Scrape onto prepared pan and spread as thinly as possible. Let cool. Break into pieces. *(Make-ahead: Store layered between waxed paper in airtight container for up to 1 month.)*

MAKES 2 LB (1 KG), ABOUT 40 PIECES.

PER PIECE: about 131 cal, 2 g pro, 5 g total fat (1 g sat. fat), 22 g carb, 1 g fibre, 3 mg chol, 69 mg sodium. % RDI: 1% iron, 1% vit A, 5% folate.

Last-Minute Gifts

❯ Cheese platters are a mainstay for the holidays. To present one as a gift, arrange a variety of specialty cheeses, dried figs, dates and apricots on a cheese board along with a knife. Cover with plastic wrap.

❯ Fill a small basket or gift bag with a wheel of Brie cheese and homemade or store-bought chutney or raspberry chipotle sauce. Include the following instructions: Spread chutney or sauce on the cheese; place on heatproof serving dish and bake in 350°F (180°C) oven until softened, about 10 minutes. Serve with flatbread.

❯ Smoked salmon is always a treat to receive. Add some to a basket along with lemons, a pepper mill, pumpernickel rounds and a bunch of dill. Throw in a bottle of chilled vodka or Champagne for extravagance.

❯ Create an antipasto collection from the deli section of the grocery store. Nestle jars of olives, tapenade, marinated artichokes and roasted peppers in a basket along with cheese and a selection of specialty breads and smoked meats.

› *Stockings to Sew*

These easy, elegant stockings are sure to entice St. Nicholas down the chimney.
Make the basic version or one with a fold-down cuff that shows off its coordinated lining.

Supplies (for each)

2 pieces of matching or coordinating medium-weight fabric, such as toile de Jouy, matelassé, jacquard, brocade or satin, each 30-inch (76 cm) square, for basic stocking, or 36 x 30 inches (91.5 x 76 cm), for cuffed stocking

.30 m coordinating grosgrain ribbon, 1½ inches (39 mm) wide

Matching thread

Brown paper

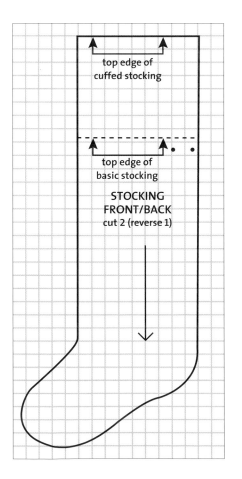

top edge of
cuffed stocking

top edge of
basic stocking

**STOCKING
FRONT/BACK**
cut 2 (reverse 1)

Instructions

Note: Finished basic stocking is approx 23⅝-inches (60 cm) long; finished cuffed stocking is approx 30¾-inches (78 cm) long.

1. Enlarge pattern as follows: On brown paper, draw grid of horizontal and vertical lines 1-inch (2.5 cm) apart. Each square on pattern grid equals a 1-inch square on paper. Draw each pattern line onto corresponding square on paper. Transfer any markings. (Seam allowance is included.) Cut out.

2. From each piece of fabric, cut stocking front and back (for basic stocking, cut top edges along broken line).

3. With right sides together and edges even, stitch same-fabric fronts and backs together using ⅜-inch (1 cm) seam allowance and leaving top edges open. Clip seam allowance at curves and turn right side out. Press under ⅜ inch around top edges. Turn lining inside out. **For basic stocking only:** Fold ribbon in half so ends are even; baste ends together to form hanging loop. With loop up, pin basted ends to wrong side of back lining between dots.

4. Matching seam lines, slip lining inside stocking. Pin together around top edge; edgestitch.

For cuffed stocking only: Fold ribbon in half so ends are even; machine-zigzag ends together to form hanging loop. With loop up, pin stitched ends to back lining between dots; topstitch through all layers. Fold down cuff.

5. Remove any basting.

Chocolate-Dipped Crystallized Ginger

Chocolate goodies are hard to beat.

| 2 oz | bittersweet or white chocolate, chopped | 60 g |
| 40 | pieces crystallized ginger | 40 |

• Line rimmed baking sheet with waxed paper; set aside.
• In heatproof bowl over saucepan of hot (not boiling) water, melt chocolate. Transfer to small bowl.
• Dip each piece of ginger halfway into chocolate. Arrange on prepared pan; refrigerate until set, about 30 minutes. *(Make-ahead: Refrigerate layered between waxed paper in airtight container for up to 2 weeks.)*

MAKES 40 PIECES.

PER PIECE: about 29 cal, trace pro, 1 g total fat (trace sat. fat), 6 g carb, trace fibre, 0 mg chol, 4 mg sodium. % RDI: 1% calcium, 10% iron, 5% vit C.

Chocolate Ginger Palettes

Crystallized ginger adds sparkle to rounds of chocolate.

| 4 oz | bittersweet or white chocolate, chopped | 125 g |
| 120 | tiny cubes crystallized ginger | 120 |

• Line rimmed baking sheet with waxed paper; set aside.
• In heatproof bowl over saucepan of hot (not boiling) water, melt chocolate. Drop by scant 1 tsp (5 mL), 1 inch (2.5 cm) apart, onto pan; tap pan on counter to spread evenly.
• Top each with 3 pieces ginger; refrigerate until set, about 30 minutes. *(Make-ahead: Refrigerate layered between waxed paper in airtight container for up to 2 weeks.)*

MAKES ABOUT 40 PIECES.

PER PIECE: about 17 cal, trace pro, 1 g total fat (1 g sat. fat), 2 g carb, trace fibre, 0 mg chol, 0 mg sodium. % RDI: 1% iron.

Cabernet Franc Wine Jelly

Thyme accentuates the herbaceous notes of Cabernet Franc. This makes a wonderful accompaniment to a cheese platter.

1¾ cups	Cabernet Franc or Merlot wine	425 mL
¼ cup	red wine vinegar	50 mL
2	large sprigs fresh thyme	2
3½ cups	granulated sugar	875 mL
1	pouch (85 mL) liquid pectin	1

• In large saucepan, bring wine, vinegar and thyme to boil over high heat. Remove from heat; cover and let stand for 20 minutes. Strain through cheesecloth-lined sieve into clean saucepan.
• Stir in sugar; bring to full rolling boil over high heat, stirring constantly. Boil for 1 minute, stirring. Remove from heat. Stir in pectin; stir for 1 minute, skimming off any foam.
• Ladle into hot ½-cup (125 mL) canning jars, leaving ¼-inch (5 mm) headspace. Wipe rims. Cover with prepared lids. Screw on bands until resistance is met; increase to fingertip tight. Boil in boiling water bath for 10 minutes. Store in cool dark place for up to 1 year.

MAKES ABOUT 4 CUPS (1 L).

PER 1 TBSP (15 ML): about 47 cal, 0 g pro, 0 g total fat (0 g sat. fat), 11 g carb, 0 g fibre, 0 mg chol, 0 mg sodium.

VARIATION

Gewürztraminer Wine Jelly: Replace Cabernet Franc with Gewürztraminer or Riesling and vinegar with lemon juice. Replace thyme with 1 strip each lime rind and Granny Smith apple peel and 2 dried apricots, halved.

Red Grapefruit Marmalade

The rich colour and vibrant flavour of this preserve is enough to brighten any holiday table.

2	large ruby red grapefruit	2
2	lemons	2
10 cups	water	2.5 L
8 cups	granulated sugar	2 L

• Scrub grapefruit and lemons in hot soapy water; rinse and let dry. Cut in half; squeeze out juice and strain into large Dutch oven to make 2 cups (500 mL).
• Pull membranes from skins; tie along with seeds in 8-inch (20 cm) square of double-thickness cheesecloth. Add bag to pot. Add water.
• Cut grapefruit and lemon skin halves crosswise into thirds; very thinly slice crosswise and add to pot. Bring to boil; reduce heat, cover and simmer until strips are very tender, about 2 hours, skimming off any foam.
• Remove and squeeze juice from bag back into pan; discard bag. Measure contents of pan; add water if necessary or cook further to reduce and make 8 cups (2 L).
• Meanwhile, place 2 small plates in freezer.
• Pour half of the fruit mixture and half of the sugar into pot; bring to boil, stirring. Boil vigorously, stirring often, until setting point is reached and ½ tsp (2 mL) dropped onto chilled plate wrinkles when pushed with fork, about 10 minutes. Let cool for 5 minutes, skimming off any foam and stirring to distribute fruit.

- Pour into hot 1-cup (250 mL) canning jars, leaving ¼-inch (5 mm) headspace. Wipe rims. Cover with prepared lids. Screw on bands until resistance is met; increase to fingertip tight.
- Repeat with remaining fruit mixture and sugar. Boil in boiling water bath for 10 minutes.

MAKES ABOUT 8 CUPS (2 L).

PER 1 TBSP (15 ML): about 52 cal, 0 g pro, 0 g total fat (0 g sat. fat), 13 g carb, trace fibre, 0 mg chol, 1 mg sodium. % RDI: 7% vit C.

Cranberry Fruit Chutney

Fresh and tangy yet sweet enough to satisfy, this burnished red condiment pairs beguilingly with turkey, ham, goose and duck. Save some for pork loin roasts and chops, too.

2 cups	lightly packed dried apricots	500 mL
2½ cups	orange juice	625 mL
1 cup	chopped dates	250 mL
½ cup	golden raisins	125 mL
½ cup	chopped preserved ginger	125 mL
2	pkg (each 12 oz/340 g) cranberries	2
1½ cups	granulated sugar	375 mL
1¼ cups	finely chopped onions	300 mL
¾ cup	corn syrup	175 mL
¾ cup	cider vinegar	175 mL
1½ tsp	mustard seeds	7 mL
¼ tsp	salt	1 mL

- Cut dried apricots into ¼-inch (5 mm) wide strips. In large Dutch oven, combine apricots, orange juice, dates, golden raisins and ginger; cover and let stand for 8 hours. *(Make-ahead: Let stand for up to 24 hours.)*
- Stir in cranberries, sugar, onions, corn syrup, vinegar, mustard seeds and salt; bring to gentle boil over medium heat, stirring often. Reduce heat to simmer; cook, stirring almost constantly, until thickened enough to mound on spoon and cranberries have popped, about 20 minutes.
- Pour into hot 1-cup (250 mL) canning jars, leaving ¼-inch (5 mm) headspace. Wipe rims. Cover with prepared lids. Screw on bands until resistance is met; increase to fingertip tight. Boil in boiling water bath for 10 minutes.

MAKES ABOUT 9 CUPS (2.25 L).

PER 1 TBSP (15 ML): about 28 cal, trace pro, 0 g total fat (0 g sat. fat), 7 g carb, 1 g fibre, 0 mg chol, 7 mg sodium. % RDI: 1% iron, 1% vit A, 3% vit C.

Apricot Jalapeño Cheese Topper

Spoon this fruity topper over a round of Brie cheese and warm just until melting. Or serve with cream cheese and crackers.

1 cup	white wine	250 mL
1 cup	chopped dried apricots	250 mL
½ cup	granulated sugar	125 mL
½ cup	water	125 mL
1	jalapeño pepper, seeded and minced	1
½ tsp	lemon juice	2 mL

• In large glass measuring cup, microwave wine at high for 1 minute or until hot. Add apricots; let stand for 1 hour. Strain into saucepan, pressing apricots to release any liquid; set apricots aside.
• Add sugar and water to pan; bring to boil over medium-high heat, stirring until sugar is dissolved. Boil until syrupy, about 10 minutes.
• Add apricots and jalapeño pepper; simmer until as thick as corn syrup, about 10 minutes. Stir in lemon juice. Let cool.
• Spoon into decorative jar and seal. *(Make-ahead: Refrigerate for up to 1 month.)*

MAKES ABOUT 1 CUP (250 ML).

PER 1 TBSP (15 ML): about 49 cal, trace pro, 0 g total fat (0 g sat. fat), 12 g carb, 1 g fibre, 0 mg chol, 2 mg sodium. % RDI: 1% calcium, 2% iron, 3% vit A.

Clementine Cranberry Sauce

When it comes to gift making, this is one of the easiest projects to tackle. It's also one of the most welcome because come Christmas dinner, everybody enjoys cranberry sauce, especially this one with a fancy twist.

6	clementines or mandarins	6
2 cups	water (approx)	500 mL
2	bags (each 12 oz/375 g) fresh or frozen cranberries	2
2 cups	granulated sugar	500 mL
¼ cup	orange-flavoured liqueur (optional)	50 mL

• Scrub clementines in hot soapy water; rinse well and let dry. Cut out stem end of each. Halve and squeeze out juice; set aside. Discard seeds. Cut skins into fine slivers.
• In large Dutch oven, bring slivered skins and water to simmer over medium heat. Reduce heat to low; cover and simmer, adding a little more water if necessary to prevent burning, until skins are tender and break easily when pressed, 30 minutes.
• Add clementine juice; bring to boil over medium heat. Stir in cranberries and sugar; return to boil. Boil vigorously until thickened and berries pop, about 5 minutes. Stir in liqueur (if using).
• Ladle into hot 1-cup (250 mL) canning jars, leaving ½-inch (1 cm) headspace. Wipe rims. Cover with prepared lids. Screw on bands until resistance is met; increase to fingertip tight. Boil in boiling water bath for 10 minutes.

MAKES ABOUT 8 CUPS (2 L).

PER ¼ CUP (50 ML): about 68 cal, trace pro, trace total fat (trace sat. fat), 17 g carb, 1 g fibre, 0 mg chol, 1 mg sodium. % RDI: 1% calcium, 1% iron, 2% vit A, 17% vit C, 1% folate.

Tarragon and Pink Peppercorn Vinegar

Tarragon's delicate citrus and licorice notes combine in this infused vinegar. Choose pretty bottles for gift giving and add a note to make a simple vinaigrette by whisking one part of this vinegar with four parts extra-virgin olive oil.

1½ cups	packed fresh tarragon sprigs	375 mL
2 tbsp	pink peppercorns	25 mL
6 cups	white wine vinegar	1.5 L

GARNISH:

	Pink peppercorns	
	Tarragon sprigs	

• Place tarragon and peppercorns in dry sterilized widemouthed 6-cup (1.5 L) jar.
• In saucepan, bring vinegar to boil; pour over tarragon and let cool to room temperature. Seal and let stand in sunny location at room temperature for 10 days, shaking jar occasionally. Strain through cheesecloth-lined sieve.
• GARNISH: Place a few peppercorns and 1 sprig tarragon in each dry sterilized bottle; pour in vinegar. Seal bottles. *(Make-ahead: Store in cool dark place for up to 6 months.)*

MAKES ABOUT 6 CUPS (1.5 L).

PER 1 TBSP (15 ML): about 2 cal, 0 g pro, 0 g total fat (0 g sat. fat), 1 g carb, 0 g fibre, 0 mg chol, 0 mg sodium. % RDI: 1% iron.

TIP:
❯ For gifts, it's best to bottle the vinegar just before giving because the tarragon naturally fades over time.

Himalayan Chai Blend

Cardamom, peppercorns, cinnamon and cloves are the most common spices in the Indian beverage chai. For maximum flavour, slurp, don't sip.

1	piece (2 inches/5 cm) gingerroot	1
8	bay leaves	8
3	cinnamon sticks, smashed	3
1 cup	black tea leaves, such as Darjeeling	250 mL
2 tbsp	fennel seeds or aniseeds	25 mL
24	whole cloves	24
12	green cardamom pods, cracked	12
1 tsp	black peppercorns	5 mL

• Cut ginger into ⅛-inch (3 mm) thick slices. Place on rack; let dry at room temperature until brittle, about 24 hours.
• Break bay leaves into small pieces. Break cinnamon sticks into 1-inch (2.5 cm) pieces.
• In bowl, mix together ginger, bay leaves, cinnamon sticks, tea leaves, fennel seeds, cloves, cardamom pods and peppercorns. Spoon into decorative bag or airtight jar.

MAKES ABOUT 16 SERVINGS.

Himalayan Chai
There are two ways to brew a cup of chai.
• To emphasize the tea: Use Darjeeling leaves. Bring ¾ cup (175 mL) water to boil; remove from heat. Add 1 tbsp (15 mL) Chai Blend to pot or teapot; steep for 5 minutes. Strain into cup. Add milk and sugar to taste.
• To emphasize the spices: In pot, bring ½ cup (125 mL) each milk and water to boil; reduce heat to simmer. Add 1 tbsp (15 mL) Chai Blend; simmer, stirring, for 5 minutes. Strain into cup. Add sugar to taste.

Limoncello

Limone, *which means* lemon *in Italian, is the refreshing note in this simple liqueur. Serve it iced from the freezer.*

8	lemons	8
1	bottle (750 mL) vodka	1
2½ cups	water	625 mL
2 cups	granulated sugar	500 mL

• Scrub lemons in hot soapy water; rinse and dry. With vegetable peeler or zester, peel off yellow rind, avoiding white pith. Place rind in 4-cup (1 L) airtight jar; pour in vodka. Seal and let stand in cool dark place for 5 days.

• In small saucepan, bring water and sugar to boil; boil gently for 15 minutes. Let cool to room temperature.

• In large measuring cup, stir together vodka mixture and sugar mixture; strain through coffee filter– or cheesecloth-lined funnel into decorative bottles. Discard lemon rind strips. Seal bottles. *(Make-ahead: Store in cool dark place for up to 1 year.)*

MAKES 6 CUPS (1.5 L).

PER 2 TBSP (25 ML): about 66 cal, 0 g pro, 0 g total fat (0 g sat. fat), 8 g carb, 0 g fibre, 0 mg chol, 1 mg sodium.

Irish Cream Liqueur

This liqueur is delicious on its own, over ice or in coffee or hot chocolate. But be careful — it's candy with a kick!

½ tsp	instant coffee granules	2 mL
2 tsp	vanilla	10 mL
1 cup	Irish whiskey	250 mL
1 cup	whipping cream	250 mL
1	can (300 mL) sweetened condensed milk	1
⅓ cup	chocolate syrup	75 mL

• In large measuring cup, dissolve coffee granules in vanilla; whisk in whiskey, cream, condensed milk and chocolate syrup. Pour into decorative bottles. Seal and refrigerate. *(Make-ahead: Refrigerate for up to 2 weeks.)*

MAKES 4 CUPS (1 L).

PER 2 TBSP (25 ML): about 91 cal, 1 g pro, 4 g total fat (3 g sat. fat), 9 g carb, 0 g fibre, 14 mg chol, 21 mg sodium. % RDI: 4% calcium, 1% iron, 4% vit A, 1% folate.

Dog's Breath Biscuits

Dogs will lick up every last crumb of these crunchy peanut butter–flavoured biscuits. For a small dog, use a smaller cutter.

½ cup	whole wheat flour	125 mL
½ cup	all-purpose flour	125 mL
1 cup	large-flake rolled oats	250 mL
¾ cup	cornmeal	175 mL
¼ cup	packed brown sugar	50 mL
2 tsp	baking powder	10 mL
½ tsp	salt	2 mL
¼ cup	butter, softened	50 mL
⅓ cup	peanut butter	75 mL
2	eggs	2
¼ cup	minced fresh mint	50 mL
¼ cup	minced fresh parsley	50 mL

• Line rimless baking sheets with parchment paper or grease; set aside.
• In bowl, whisk together whole wheat and all-purpose flours, rolled oats, cornmeal, sugar, baking powder and salt.
• In separate bowl, beat butter with peanut butter; beat in eggs, 1 at a time. Stir in flour mixture, mint and parsley to make soft dough. Divide in half; wrap and refrigerate until firm, about 1 hour. *(Make-ahead: Refrigerate for up to 2 days.)*
• On lightly floured surface, roll out dough to ½-inch (1 cm) thickness. Using 4-inch (10 cm) bone-shaped cookie cutter, cut out shapes. Arrange on prepared pan; bake in centre of 325°F (160°C) oven until golden and firm, 35 to 40 minutes. Transfer to rack; let cool. *(Make-ahead: Store in airtight container for up to 2 weeks.)*

MAKES ABOUT 12 DOG BISCUITS.

For the Birds

For an easy project, mix up a batch of bird food to put outside. Then sit by the window and wait for the feast to begin.

Peanut Butter Pinecones
Lay 2 pieces of waxed paper on work surface. In centre of 1, spoon about 1 tbsp (15 mL) peanut butter; on the other, sprinkle about 3 tbsp (50 mL) birdseed.
• Roll 5-inch (12 cm) pinecone in peanut butter until coated; roll in birdseed. Spoon extra birdseed into spaces.
• Tie twine around tip of cone; tie other end around tree branch just outside window.

MAKES 1 PINECONE.

Suet Cakes
Suet attracts all sorts of insect-eating birds. The fat is a good source of energy and heat – just what birds need in winter.
• Line 6 muffin cups with paper liners; set aside.
• In top of double boiler, melt 2 cups (500 mL) suet. Stir in ¼ cup (50 mL) each birdseed and other treat (such as raisins, peanut butter, nuts, seeds or crushed eggshells).
• Divide among prepared cups. Refrigerate until hard.
• Remove from paper cups. Poke hole through centre, thread twine through hole and attach to tree. Freeze any leftover cakes.

MAKES 6 CAKES.

A

B

ABOUT OUR NUTRITION INFORMATION

To meet nutrient needs each day, moderately active women 25 to 49 need about 1,900 calories, 51 g protein, 261 g carbohydrate, 25 to 35 g fibre and not more than 63 g total fat (21 g saturated fat). Men and teenagers usually need more. Canadian sodium intake of approximately 3,500 to 4,500 mg daily should be reduced.

Percentage of recommended daily intake (% RDI) is based on the highest recommended intakes (excluding those for pregnant and lactating women) for calcium, iron, vitamins A and C, and folate.

    Figures are rounded off. They are based on the first ingredient listed when there is

a choice and do not include optional ingredients or those with no specified amounts.

Abbreviations:
cal = calories
pro = protein
carb = carbohydrate
sat. fat = saturated fat
chol = cholesterol

FOOD

Recipes not listed were developed in
The Canadian Living Test Kitchen.

Donna Bartolini
Roast Beef and Horseradish Phyllo Cups, 3; Shrimp and Avocado Salad Phyllo Cups, 3; Thai Crab Salad Phyllo Cups, 5; Earl Grey Pots de Crème, 99; Mini Tiramisu, 101; Lemon Semifreddo with Coffee Syrup, 102; Panpepato Bars, 157; Winter Gingerbread Village, 183

Pam Collacott
Ginger Star Wreath Centrepiece, 185

Cynthia David
Swedish Saffron Bread, 168

Carol Ferguson
Reverse Nanaimo Bars, 154

Christine Grimes
Sesame Shrimp with Wasabi Sauce, 23

Jan Main
Crunchy-Top Cranberry Muffins, 175

Dana McCauley
Pignoli, 150

Rose Murray
Tandoori Spice Blend and Tandoori Chicken, 203

Daphna Rabinovitch
Pistachio Thumbprints with White Chocolate, 129; Vanilla Cookie Snowmen, 130

Lucie Richard
Treescape Candle Base, 180

Emily Richards
Fritto Misto, 93; Romano Brunch Braid, 172

Adell Shneer
Turkey Phyllo Strudel, 93; Chocolate Butterscotch Babka, 169

Linda Stephen
Peanut Butter Nanaimo Bars, 156; Gluten-Free Sticky Toffee Squares, 161

Susan Van Hezewijk
Speculaas, 140

Nicole Young
Nut Brittle, 210; Dog's Breath Biscuits, 223

CRAFTS

Lisa Aiken
Snacks for Santa and His Team, 90; Branching Elegance, 170; Twig Tree, 170

Eva Cooney
Traditional Mantelscape, 30; Dress Up the Dining Table (floral arrangements), 80

Anthony Costa
Contemporary Mantelscape, 31

Ronda Dahlke
Ornamental Wreath, 7

Heather Gilmour
Beaded Moss Tree, 105

Steven Howard
Vintage Mantelscape, 31

Dorotea Kemenczy
Beaded Initials, 49; Embroidered Table Linens, 49; Monogrammed Ornaments, 49; Christmas Crackers, 73; Gilded Candles, 118; Rectangular Wreath, 149

Carole Lawrence
Ribbon Wreath, 21

Sabrina Linn
Stockings to Sew, 212

Courtesy of Offray
A Gala Ball, 126

Wendy Relmer
Dress Up the Dining Table (table settings), 80

Michele Rose
Hand-Painted Candle Holders, 126

Renée Schwarz
O Little Town, 144; Snowman Ornament, 186; Paper Chain of Snow People, 196

Kate Seaver
How to Decorate a Tree, 62; Recycle and Refresh Old Ornaments, 63

Jennifer Spratley
A Frosty Fireplace, 12; Pinecone Place Cards and Bow-Tied Chairs, 67

Courtesy of Wrights
Wine-Bottle Gift Bags, 204

PHOTOGRAPHY
Michael Alberstat
  page 195
Christopher Campbell
  pages 20, 55, 89, 110, 111 and 207
Paul Chmielowiec
  page 7
Christopher Dew
  pages 56 and 57
Yvonne Duivenvoorden
  pages 4, 5, 11, 14, 21, 22, 34, 49, 51,
  52, 60, 69, 76, 79, 86, 95, 100, 103, 106, 109,
  113, 116, 120, 125, 126, 130, 134, 137, 139,
  149, 155, 162, 166, 173, 178, 182, 188, 192,
  200, 211, 213, 214 and 222
Geoff George
  page 25
Michael Graydon
  pages 30 and 31
Donna Griffith
  pages 80 and 81
Daniel Harrison
  pages 12, 45, 49, 56, 57, 62, 63, 73, 90,
  118, 144, 170 and 180
Gabor Jurina
  page 204
Michael Kohn
  pages 21 and 73
Edward Pond
  page 218
Ted Yarwood
  pages 12, 67 and 105

ILLUSTRATION
Katy Dockrill
  page 149

FOOD STYLING
Julie Aldis
  pages 4, 34, 106, 137, 139, 155 and 162
Donna Bartolini
  pages 22, 130, 180, 182 and 192
Lucie Richard
  pages 14, 109, 113, 188, 200, 211 and 214
Claire Stancer
  pages 51, 52, 69, 76, 79, 86, 95, 100,
  103, 120, 125, 134, 166, 195 and 218
Claire Stubbs
  pages 11, 60, 116, 173, 178 and 222

PROPS STYLING
Marc-Philippe Gagné
  pages 109, 188 and 192
Karen Kwinter
  pages 45, 49, 90 and 118
Oksana Slavutych
  pages 4, 11, 14, 22, 34, 49, 51, 52, 60, 69, 76,
  79, 86, 95, 100, 103, 106, 113, 116, 120, 125,
  130, 134, 137, 139, 155, 162, 166, 173, 178,
  182, 195, 200, 211, 213, 214, 218 and 222